FLOYD CLYMER'S MOTORCYCLIST'S LIBRARY

The Book of the
ROYAL ENFIELD

A COMPLETE GUIDE FOR OWNERS OF ROYAL ENFIELD MOTOR-CYCLES (COVERS SINGLES AND VEE TWINS FROM 1937 TO 1953 INCLUSIVE)

BY

W. C. HAYCRAFT, F.R.S.A.

ANNOUNCEMENT

By special arrangement with the original publishers of this book, Sir Isaac Pitman & Son, Ltd., of London, England, we have secured the exclusive publishing rights for this book, as well as all others in THE MOTORCYCLIST'S LIBRARY.

Included in THE MOTORCYCLIST'S LIBRARY are complete instruction manuals covering the care and operation of respective motorcycles and engines; valuable data on speed tuning, and thrilling accounts of motorcycle race events. See listing of available titles elsewhere in this edition.

We consider it a privilege to be able to offer so many fine titles to our customers.

FLOYD CLYMER
Publisher of Books Pertaining to Automobiles and Motorcycles

2125 W. PICO ST.   LOS ANGELES 6, CALIF.

INTRODUCTION

Welcome to the world of digital publishing ~ the book you now hold in your hand, while unchanged from the original edition, was printed using the latest state of the art digital technology. The advent of print-on-demand has forever changed the publishing process, never has information been so accessible and it is our hope that this book serves your informational needs for years to come. If this is your first exposure to digital publishing, we hope that you are pleased with the results. Many more titles of interest to the classic automobile and motorcycle enthusiast, collector and restorer are available via our website at www.VelocePress.com. We hope that you find this title as interesting as we do.

NOTE FROM THE PUBLISHER

The information presented is true and complete to the best of our knowledge. All recommendations are made without any guarantees on the part of the author or the publisher, who also disclaim all liability incurred with the use of this information.

TRADEMARKS

We recognize that some words, model names and designations, for example, mentioned herein are the property of the trademark holder. We use them for identification purposes only. This is not an official publication.

INFORMATION ON THE USE OF THIS PUBLICATION

This manual is an invaluable resource for the classic motorcycle enthusiast and a "must have" for owners interested in performing their own maintenance. However, in today's information age we are constantly subject to changes in common practice, new technology, availability of improved materials and increased awareness of chemical toxicity. As such, it is advised that the user consult with an experienced professional prior to undertaking any procedure described herein. While every care has been taken to ensure correctness of information, it is obviously not possible to guarantee complete freedom from errors or omissions or to accept liability arising from such errors or omissions. Therefore, any individual that uses the information contained within, or elects to perform or participate in do-it-yourself repairs or modifications acknowledges that there is a risk factor involved and that the publisher or its associates cannot be held responsible for personal injury or property damage resulting from the use of the information or the outcome of such procedures.

WARNING!

One final word of advice, this publication is intended to be used as a reference guide, and when in doubt the reader should consult with a qualified technician.

PREFACE

ROYAL ENFIELD motor-cycles are designed and manufactured by The Enfield Cycle Co., Ltd., of Redditch, a firm which has specialized in high-grade motor-cycle production for some fifty years. During the Second World War tens of thousands of bicycles and motor-cycles were delivered to the Armed Forces.

Among the motor-cycles supplied to the Airborne Forces was a remarkably tough "go anywhere" lightweight two-stroke model (WD/RE) having a 125 c.c. unit-construction engine and gearbox. Many of these lightweights, nicknamed "Flying Fleas" by the troops, were parachuted into enemy territory and behaved splendidly. It is not surprising, therefore, that a civilian version (Model RE) has been in continuous production since the termination of hostilities.

Other Royal Enfields (type WD) delivered to the Armed Forces were the 248 c.c. S.V. Model WD, the 346 c.c. S.V. Model WD/C, and the 346 c.c. O.H.V. Model WD/CO. Since the war these ex-military machines have shed their drab khaki and emerged on the roads in various colour schemes after being thoroughly reconditioned by various motor-cycle dealers. Thousands are now in private ownership.

Model WD/CO is similar to the civilian Model CO produced for export during 1945–6. *All ex-military machines (WD) and "export" models are dealt with in the present edition, which also covers all* 1937–9 *singles and Vee twins. The* 1946–8 *range (Models G, J, J2, RE) is fully dealt with, and the same applies to the* 1949 *range (Models G, J2, RE), with the exception of the brand-new spring frame* 346 *c.c. "Bullet" model, and the spring frame* 500 *c.c. vertical twin.* Both these new models have entirely new engines. When these new machines become very popular it is hoped to include appropriate instructions.

The fifth edition of this handbook is a great improvement on all earlier editions. Much new matter has been added and all data concerning carburation, ignition, lubrication, and lighting equipment have been carefully checked and brought right up to date.

PREFACE

The objective of the book is to assist Royal Enfield owners to obtain trouble-free running at minimum expense. In these days of shortages and increased prices, keeping your machine well tuned and in sound condition is *essential* in order to obtain maximum m.p.g. and m.p.£.!

Owners of 1950-3 Royal Enfields (Models G, J2, RE) should carefully note the following. The instructions given in this edition for the 1949 four-stroke O.H.V. Models G, J2 apply to the 1950-3 Models G, J2 except in regard to: (*a*) the stripping down of the modified (1951-3) front forks (which have a facia for the speedometer) and (*b*) the renewal of the headlamp main bulb. The 1951-3 models require a 6-volt, 30/30 watt double-filament main bulb (Lucas).

The instructions for the 1949 two-stroke Model RE apply also to the 1950 Model RE except in regard to the front forks. Telescopic-type forks were fitted for 1950 (see page 80) and the 1951-3 machines have been redesigned throughout and are now known as Model RE2.

In conclusion I give my sincere thanks to The Enfield Cycle Co., Ltd. for their valuable assistance in connection with the compiling of this edition, which it is hoped will prove of real practical assistance to owners of an increasingly popular make of motor-cycle.

W. C. H.

CONTENTS

CHAP.		PAGE
I.	HANDLING A ROYAL ENFIELD	1
II.	OBTAINING GOOD CARBURATION	19
III.	CARE OF IGNITION SYSTEM	42
IV.	ALL ABOUT LUBRICATION	60
V.	CARE OF LIGHTING EQUIPMENT	81
VI.	GOOD TYRE MILEAGE	100
VII.	ADJUSTMENTS AND OVERHAULING	107
	INDEX	165

CHAPTER I

HANDLING A ROYAL ENFIELD

THIS chapter is mainly for novices and deals with the handling of a Royal Enfield motor-cycle rather than the technique of driving on the road and the cultivation of road sense. It is assumed that you are the owner of a brand-new four-stroke or two-stroke model (Figs. 1–3, 6), or else have just bought a good second-hand mount and are about to get on the road.

FIG. 1. AN ATTRACTIVE AND ECONOMICAL UTILITY MOUNT FOR SHORT OR LONG JOURNEYS—THE 125 C.C. MODEL RE2 TWO-STROKE

The two-stroke "RE" engine has a bore and stroke of 53·79 mm. × 55 mm., and a compression ratio of 5·5 to 1. Unit construction of the engine and gearbox and Miller lighting are specified, and the total weight is only 140 lb. Finish is in silver-grey and the price is remarkably low. Maximum speed is 45–50 m.p.h. and fuel consumption 120–150 m.p.g. A spring-frame 148 c.c. model is also available

Before Getting on the Road. The law insists that prior to riding on the public highway you shall comply with certain preliminaries. Various forms can be obtained from a Post Office (see below) and must be carefully and truthfully filled in. Here are seven vital preliminaries which you must attend to—

1. Take out an insurance policy to cover all *third-party* risks, and obtain cover note or "certificate of insurance." If your motor-cycle is valuable, it is advisable to insure it also against damage, fire, and theft by taking out a full comprehensive insurance policy. Note that a passenger is *not* insured.

FIG. 2. IN CAPABLE HANDS THE ROYAL ENFIELD CAN BE RIDDEN SAFELY ALMOST ANYWHERE
(*W. J. Brunell, Paignton*)

Above is shown Mr. C. N. Rogers demonstrating in no uncertain manner the surging power and stability of a 346 c.c. model in the 1947 West of England Trial. Observe the natural poise and unruffled attitude of the rider as he takes "rough stuff" in his stride. Mr. C. N. Rogers was also a member of the team which won the International Six Day's Trophy held in Italy in September, 1948

2. Obtain a "provisional" or driving licence (Form D.L. I).

3. Obtain the registration licence and registration book (Form R.F. 1/2),* or renew the licence (Form R.F. 1/A). 125 c.c. and 225 c.c. two-strokes are taxed at the rate of 17s. 6d. and £1 17s. 6d., respectively. Machines of over 250 c.c. are taxed at the rate of £3 15s. per annum, with an additional duty of £1 5s. per annum where a sidecar is attached.

4. Keep the registration book in a safe place, and return it to

Fig. 3. Suitable for Most Purposes—The 346 c.c. O.H.V. Model G Four-stroke

Characteristics of Model G are its compactness, luxurious equipment, extreme flexibility, and power. Maximum speed is 65-70 m.p.h. The engine has a bore and stroke of 70 mm. × 90 mm. and a compression ratio of 6 to 1. Included in the specification are D.S. lubrication, an Amal carburettor, cradle type frame, telescopic front forks, four-speed Albion gearbox, cush-drive rear hub, "Magdyno" lighting (with C.V.C.), etc. Fuel consumption is 75-80 m.p.g. See also pages 17, 18

the Registration Authorities for amendment if you change your address, if you attach a sidecar, or if you sell the machine.

5. If you are not eligible for an actual driving licence, attach "L" plates to the front and rear of the machine. They must not obscure the index letters or registration numbers.

6. Where a pillion rider is carried, see that the passenger sits *astride* a proper pillion seat securely *fixed* to the machine and is the holder of a current driving licence if you are a "learner."

7. Fit a speedometer (if mount licensed *after* 1st Oct., 1937).

---

* On most Royal Enfields the frame and engine numbers which require to be included on Form R.F. 1/2 are situated on the near-side of the head lug and the near-side of the crankcase (just below the cylinder base), respectively. On the 125 c.c. two-strokes, however, both numbers are on the off-side, the engine number being on the flywheel magneto housing.

Can You Obtain a Driving Licence? You can if you have reached the age of 16 and have complied with one of the following three conditions—
1. Have passed an official driving test (Form D.L. 26).
2. Have held a driving licence prior to 1st April, 1934.
3. Have obtained exemption from the prescribed driving test under the provisions of the Road Traffic (Driving Licences) Act, 1947.

Familiarize Yourself With Controls. It is assumed that you understand the functions of the various controls provided on a motor-cycle and have an elementary knowledge of the basic principles of the four-stroke or two-stroke engine, including carburation and ignition. Basic principles are beyond the scope of this handbook, which deals specifically with Royal Enfield machines.

If you are unaccustomed to the Royal Enfield control layout you should before attempting to start up or get on the road, familiarize yourself with the disposition of the various levers, pedals, and switches. Also reflect on their functions, and effect of operating them with the engine running and while riding.

The control layouts on the 1937 and later four-stroke single-cylinder and twin-cylinder models are shown in Figs. 4 and 4A. There are certain slight variations on different models and these are referred to beneath the control layout illustrations. Some important points concerning the controls should be noted.

All controls, including the gear-change pedal and the rear brake pedal, are adjustable and if the existing arrangement does not suit your individual physical requirements, the handlebars, footrests, and control levers (see page 133) should be adjusted until the most convenient and comfortable positions are obtained. For lighting switch positions, see pages 89–91.

Controls on Four-stroke Models. The handlebar controls (see Figs. 4 and 4A), with few exceptions, are operated by *inward* movement (i.e. towards the rider). Do not use the exhaust valve lifter except for starting up, stopping the engine ("Magdyno" models), and when descending a steep hill with a treacherous road surface. Except when effecting a start, the air lever and ignition control should be kept wide open and fully advanced respectively. It is permissible, however, to retard the ignition control slightly, and temporarily to give slightly less air (on a coldish engine) to prevent the engine "knocking" under a severe load such as may be imposed when accelerating suddenly or when hill climbing. But always make full and timely use of the Albion four-speed gearbox.

A foot gear-change pedal is provided on all models except the

1937–9 Big Twins and some of the earlier four-stroke singles (e.g. Model T). To show clearly which gear is engaged, an indicator

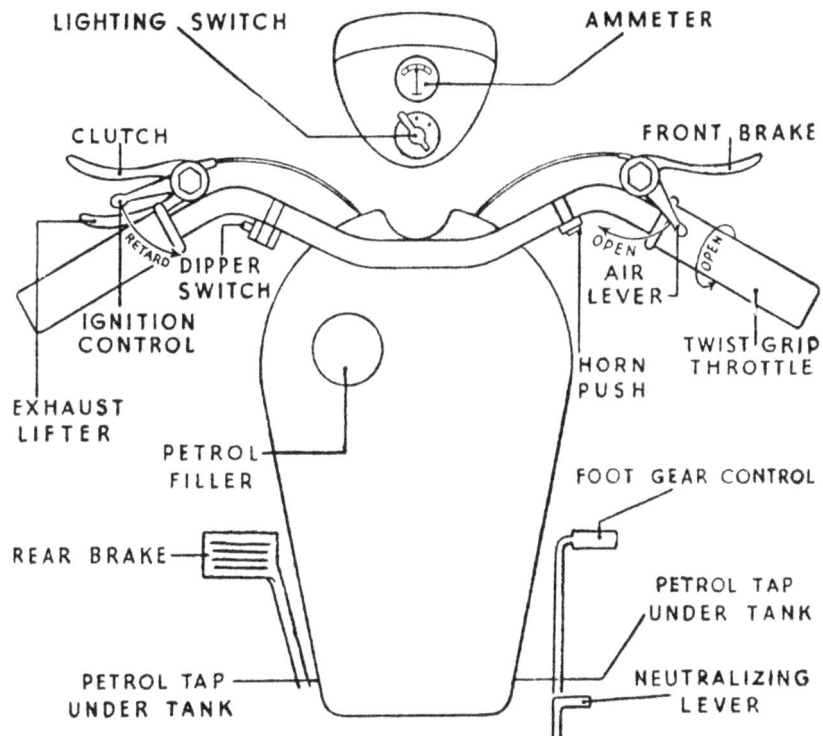

FIG. 4 CONTROL LAYOUT ON MOST SINGLE-CYLINDER "MAGDYNO" MODELS (1937 ONWARDS)
(*The Enfield Cycle Co., Ltd.*)

The neutralizing lever shown is fitted only on the post-war Models G, J, and J2. An exhaust valve lifter is not provided on 250 c.c. models, some earlier types of which have hand instead of foot gear control. On certain machines the ignition control is moved outwards (not inwards as indicated) to retard the ignition. The control layout on the coil ignition models is similar to that of the "Magdyno" models, except that a warning light and ignition switch are incorporated on the headlamp, the ignition switch usually comprising a detachable key located in the centre of the lighting switch. On some 1937 Royal Enfields the ammeter, lighting switch, and ignition switch (coil models) are neatly mounted in a panel on top of the petrol tank. In the case of the 1939 Model G, "350 Bullet" and the "500 Bullet" Model J2 an oil pressure gauge is also included on the tank panel. No dipper switch is provided on Model WD/CO, this machine having a four-position lighting switch

is fitted to the foot-operated control. On 1946 and later Models G, J, and J2 a neutralizing lever (Fig. 5) is also fitted to facilitate selecting "neutral."

Where a neutralizing lever is not fitted it is necessary in order to obtain "neutral" from first or second gear to move the foot gear-change pedal down or up *half* the amount necessary to engage the next gear. To make an upward gear change, the pedal is pressed *downward* with the toe, and to make a downward change (i.e. to a lower gear) the pedal is *raised* with the toe of the foot. On all Albion gearboxes a hairpin-shaped piece of

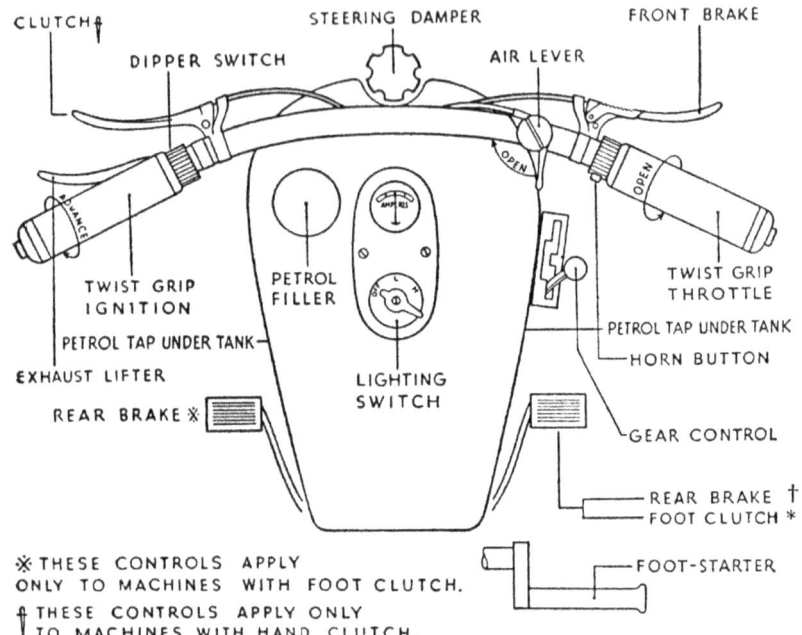

Fig. 4a. Control Layout on the Twin-cylinder S.V. Models K and KX (1937 to 1939)
(*The Enfield Cycle Co., Ltd.*)

On the 1939 Big Twins an ignition lever instead of twist-grip control is provided, and this retards the ignition by *inward* movement. On all 1938-9 models the ammeter and lighting switch are incorporated on the headlamp. The positions of the clutch and rear brake controls vary as indicated in the illustration

flat spring-steel returns the foot-change pedal automatically to the horizontal position after each gear change is made.

Controls on Two-stroke Models. The control layout (not illustrated) on the 1937 and later 225 c.c. Model A and the postwar 125 c.c. Models RE and WD/RE is simpler than on the four-stroke models. A single-lever Amal carburettor is fitted and no separate air lever is therefore provided, the throttle being controlled by means of a twist-grip on the right-hand side of the handlebars. The throttle is opened by *inward* movement of the twist-grip. No ignition control is included, but Model A has an ignition key fitted in the centre of the lighting switch (see page 89).

To switch the ignition on or off the ignition key is turned clockwise or anti-clockwise respectively.

On Models RE and WD/RE an air filter is provided behind the carburettor. Movable shutters on the filter enable it to be used as an air strangler for starting up purposes. Models RE and WD/RE also have a compression-release valve; it is operated by a small trigger-type lever on the near-side of the handlebars.

Models RE, WD/RE, and A have the clutch and the front brake operating lever situated on the near- and off-side ends of the handlebars respectively. Operation of the rear brake is by means of a toe-actuated pedal on the near-side. The kick-starter is, of course, located on the off-side of the gearbox.

Hand control of the three-speed gearbox is included, the quadrant being secured to the off-side of the tank. The quadrant has four notches, "neutral" position being between first (bottom) gear and second gear (which is the central position). On Models RE, WD/RE first and third (top) gears are obtained by moving the gear-change lever right forward and right back respectively. On Model A first and third gears are selected by moving the gear lever right back and right forward respectively.

The Compression-release Valve. It is not normally necessary to use the compression-release when starting up Model RE or WD/RE. This release valve does, however, serve three useful purposes.

1. If the clutch is worn or thoroughly impregnated with oil it may tend to slip when kick-starting the engine, though it will never slip when the engine is driving the machine. Any tendency to clutch slip when kick-starting the engine can be overcome by lifting the decompressor.

2. When descending very steep hills in bottom gear, as in Reliability Trials, the use of a decompressor will prevent the compression of the engine from locking the rear wheel.

3. Kicking the engine over with the decompressor lifted and the petrol turned off will usually clear an engine which has become flooded with petrol during failure to start caused by a dirty sparking plug or incorrectly adjusted contact-breaker.

Starting Up (All Four-stroke Models). First check that the oil tank (integral with the crankcase on all models) is replenished with suitable engine oil to the correct level (see page 68), and that there is sufficient petrol in the fuel tank.* It is assumed that the gearbox is properly replenished (page 74).

* On most Royal Enfields the petrol and oil tank filler caps are opened by turning the cap anti-clockwise until the catch is felt, pushing the cap down, and then turning it anti-clockwise as far as possible and lifting the cap off. To tighten the cap, push it down and then turn clockwise to the maximum extent.

If replenishment of the fuel tank is necessary, it is best to top up with No. 1 grade of a good brand of petrol, except perhaps in the case of a 1939 "350 Bullet" with high compression piston where it is advisable to use an ethylized fuel. The general use of anti-knocking fuels containing "lead" is to be deprecated, as such fuels tend to make the rider lazy in regard to changing gear. This form of neglect reacts most unfavourably on both the engine and transmission.

Most Royal Enfields are provided with two petrol taps under the tank. Where two taps are provided, turn on the *off-side* tap only so as to maintain a reserve supply of petrol. Should it be necessary to run on the reserve compartment, replenish the fuel tank immediately afterwards, and shut the reserve tap. To turn on either petrol tap, pull the knob away from the body of the petrol tap. To close a tap, push the knob inwards.

Check that the foot gear-change lever is in the "neutral" position as shown by the gear indicator, and adjust the engine controls for starting up. Open the throttle slightly by turning the twist-grip inwards about *one-eighth* of its total movement. Partly close the air lever. If the engine is stone cold it can be closed almost completely. If, on the other hand, the engine is warm, the air lever may be kept nearly half open. Retard the ignition control slightly (say one-third). The best control setting varies slightly for different machines, but that giving the quickest start can soon be found from experience. On a coil ignition model switch on the ignition by turning the ignition key clockwise.

Before starting up a cold engine momentarily depress the tickler on the lid of the carburettor float chamber, so as to fill the chamber completely. But avoid excessive "flooding" which wastes fuel and causes an over-rich mixture.

Except on 250 c.c. models having no exhaust valve lifter, raise the exhaust valve lifter and depress the kick-starter smartly downwards with the foot, releasing the exhaust valve lifter when the kick-starter crank is about half way down. An experienced rider can generally make an immediate start, but it may take a little time for the novice to master the knack of releasing the exhaust valve lifter at exactly the right moment. If the engine refuses to start at the second kick, try the effect of varying the throttle opening slightly.

Immediately the engine fires, advance the ignition control fully and open the air lever, not too rapidly, to its full extent. Adjust the throttle so that the engine warms up moderately fast and circulates the oil properly. Never permit a cold engine to race unless you are sure that the oil circulation is normal as verified by watching the flow from the oil return pipe (see page 68). Avoid permitting the engine to "tick-over" slowly, as this involves slow working of the oil pump and an abnormally low running temperature, possibly giving rise to condensation of fuel internally.

Starting Up (125 c.c. Models RE., WD/RE Two-stroke).

Verify that the tank is properly replenished with a mixture of petrol and engine oil. Suitable engine oils to use and the correct proportions for the petroil mixture are dealt with on page 61. As regards petrol, use No. 1 grade of a good brand, and do not try benzole-mixture or ethylized fuels.

Push the machine off its centre stand and check that the hand gear-change lever is in the "neutral" position (i.e. between first and second gears). Open the fuel tap and depress the tickler on the lid of the float chamber until petroil begins to overflow from the vent hole in the top of the float chamber.

If the engine is *cold*, also close the strangle shutters of the air filter attached to the air-intake of the carburettor. It is essential to obtain a *rich* mixture for starting, because some of the fuel condenses inside the crankcase, and this has a weakening effect.

If a *hot* engine has been left standing for a few minutes, it is advisable to enrich the mixture slightly by *half* closing the strangler, but in this instance do not "flood" the carburettor. An alternative method for starting a *warm* engine is to keep the strangler wide open and slightly "flood" the carburettor. It is important in any event not to close the strangler completely, otherwise the mixture will be so rich that starting may be virtually impossible, and each kick of the starter will make matters worse.

Where the engine has not been allowed to cool down and is *quite hot*, avoid "flooding" the carburettor, and keep the strangler wide open. Unless this is done, the mixture will be excessively rich and considerable trouble may be experienced in effecting a start.

Open the throttle slightly by turning the twist-grip inwards about *one-quarter to one-half* of its total movement. Then operate the kick-starter smartly. The engine should respond after not more than three or four attempts at starting.

After the 125 c.c. engine has started, run it up for a few moments with the strangler partially* closed and throttle up the engine two or three times so as to enable the petroil mixture to be sucked into the crankcase. Afterwards open the strangler shutters. When low thermometer readings prevail, it may be necessary to keep the strangler partly closed for about a quarter of a mile to ensure good combustion and even firing, as condensation of fuel occurs in the crankcase. See also notes on page 10.

* The strangler must be kept partially open once the engine has started, otherwise the sparking plug may become wet due to excess fuel.

Difficulty in Starting (Models RE., WD/RE). Should the clutch slip when kicking the engine over, ease the piston past compression by raising the compression-release valve by means of the trigger-type lever on the near-side of the handlebars. Close the valve as soon as a start is effected.

In the unlikely event of trouble being experienced in effecting a start with the kick-starter, it is often possible to get going by pushing off with the compression-release valve raised and first gear engaged. Close the compression-release valve as soon as the machine attains a speed equivalent to a fair walking pace. Temporarily disengage the clutch immediately the engine fires. When obstinate starting trouble occurs, it is advisable forthwith to—

1. Check the gap between the sparking plug electrodes (see page 43).
2. Verify the contact-breaker gap (see page 52). An incorrect gap will alter the ignition timing of the engine.
3. Inspect the h.t. lead and plug insulation. There must be no trace of water which is liable to cause shorting.
4. Make quite sure that the h.t. lead is pushed well down into the ebonite bush on the flywheel cover.

Flooding of Crankcase (Models RE., WD/RE). Should the crankcase of a 125 c.c. two-stroke model become "flooded" with petrol mixture, it may be found impossible to effect a start until the surplus has been removed. Except on the earliest engines, a drain plug will be found beneath the crankcase. In fact, two plugs are provided, but the larger one is for draining the gearbox. After draining off the excessive petrol mixture, clean the plug, and start up. It is preferable to do this by pushing off in first gear (see previous paragraph).

Starting Up (225 c.c. Model A Two-stroke). If replenishment of the fuel tank is necessary, top up with a petrol mixture consisting of No. 1 grade of petrol and suitable engine oil, mixed in the correct proportions (see page 61). Verify that the gear lever is in the "neutral" notch of the quadrant (between first and second gears).

Open the fuel tap and if the engine is *cold* slightly "flood" the carburettor by depressing the tickler on the float chamber lid until petrol begins to overflow from the top of the float chamber. Do not "flood" the carburettor if the engine is already warmed up. Switch on the ignition by turning the ignition switch in the centre of the lighting switch *clockwise*.

With your Model A on its stand, turn the engine over smartly with the kick-starter. It should fire at the first or second kick. If it remains dormant, try the effect of "flooding" the carburettor

HANDLING A ROYAL ENFIELD

again, and perhaps using a slightly wider throttle opening, but avoid too much throttle as this will hinder rather than facilitate quick starting.

Moving Off. It is assumed you have attended to preliminaries and have read and understand the Highway Code. Ease the machine off its stand with the engine running and the gear-change lever in "neutral." Then while astride the saddle, fully disengage the clutch and engage first gear. Where foot gear control is provided, raise the pedal to its full extent with the instep of the foot and then release the pedal. If hand gear control is specified (Big Twins and two-strokes), pull the gear lever right back. In the case of the 125 c.c. Models RE, WD/RE, however, push the gear lever right forward. If first gear does not readily engage, move the machine slightly backwards or forwards while operating the gear control, until proper engagement is obtained.

To move off, gradually open the throttle by turning the twist-grip *inwards* and simultaneously engage the clutch by releasing the handlebar lever. As the clutch plates "bite," the machine will begin to move forward and gather momentum. On taking up the load the engine speed tends to fall and this tendency must be countered by progressively opening the throttle so as to accelerate the engine and further increase the speed of the machine. A smooth take-off without jerk or transmission snatch is soon mastered and the correct co-ordination of the controls required to ensure this quickly becomes an instinctive procedure.

Changing Up. When a sufficient speed has been attained (approximately 10 m.p.h.), disengage the clutch, simultaneously close the throttle slightly, pause a second, and then engage second gear by *depressing* the foot gear-change pedal with the toe *to its full extent* and then releasing it. A firm and decisive movement is required, but force must *not* be used on the pedal. If hand gear control is fitted, move the gear-change lever (backwards on Models RE, WD/RE, and forwards on Model A) into the second gear quadrant notch after slightly closing the throttle and disengaging the clutch. As soon as second gear has been engaged, gradually re-engage the clutch and again throttle up the engine so as to take up the load and increase the speed of the machine.

To engage in turn third and fourth gears (three gears provided on two-strokes), repeat the gear changing procedure in the manner just described for second gear at road speeds of approximately 20 m.p.h. and 30 m.p.h. respectively. Speeds 5 m.p.h. higher are advised for the pre-war Model G "350 Bullet." The optimum road speeds at which gear changes should be made depend, of course, on whether the road is level or not. The approximate figures quoted are for driving on the level. Gear changing on an upward gradient calls for the changes to be made at somewhat higher road speeds. A commendable feature of all Royal Enfield (Albion) gearboxes is that all gears are actuated by a *single* striking fork. This renders impossible the simultaneous engagement of two gears, irrespective of how much wear has occurred inside the gearbox.

Endeavour to make all gear changes smoothly and silently, and avoid fierce acceleration, which is unkind both to the tyres and transmission. Once you are cruising comfortably in top gear, always keep the air lever wide open and the ignition lever fully advanced. In the case of Models RE, WD/RE, however, it is advisable when starting off in cold weather to keep the strangler shut (see page 9), and where Model A is concerned to keep the air lever partly closed until the engine has properly warmed up.

Changing Down. To change down into a lower gear, disengage the clutch, leaving the throttle open, pause a second, and then *raise* the foot gear-change pedal *fully* to obtain the next lower gear. As soon as the lower gear has been engaged, gradually re-engage the clutch, release the gear-change pedal, and adjust the throttle opening to suit the prevailing conditions of road and load.

Where hand gear control is provided, move the gear-change lever (forward on Models RE, WD/RE, and backward on Model A) into the required quadrant notch with the clutch disengaged and the throttle open. As in the case of changing up, practice soon enables smooth, silent, and precise changes to be made. Practise gear changing on a quiet road where there is little risk of sudden emergencies occurring.

Hill Climbing. This demands good power output and therefore the engine revolutions (r.p.m.) must be kept reasonably high. Always make full use of the three- or four-speed gearbox provided and change down in good time. On no account permit the engine to labour on a hill and never try and force an unwilling mount up a steep hill in top gear. This amounts to gross ill-treatment.

Just prior to negotiating a hill it is desirable to increase the speed and momentum of the machine by giving it plenty of throttle. Increase the throttle opening as the gradient increases and very gradually retard the ignition control and/or give slightly less air as soon as a slight metallic noise or "knocking" (perhaps a "rattling" sound on a two-stroke) warns you that the engine is beginning to labour. Retarding the ignition, however, reduces the power output, and a change down to a lower gear should be made while the machine still has plenty of momentum.

If a change down is made in good time, a fast climb is possible and further changes down higher up on the gradient may be rendered unnecessary. After a change down has been made, advance the ignition control if this has been previously retarded, and open the air lever fully if this has been partially closed to

FIG. 5. NEUTRALIZING LEVER ON 1946 AND LATER FOUR-STROKE MODELS
(*The Enfield Cycle Co., Ltd.*)
This view also shows the gear-change indicator, but the pedal of the foot gear-change lever is "off the picture." To obtain "neutral" quickly from fourth, third or second gears, it is only necessary to disengage the clutch and press the neutralizing lever down against its stop

prevent "knocking." All normal undulating roads and many main road hills can be tackled in top gear if judicious use is made of the throttle.

It should be noted that at the lower road speeds, two-stroke engines pull somewhat better on three-quarter throttle rather than full throttle. Therefore if power declines when near the crest of a hill on full throttle, it is sometimes possible to coax the machine over the remaining portion by slightly closing the throttle. But change down immediately if there is any tendency to labour. On Model RE it is best to change down from top to second at 20–25 m.p.h., and from second to first at 10–12 m.p.h.

To Obtain " Neutral." Where a neutralizing lever (Fig. 5) is fitted (i.e. on 1946 and later four-stroke models), to obtain "neutral," the following simple procedure is necessary. Disengage the clutch with the machine in motion and then depress the neutralizing lever with the right foot to its *full extent*. The above is applicable to obtaining "neutral" from all gears except first (bottom) gear. To obtain "neutral" from bottom gear you must engage second gear before disengaging the clutch and fully depressing the neutralizing lever.

Where a neutralizing lever is not fitted, it is necessary in order to obtain "neutral" from first or second gear to declutch and move the foot gear-change pedal down or up *half* the amount necessary to engage the next gear. If hand control is fitted, declutch and move the gear-change lever into the "neutral" notch of the quadrant. Before engaging "neutral" the throttle should, of course, be nearly closed to prevent the engine racing.

Stopping the Machine. To bring a Royal Enfield to a normal stop on the road, close back the throttle twist-grip completely, progressively and simultaneously apply *both* brakes, and before coming to a standstill disengage the clutch and obtain "neutral" (see previous paragraph).

On machines having no carburettor throttle stop provided (e.g. Model RE two-stroke) or on machines where a throttle stop is provided but is set to allow the throttle to close completely, it is necessary when making a temporary halt in traffic to open the throttle slightly before disengaging the clutch. This will prevent the engine stalling.

When slowing up prior to coming to a standstill, always make a habit of applying the front and rear brakes together, as this reduces the tendency for skidding and also minimizes and equalizes the wear of the brake shoe linings. Never indulge in the truly pernicious habit of using the clutch or exhaust valve lifter for slowing up!

For controlling speed, learn to "drive on the throttle" and use the brakes as infrequently and lightly as possible. Reserve their full use for steep hills and "jaywalking" dogs and pedestrians. In connection with hills, it should be noted that closing the throttle and opening the air lever wide acts as a powerful brake which can be supplemented by the internal expanding brakes.

Controlling speed by "driving on the throttle" saves both tyres and transmission. Only poor quality riders keep "jumping on the brakes" and such riders get unnecessary repair bills and frayed nerves also.

Stopping the Engine. Amal carburettors provided on Royal Enfields (excluding Model RE) have a throttle stop designed and (usually) adjusted to enable the engine to idle when the throttle twist-grip is turned right back. To stop the engine after stopping the machine it is necessary (unless the throttle stop is adjusted to close the throttle completely) to raise the exhaust valve lifter. However, in the case of the earlier 250 c.c. four-stroke models and on the two-stroke machines, there is no exhaust valve lifter.

To stop a 250 c.c. four-stroke engine (minus exhaust valve lifter) switch off the ignition where coil ignition is fitted; if "Magdyno" ignition is specified on a 250 c.c. engine, close the throttle completely (with the throttle stop set to give complete closing), or alternatively stop the engine by fully retarding the ignition and opening the throttle suddenly. On Model RE two-stroke (minus throttle stop), close the throttle completely, or on Model A two-stroke (with throttle stop) switch off the ignition. On Model A it is desirable to set the throttle stop so that the throttle closes completely, thereby preventing a tendency for erratic running when travelling fast downhill.

Parking the Machine. To prevent loss by theft, park the machine in an authorized car park, or else place it in a position where an eye can be kept on it, or padlock it. If the machine is left by the kerbside after dark, turn the lighting switch on a "Magdyno" model to the "L" or "LOW" position, as the pilot bulb consumes less current than the double-filament main bulb. With a Miller coil ignition model, turn the switch to the "PK" position. This switches on the parking lights and also switches off the ignition. On Model RE two-stroke, move the switch over to the extreme left to illuminate the parking lights (see page 91).

When parking a four-stroke coil ignition machine or a Model A two-stroke, be sure to switch off the ignition by means of the ignition switch in the centre of the lighting switch, otherwise the battery will discharge through the contact-breaker if the contacts happen to be closed. The warning lamp will show *red* if the ignition has accidentally been left on after stopping the engine other than by means of the ignition switch.

If it is intended to park a two-stroke machine for several hours in cold weather, it is advisable to turn off the petrol tap and then run the engine up until the contents of the float chamber are exhausted. This will prevent oil accumulating in the jets (one on Model RE) of the carburettor and possibly choking them.

It is a good plan to turn off the fuel tap a short distance before the end of each run. This undoubtedly facilitates starting up.

The petrol evaporates in the float chamber and causes the petroil mixture contained therein to become somewhat "heavy" for starting if the above precaution is not taken. It is, of course, not essential to do this.

Running-in (All Four-stroke Engines). If you are the lucky owner of a brand new shining Royal Enfield or have a second-hand machine with reconditioned engine, go very steady for about the first 500 miles. By doing so you will obtain the maximum life from your engine, plus a performance which will increase with the mileage. Neglect to run-in your engine carefully during the first 500 miles may *permanently* spoil its efficiency.

The essence of proper running-in is *progressively* to increase the work imposed on the engine, and to keep the piston as cool as possible by avoiding excessive throttle openings for excessive periods.

To reduce the risk of piston seizure during the vital running-in period and to enable close limits to be used (to prevent piston "slap"), the piston on Royal Enfield machines is formed slightly oval. But this ovality in no way absolves you from the onus of careful running-in. During running-in, observe the following points—

1. Pay special attention to correct lubrication (see Chapter IV).
2. Do not permit the engine to idle with the machine stationary for more than a minute or two.
3. See that the engine does not labour on hills. Change to a lower gear in good time (see page 12).
4. Avoid running the engine too fast in the lower gears.
5. After covering several hundred miles* (when some bedding-down occurs), check the adjustments of the tappets, contact-breaker, and the brakes, and clutch (see appropriate paragraphs of Chapter VII).
6. Do not exceed 30 m.p.h. (25 m.p.h. on 250 c.c. S.V. machines) during the first 200 miles.
7. Avoid using more than *half* throttle until 500 miles have been covered.
8. After covering 500 miles it is advisable to facilitate the bedding-down of the piston thrust faces by undertaking *short* speed bursts. Increase their duration *progressively* until the engine begins to thrive on larger throttle openings, but use discretion throughout.
9. After running-in is completed it is permissible to step up the throttle openings gradually, but avoid using full throttle on the level or uphill until you have ridden for about 1000 miles.

* A free service scheme is now available for owners of new machines bought in the U.K.

Running-in (Two-stroke Engines). Two-stroke engines, like four-stroke engines, must be properly run-in, but they are somewhat less likely to overheat due to smaller capacity, the use of petroil lubrication, and the fact that the firing impulses are more even. The following points should be observed during the running-in period of 200-300 miles.

1. See that the petroil mixture is correct, and mix slightly

Fig. 6. A Fast Twin-port Job—The 499 C.C. O.H.V. Model J2

This well equipped machine has acceleration and maximum speed appreciably greater than those of Model G

more engine oil with the petrol during the running-in period (see page 61).

2. Do not exceed 30 m.p.h. in top gear.
3. Do not exceed 20 m.p.h. in second gear.
4. Do not exceed 10 m.p.h. in first (bottom) gear.
5. See that the engine does not labour, and make full use of the gearbox.
6. After covering 200 miles it is permissible to step up the speed gradually.

Colloidal Graphite for Running-in. During the running-in of a four-stroke engine it is beneficial to mix Acheson's Colloidal Graphite with the engine oil in the proportions of *one pint* to one gallon of oil. This makes for cooler running and protects the bearing surfaces from metal pick-up. It is also beneficial to the valves. It is possible to obtain the compound from most large garages.

If the Piston Seizes. Should there be the slightest tendency for the piston to seize during the running-in period or subsequently, it is important to take *immediate* action. If too much throttle has been given for too long and the engine begins to slow up due to incipient seizure, declutch instantly, close the throttle, and allow the engine to cool down for several minutes. If this action is taken, it is unlikely that damage will occur, and the piston should free itself automatically.

If an actual seizure does occur, remove the piston and have

Fig. 7. A Spring Frame Sports Model of New Design—The 346 C.C. "Bullet" (Standard)
Introduced in 1949, this mount is obtainable to standard or trials specification

it closely inspected by a competent mechanic. It may be necessary for him to ease down some "high spots" and to eradicate any slight smearing of the piston surface in the vicinity of the piston ring lands. Do not attempt this work yourself unless highly skilled, otherwise the last state of the piston may be worse than the first.

General Driving Hints. Always drive with due consideration for all other road users and conform with the law both in letter and spirit. Avoid excessive noise, and ride in a state of constantly expecting the unexpected. Selfishness, carelessness, or lack of road sense by one or more of the parties concerned are the causes of most accidents. The great majority of accidents *could* be avoided by the use of ordinary common sense and by observance of the advice given in the Highway Code. Considerations of space do not permit the author delving into legal matters or driving tactics.

CHAPTER II
OBTAINING GOOD CARBURATION

THIS chapter deals with the working, tuning, and maintenance of the different types of carburettors fitted to 1937 and later Royal Enfield machines.

Types of Carburettor Fitted. Three types of Amal instruments have been fitted, and an understanding of their functioning is necessary in order to tune them intelligently. The three types are—
 1. Two-lever needle-jet type (fitted to all machines except where carburettors (2) and (3), below, are specified).
 2. Two-lever non-needle jet type (1937–9 Models A and T).
 3. Single-lever needle-jet type (fitted to the 1946–50 Model RE two-stroke).

It should be observed that the war-time version of Model RE (i.e. the "Flying Flea") supplied to the Airborne Forces was fitted with a Villiers single-lever needle-jet carburettor. In view of the fact that a considerable number of Model WD/RE two-strokes, originally supplied to the Forces, are now in civilian hands after being reconditioned, it has been thought desirable to deal with the Villiers (type 3/2) carburettor in addition to the three above-mentioned Amal carburettors fitted to all other models.

TWO-LEVER NEEDLE-JET AMAL

Details of Instrument. The following description should enable the reader to comprehend its working. Referring to Fig. 8, A is the carburettor body or mixing chamber, the upper part of which has a throttle valve B, with taper needle C attached by the needle clip. The throttle valve regulates the quantity of mixture supplied to the engine. Passing through the throttle valve is the air valve D, independently operated, and serving the purpose of obstructing the main air passage for starting and mixture control.

Secured to the underside of the mixing chamber by the union nut E is the jet block F, and interposed between them is a fibre washer to ensure a petrol-tight joint. On the upper part of the jet block is the jet block barrel H, forming a clear through-way. Integral with the jet block is the pilot jet J, supplied through the passage K. The adjustable pilot air passage communicates with a chamber from which issues the pilot outlet M and by-pass N.

An adjusting screw (TS, Fig. 8A) is provided on the mixing chamber, by which the position of the throttle valve for tick-over

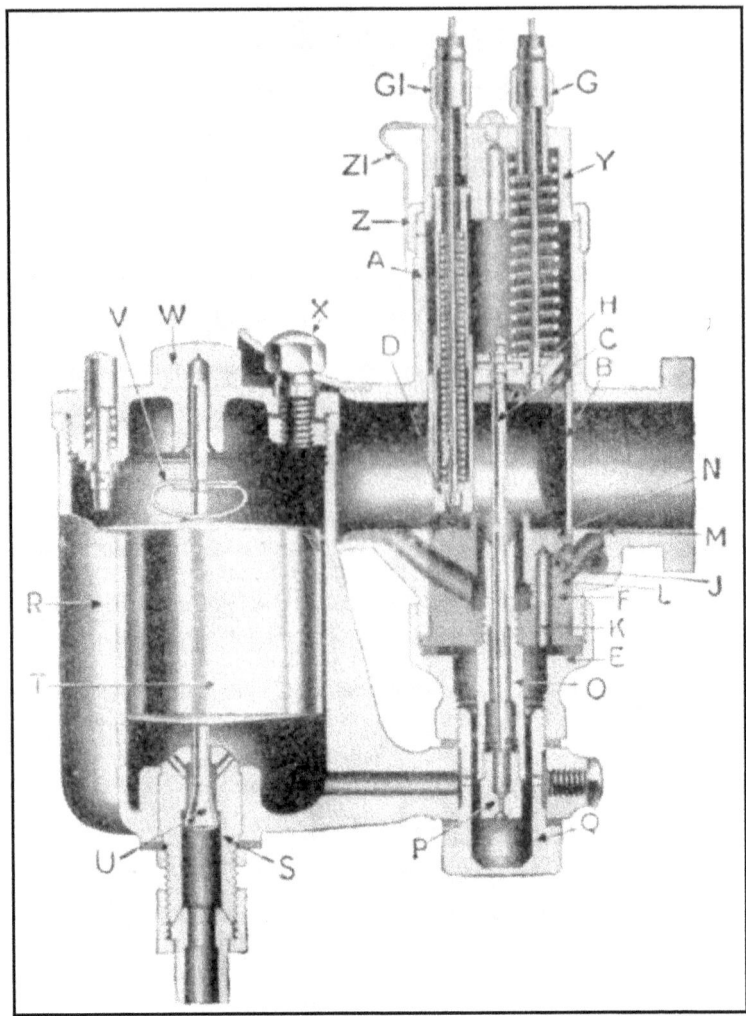

FIG. 8. SECTIONAL VIEW OF TWO-LEVER NEEDLE JET AMAL CARBURETTOR

KEY TO FIG. 7

A = Mixing chamber
B = Throttle valve
C = Jet needle and clip
D = Air valve
E = Mixing chamber union nut
F = Jet block
G = Cable adjuster for throttle valve
G1 = Cable adjuster for air valve
H = Jet block barrel
J = Pilot jet
K = Passage to pilot jet
L = Pilot air passage
M = Pilot outlet
N = Pilot by-pass
O = Needle jet
P = Main jet
Q = Jet plug
R = Float chamber
S = Connexion for float chamber
T = Float
U = Float needle
V = Float needle bow clip
W = Float chamber cover
X = Float chamber lock screw
Y = Mixing chamber cap
Z = Lock ring for above
Z1 = Locking spring

OBTAINING GOOD CARBURATION

is regulated independently of cable adjustment G. The needle jet O is screwed in the underside of the jet block, and carries at its bottom end the main jet P. Both these jets are removable when the jet plug Q, which bolts the mixing chamber and the float chamber together, is removed. The float chamber R, which has bottom feed, consists of a cup, fed with petrol through connection S, containing a float T, and the needle valve U attached by the clip V. The float chamber cover has a lock-screw X for security.

How it Works. With petrol tap on, petrol will flow past the needle valve U until the quantity of petrol in the chamber R is sufficient to raise the float T, when the needle valve U will prevent a further supply entering the float chamber until some in the chamber has already been used up by the engine. The float chamber having been filled to its correct level, the fuel passes along the passages through diagonal holes in the jet plug Q, when it will be in communication with the main jet P and the pilot feed hole K; the level in these being, obviously, the same as that maintained in the float chamber.

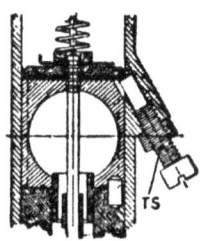

FIG. 8A. AMAL THROTTLE STOP

Imagine the throttle valve B very slightly open. As the piston descends, a partial vacuum is created in the carburettor, causing a rush of air through the pilot air hole L, and drawing fuel from the pilot jet J. The mixture of air and fuel is admitted to the engine through the pilot outlet M. The quantity of mixture capable of being passed by the pilot outlet M is insufficient to run the engine; this mixture also carries excess of fuel. Consequently, before a combustible mixture is admitted, throttle valve B must be slightly raised, admitting a further supply of air from the main air-intake. The farther the throttle valve is opened, the less will be the depression on the outlet M, but, in turn, a higher depression will be created on the by-pass N, and the pilot mixture will flow from this passage as well as from the outlet M. As the throttle valve is farther opened the fuel passes the main jet P, and this jet governs the mixture strength from three-quarter to full throttle. For intermediate throttle positions, the jet needle C working in the needle jet O is the governing factor. The farther the throttle valve is lifted, the greater the quantity of air admitted to the engine, and a suitable graduation of fuel supply is maintained by means of the taper needle. The air valve D, which is cable-operated on the two-lever carburettor, has the effect of obstructing the main through-way, and, in consequence, increasing the depression on the main jet, enriching the mixture. The cable for the air valve, like that for the throttle valve, has an adjuster which is shown at *GI* in Fig. 8.

Is Mixture Correct? When the mixture is correct, maximum all-round performance is obtained, carbon formation is slow, the exhaust note is crisp, and its smell inoffensive. The flame at the open exhaust port is small and *whitish-blue* in colour.

An over-rich mixture gives a *yellowish* flame at the exhaust port and there is generally considerable black smoke. Power output may be good but fuel consumption is high and carbon formation rapid. Other likely symptoms of an over-rich mixture are a tendency for eight-stroking, some overheating, heavy and

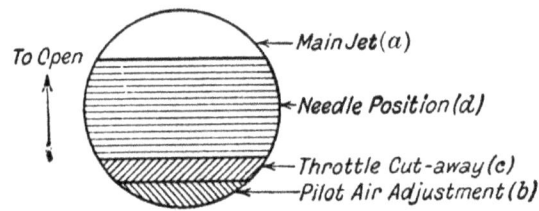

FIG. 9. RANGE AND SEQUENCE OF ADJUSTMENTS—AMAL TWO-LEVER NEEDLE-JET CARBURETTOR

lumpy running, and a tendency for petrol to spray from the carburettor and for the sparking plug to get dirty. If the air lever is closed slightly, the engine may choke.

An excessively weak mixture gives a *light-blue* flame at the exhaust port, poor acceleration, indifferent power output, bad slow-running, a tendency to misfire or eight-stroke, and often severe overheating, "knocking," and spitting-back at the carburettor. A generally sluggish performance may be observed to improve by closing the air lever slightly. From the above summary of undesirable symptoms, the importance of running on a correct mixture (especially these days) needs no emphasis.

Tuning Two-lever Needle-jet Carburettor. Should the setting not give entire satisfaction for particular requirements, there are four separate ways of rectifying matters as given herewith, and the adjustment should be made in this order: (*a*) Main jet (three-quarters to full throttle); (*b*) Pilot air adjustment (closed to one-eighth throttle); (*c*) Throttle valve cut-away on the air-intake side (one-eighth to one-quarter throttle); (*d*) Needle position (one-quarter to three-quarters throttle). The diagram (Fig. 9) clearly indicates the part of the throttle range over which each adjustment is effective. Do not alter the carburettor setting without good reason.

OBTAINING GOOD CARBURATION

(*a*) **Main Jet.** This controls the fuel supply when the throttle is more than three-quarter open, but at smaller throttle openings, though the fuel supply passes through the main jet, the quantity is decreased by the metering effect of the needle in the needle jet. All jets are numbered after exact calibration, so that the number of a jet is precise identification as regards discharge. The higher the number, the greater is the discharge. On no account should a jet be reamed oversize if its orifice is too small. Always obtain a new jet of the correct size (and of Amal manufacture) To remove the main jet, remove the jet plug Q (Fig. 8) and unscrew (with an Amal jet key) the main jet from the needle jet, holding the latter with a spanner if the jet is tight.

(*b*) **Pilot Air Adjustment Screw.** The small adjusting screw at the base of the mixing chamber controls the mixture strength for idling and for initial throttle openings. By metering the quantity of air mixing with the fuel, it regulates the suction imposed on the pilot jet.

(*c*) **Throttle Valve Cut-away.** To influence the depression on the main fuel supply, the atmospheric side of the throttle valve is cut-away. This provides a means of tuning between the pilot and needle jet range of throttle opening. A number marked on the throttle indicates the amount of cut-away. For instance, 6/3 indicates a type 6 throttle valve with No. 3 cut-away. By fitting a throttle valve with smaller or greater cut-away, the mixture is enriched or weakened respectively.

(*d*) **Needle Position and Needle Jet.** The needle attached to the throttle valve is tapered and therefore permits more or less fuel to pass through the needle jet according to whether the throttle valve is raised or lowered, throughout the range of

CARBURETTOR SETTINGS FOR 1946-9 FOUR-STROKES

Enfield Model (c.c.)	Date of Model	Main Jet Size	Throttle Valve	Needle Position
CO* (346)	1946	130	6/4	2
G (346)	1946-9	130	6/4	3
J* (499)	1946-8	140	6/4	3
J2* (499)	1947-9	170	6/4	2

* These three machines have been produced in considerable quantity for export purposes. Model CO is the civilian version of the 1941-5 military machine, Model WD/CO. On the 1948 Model J fit a 150 main jet.

throttle opening, except at nearly full throttle or during tickover. A standard size needle jet is fitted, and this should not be changed unless *alcohol* fuels are used.

It is possible to adjust the position of the taper needle relatively to the throttle opening by securing it to the throttle valve with the needle clip spring in a certain groove, of which there are several. The effect of lowering or raising the needle is to weaken or enrich the mixture at throttle openings from $\frac{1}{4}$ to $\frac{3}{4}$ full throttle. Heavy fuel consumption on a machine used for a long time may often be remedied by altering the needle position (see page 27) or renewing the needle and jet.

(*e*) **Throttle Stop Screw.** But for this little screw there might be the deuce of a job in keeping the engine running in traffic halts. Adjust it so that it props up the throttle valve when the throttle twist-grip is shut right off.

(*f*) **Air Valve.** Normally this must always be kept wide open. Close it for starting and slightly close it when the engine is running cold.

Tuning Sequence. The two-lever needle-jet Amal carburettor (see Fig. 8) should be tuned as described below in that order. It is best while tuning to select a quiet road with a slight up gradient, so as to impose a slight load when testing. Reference should be made to Fig. 10 when reading the tuning instructions.

1st—Main Jet (with Throttle in 1st Position). Test the engine for full throttle; if when at full throttle the power seems better *with the throttle less than wide open* or with the air valve closed slightly, the main jet is too small. If the engine runs "heavily," the main jet is too large. If testing for speed work, note that the jet size is rich enough to keep the engine cool, and to verify this examine the sparking plug by taking a fast run, declutching, and stopping the engine quickly. If the plug body at the end has a bright black appearance, the mixture is correct; if sooty, the mixture is rich; or if a dry grey colour, the mixture is too weak and a larger size jet is necessary.

2nd—Pilot Jet (with Throttle in 2nd and 5th Positions). With the engine idling too fast with the twist-grip shut off and the throttle slide shut down on to the throttle stop screw, and the ignition set for best slow running: (1) Loosen the throttle stop screw nut and screw down until the engine runs slower and begins to falter; then screw the pilot air adjustment screw in or out to make the engine run regularly and faster. (2) Now gently lower the throttle

OBTAINING GOOD CARBURATION

stop screw until the engine runs slower and just begins to falter. Then lock the nut lightly and begin again to adjust the pilot air screw to obtain the best slow running; if this second adjustment makes the engine run too fast, go over the adjustment again a third time. Finally, lock up tight the throttle stop screw nut without disturbing the position of the screw.

3rd—Throttle Cut-away (with Throttle in 3rd Position). If, as you move off from the idling position, there is objectionable spitting from the carburettor, slightly enrich the pilot mixture by

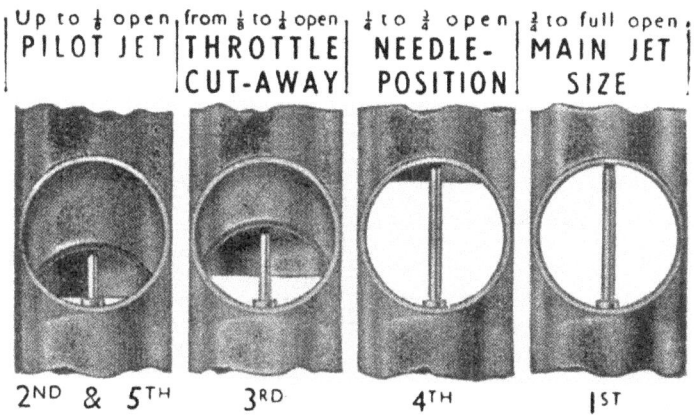

FIG. 10. PHASES OF AMAL TWO-LEVER NEEDLE-JET CARBURETTOR THROTTLE OPENINGS

screwing the air screw in about half a turn, but if this is not effective, screw it back again and fit a throttle with a smaller cut-away. If the engine jerks under load at this throttle position and there is no spitting, either the throttle needle is too high or a larger throttle cut-away is required to cure the richness.

4th—Needle Position (with Throttle in 4th Position). The needle controls a wide range of throttle opening and also the acceleration. Try the needle in as low a position as possible, viz. with the clip in a groove as near the end as possible; if acceleration is poor, and with the air lever partially closed the results are better, raise the needle by two grooves; if very much better, try lowering the needle by one groove and leave it in the best position.

NOTE. If the mixture is still too rich with the clip in groove No. 1 nearest the end—the *needle jet* probably wants replacement because of wear. The needle itself never wears out.

5th—Final. Check over the idling again for final touches until a perfect tick-over is obtained.

CARBURETTOR SETTINGS FOR 1937–49 TWO-STROKES

Enfield Model (c.c.)	Date of Model	Main Jet Size	Pilot Jet	Jet Needle
A (225)	1937–9	70	25 or 30	—
RE (125)	1945–9	90	—	Position 3
WD/RE* (125)	1939–45	1	—	Taper: $2\frac{1}{2}\%$

* This is the machine supplied to the Airborne Forces during the war and known as the "Flying Flea." It has a Villiers carburettor, unlike all other Royal Enfields, which have Amal carburettors fitted.

CARBURETTOR SETTINGS FOR 1937–45 FOUR-STROKES*

Enfield Model (c.c.)	Date of Model	Main Jet Size	Throttle Valve	Needle Position
D (248)	1939	75	4/5	3
DC (346)	1939	85	4/5	3
G (346)	1937–8	150	6/4	3
G2 (346)	1937	170	6/3	3
H (570)	1937	120	5/5	3
H, HM (570)	1938–9	140	6/3	3
L (570)	1937–9	140	6/3	3
J, JM (499)	1937–8	140	6/3	3
J2 (499)	1937	140	6/3	3
JF "500 Bullet"	1937–8	200	29/4	2
J2 "500 Bullet"	1938–9	200	29/4	2
J2 "500 Bullet"	1938	170	6/4	2
J2 "500 Bullet"	1939–40	150	6/4	2
"250 Bullet"	1937–8	120	5/4	3
"350 Bullet"	1937–8	170	6/4	3
G "350 Bullet"	1939	140	6/4	3
K, KX (1140)	1937–9	140	6/4	3
B, BM (248)	1937–8	75	4/5	3
C (346)	1937–9	85	4/5	3
BCO, CO, CM (346)	1938–9	85	4/4	2
S, SM, S2 (248)	1937–9	75	4/4	2
SF (248)	1939	75	4/4	2
T, TM (148)	1937–9	55	3 Std.	p. 15
WD (248)	1939–40	75	4/5	3
WD/C (346)	1939–41	85	4/5	3
WD/CO (346)	1941–5	130	6/4	3

* Models DC and BCO were made for the export market and correspond to Models D and CO respectively. Four-valve cylinder heads are fitted to the 1937–8 JF and 1938–9 J2 "500 Bullets." A box-type air cleaner is fitted to the carburettor on the 1939 Models L, J2, and G "350 Bullet" (see text on page 40). Models WD, WD/C, WD/CO are military models, many of which have been made available to the public since 1945, either unused or reconditioned.

Note Regarding Needle Position. It should be observed that all references in the text and accompanying carburettor settings regarding the needle position (e.g. No. 3) apply to the needle groove in which the spring clip is fitted counting *from the top of the needle*.

Excessive Petrol Consumption. Should the engine lap up fuel to an excessive extent, bear in mind the adverse effect of binding brakes, incorrect tappet adjustment, dry or excessively tight transmission chains, a slipping clutch, etc. Also look for any petrol leakage from the petrol tank, tap, and float chamber. A badly carbonized engine will also raise the petrol consumption.

If there are none of the above fairly obvious defects, check the slow-running adjustment and try the effect of lowering the jet needle in the needle-jet *one notch*. Do not endeavour to economize by reducing the size of the main jet below the recommended size. This jet takes effect only when the machine is being ridden at more than half full throttle.

Maintenance of Two-lever Needle-jet Carburettor. Periodical cleaning is necessary to maintain efficient functioning of the carburettor, and should be carried out in the following sequence.

Disconnect petrol pipe. Unscrew the jet plug Q (Fig. 8) and remove float chamber complete. With box or set spanner, slacken the mixing chamber union nut E. Mixing chamber complete may now be removed from engine, either by unscrewing the clip pin (on early models) or the bolts (if flange fitting). Unscrew mixing chamber lock ring Z, after releasing the locking spring Z1, and remove the mixing chamber cap Y. Then withdraw the throttle valve B, jet needle C, and air valve D. Remove main jet P and needle jet O. Mixing chamber union nut E may then be removed and jet block pushed out. If this is obstinate, tap gently, using a wooden stump inside the mixing chamber. Unscrew float chamber cover W and slacken lock screw X. Withdraw the float by pinching the clip V inwards, and at the same time pull gently upwards.

Generally it is sufficient to wash all the parts in clean petrol, but if the carburettor has had extended service, check the following.

(*a*) FLOAT CHAMBER NEEDLE U. If a distinct shoulder is visible on the point of seating, renew needle as soon as convenient.

(*b*) THROTTLE VALVE. Test in mixing chamber, and if excessive play is present it is advisable to renew valve without delay.

(*c*) THROTTLE NEEDLE CLIP. This part must securely grip needle. *Free rotation must not take place*, otherwise the needle groove will become worn and necessitate a new part being fitted. *Be sure to refit the clip in the same groove.*

(*d*) JET BLOCK *F*. If trouble has been experienced with erratic "idling," ascertain by means of a fine bristle that the pilot jet *J* is clear, and that the pilot outlet *M* in the mixing chamber *A* is unobstructed.

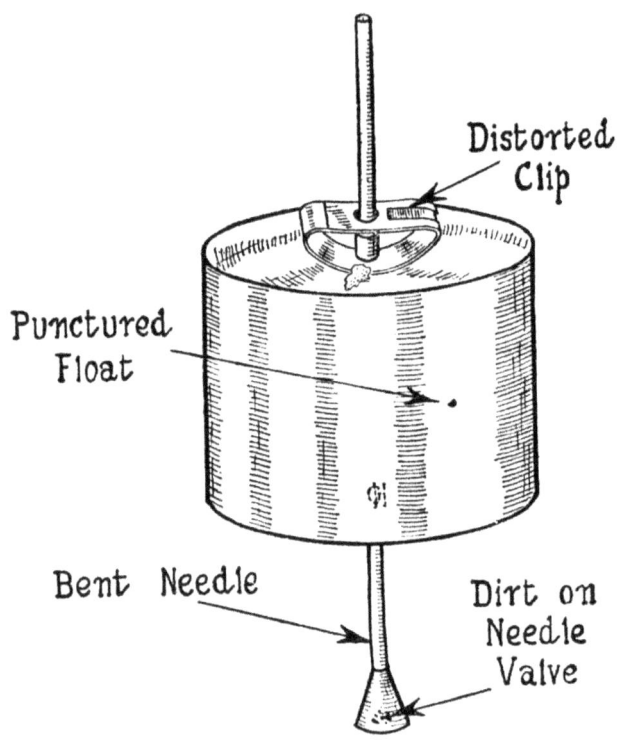

FIG. 11. CAUSES OF "FLOODING" (STICKING "TICKLER" ALSO POSSIBLE)

To Reassemble. Refit jet block *F* with washer on underside, and screw on lightly mixing chamber union nut *E*. Screw in needle jet *O* and main jet *P*. Open air lever $\frac{7}{8}$ in., the twist-grip half-way; grasp the air valve *D* between the thumb and the finger; *make sure that the needle enters the centre hole in the adaptor top.* Slightly twist the throttle valve *B* until it enters the adaptor guide, when on pushing down the valves the air valve should enter its guide. If not, slightly move the mixing chamber cap *Y*, when the air valve will slide into place. Screw on mixing chamber lock ring *Z*. *No brute force is necessary.* Afterwards secure with the locking spring *Z1*. Check that the throttle and air valves close freely.

Attach carburettor to the cylinder head, pushing right home; first examine washer if flange fitting. Refit float T and needle U, holding the needle head against its seating by means of a pencil until the float and the bow clip V are slipped into position. Make sure that the clip enters the groove provided. Screw on the float chamber cover W tightly and lock in position by means of the lock screw X. Fit the jet plug Q in float chamber with one washer above and one below the lug. Screw the jet plug into mixing chamber and lock securely. Clean petrol pipe and filter if fitted.

TWO-LEVER NON-NEEDLE AMAL

How it Works. With the petrol tap turned on (see Fig. 12) petrol will flow past the needle valve P until the quantity of petrol in the float chamber G is sufficient to raise the float O, when the needle valve P will prevent a further supply entering the float chamber. The action of the float can readily be understood, for, as the quantity of fuel in the float chamber is used, the float O will drop, carrying with it the needle P, and admitting a further supply. Thus, automatically, the petrol level is kept constant. In connection with the float chamber, it must be clearly understood that any alteration to the standard level can only have detrimental results.

The float chamber having filled to its correct level, the fuel passes along the passages through the diagonal holes in the jet plug H, when it will be in communication with the main jet D and the pilot jet C, the level in these jets being, obviously, the same as that maintained in the float chamber.

Imagine the throttle valve K very slightly open. As the piston descends, a partial vacuum is created in the carburettor, causing a rush of air through the through-way A, and drawing fuel from the pilot jet C. The pilot jet, being situated immediately beneath the base of the throttle valve, is subjected to a heavy depression, so as to obtain the necessary mixture for "idling" and small loads.

In the case of the main jet D, which is the longer of the two, and situated near the carburettor air intake, at small throttle openings it is inoperative, and the mixture is governed entirely by the size of the pilot jet C.

The throttle K being almost closed, it will be seen that the pilot jet C is situated in an extremely restricted area. In consequence, the passage of the air from the main through-way will be restricted, and at the same time a high depression will exist on the pilot C. At this position of the throttle, it will readily be seen that not only is the main jet D shrouded by the throttle valve, but also the area of the mixing chamber in which it is housed is infinitely bigger than the area of the through-way exposed to the suction of the engine, in consequence of which no fuel is drawn from the main jet.

As the throttle valve K is raised, the area immediately above the pilot jet C is increased, and in consequence the suction or

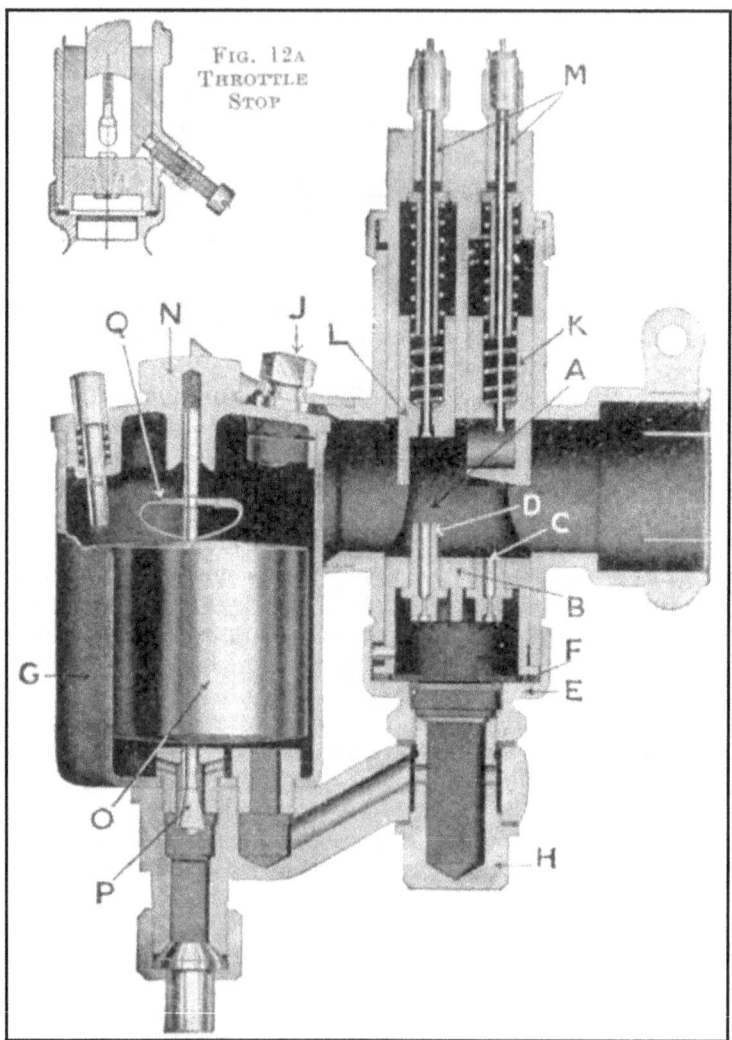

Fig. 12. Sectional View of Amal Two-lever Non-needle Carburettor
(*Amal, Ltd.*)

depression on this jet diminishes, and at the same time increases on the main jet, so a balance between the two jets is obtained throughout the whole range.

OBTAINING GOOD CARBURATION

Tuning Non-needle Carburettor. There are three ways in which the quality of the mixture can be varied, and these are given hereunder in the order in which the adjustments should be made.

(a) Main jet (affects the mixture from $\frac{5}{8}$ to full throttle).
(b) Pilot jet (affects the mixture from closed to $\frac{1}{4}$ throttle).
(c) Throttle valve cut-away (affects mixture from $\frac{1}{4}$ to $\frac{5}{8}$ throttle).

The diagram shown in Fig. 13 clearly indicates the part of the throttle range over which each adjustment is effective.

(a) *Main Jet.* Fit the smallest size main jet which gives maximum speed. For touring conditions I advise this to be obtained with the air lever three-quarter open.

(b) *Pilot Jet.* This affects "slow running" and slow pulling

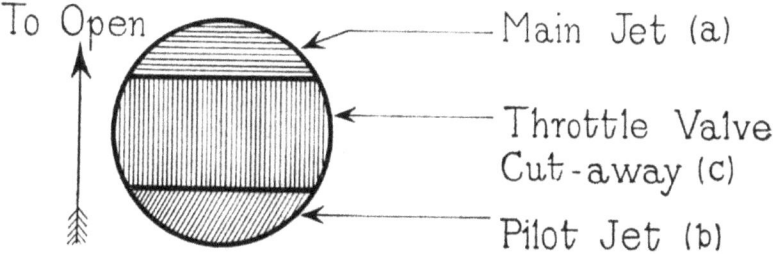

FIG. 13. RANGE AND SEQUENCE OF ADJUSTMENTS—AMAL NON-NEEDLE CARBURETTOR.

only, and the smallest size should be selected which gives the best "idling." At the same time, care must be taken not to reduce the size of the pilot jet unduly, otherwise difficulty will be experienced in obtaining a correct blend with the main jet.

Blend of Main and Pilot. If any trouble is experienced due to a weak spot between the pilot and main jet, it can usually be cured by increasing the pilot jet one size.

(c) *Throttle Valve Cut-away.* Richness at $\frac{3}{8}$ to $\frac{5}{8}$ throttle can be rectified by fitting a "cut-away" throttle valve. The standard cut-aways are from O, which is flat bottom, to No. 5, which is cut away $\frac{5}{16}$ in.

Starting Up. With a *cold engine*, depress the carburettor tickler, close air valve, open throttle about one-eighth, ignition about three-quarter advanced, when, if the ignition system is in good order, no difficulty should be experienced in obtaining an "easy start." With a *warm engine* it is unnecessary to flood carburettor, but the air lever should be closed. If the float chamber is unduly flooded, excessive richness of mixture will prevent the engine starting. Open throttle fully and revolve the engine smartly until excess of fuel is exhausted; then proceed as before, without again flooding.

Maintenance of Amal Non-needle Carburettor. To keep the carburettor in thoroughly efficient working order it is important to clean it occasionally, as various impurities find their way into the instrument. The best method of cleaning the carburettor and one which the author always adopts is to strip it right down and clean the various parts in petrol. Should any parts appear worn they should be renewed at once, otherwise it is foolish to expect perfect carburation. For instance, renew the needle valve of the float chamber if a distinct ridge is present on the head where it seats; similarly replace the throttle valve if much side play is present; again fit a new mixing chamber union nut if there is any suspicion of this being in any way worn or damaged. Before reassembling clean the filter situated beneath the jets and when reassembling avoid using any brute force to tighten any nuts. Ascertain that the needle enters the top of the float chamber lid easily, that the mixing chamber is quite vertical and pushed tight home, that the washer on flange fitting instruments is in sound condition and that the jets are properly fitted.

When Ordering Spares. Always quote the number which is stamped on the side of the mixing chamber. This will ensure the correct part being sent and will obviate much bother on both the part of the rider and the manufacturer.

SINGLE-LEVER NEEDLE-JET AMAL

This Amal carburettor which has a choke bore of $\frac{11}{16}$ in. (indicated at F in Fig. 14) is specially designed for small-capacity engines, and the throttle controls the mixture automatically according to the engine speed. A sectional view of the instrument is shown in Fig. 14. The carburettor fitted to Model RE incorporates an air filter and strangler (not illustrated).

How It Works. Referring to Fig. 14, on turning on the fuel tap, fuel enters the float chamber (23) through the top of the cover (9) to which the feed pipe is connected by means of the union nut (8). The float E, the attached needle I, and the needle seat A maintain a constant level of fuel in the float chamber. Fuel flows at this level to the main jet (21) and the needle jet (18) via the feed passage D. The passage C enables any trapped air to escape into the top of the float chamber whose cover has an air-vent hole B. A drain hole is provided at G on the side of the mixing chamber so as to liberate any excess fuel caused by "flooding."

OBTAINING GOOD CARBURATION

For normal running the main jet (21) feeds the engine through the needle jet (18). The taper on the needle (19) passing through the needle jet regulates the mixture at the smaller throttle

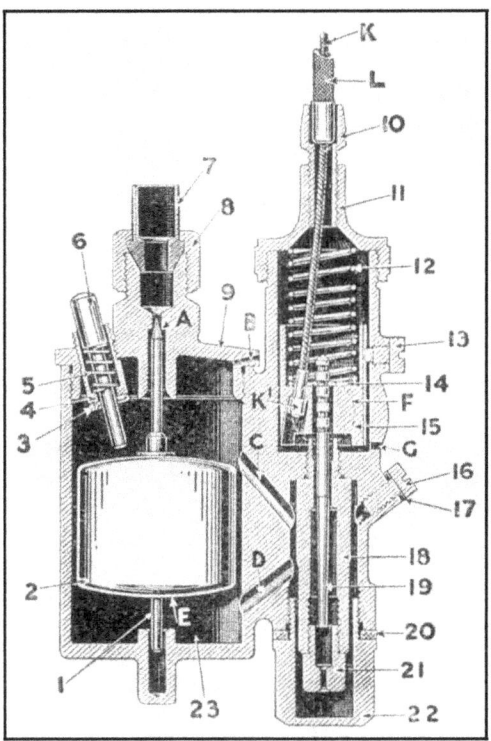

Fig. 14. Sectional View of Single-lever Needle-jet Amal Carburettor

(*Amal, Ltd.*)

 1 = Float needle
 2 = Float
 3 = Cotter for tickler
 4 = Bush for tickler
 5 = Tickler spring
 6 = Tickler
 7 = Feed pipe union nipple
 8 = Feed pipe union nut
 9 = Float chamber cover
10 = Cable adjuster
11 = Mixing chamber cap
12 = Throttle return spring
13 = Throttle valve location screw
14 = Jet needle clip
15 = Throttle valve
16 = Feed hole screw
17 = Feed hole washer
18 = Needle jet
19 = Jet needle
20 = Washer for jet plug
21 = Main jet
22 = Jet plug
23 = Float chamber

openings, and varying the vertical position of the taper in the needle jet is the means whereby the mixture can be enriched or weakened at different throttle openings. The throttle valve (15) is operated by the control cable *K* and has a location screw engaging a vertical groove in the slide.

A circular spring clip (14), held down by the throttle spring (12), locates the needle (19) in the throttle valve (15). The particular groove in which the clip fits determines the vertical position of the taper needle in the needle jet.

The parallel portion of the jet needle (19) entering the bore of the needle jet (18) regulates the fuel supply for idling purposes. Obviously the difference between the two diameters is very small and only a small amount of fuel is permitted to pass. Owing to this restriction and the use of petroil lubrication, it is possible for slight gumming-up to occur occasionally. Opening the throttle quickly clears any obstruction of this kind.

Is Mixture Correct? Reduced pulling capacity accompanied by a proneness for the engine to cut out or "spit back" on turning up the twist-grip indicates that the mixture is *weak*. A tendency for high fuel consumption and excessive four-stroking, on the other hand, shows that the mixture is *over-rich*. It should be noted, however, that some degree of four-stroking is normal for any two-stroke engine when running on small throttle openings, also that the choking of the exhaust system can cause the engine to four-stroke when running fast on large throttle openings.

When riding a Model WD/RE or Model RE after starting up from cold, symptoms of a weak mixture are likely to be present for about the first 300 yards (farther in cold weather) due to the condensation of fuel in the crankcase. Subsequently there may be temporary symptoms of an over-rich mixture due to the vaporizing of the condensed fuel in the crankcase. It is therefore advisable when making a trial run, with a view to testing carburation, to observe the behaviour of the engine after three to five miles have been covered.

Excessive Fuel Consumption. Where excessive fuel consumption (considerably less than 100 m.p.g.) occurs, it is advisable before checking up on the carburettor setting to make sure that there are no leaks from the carburettor itself, the fuel pipe, tap, or the tank. Tell-tale oil smears caused by leaking petroil mixture should enable the source of leakage to be tracked down readily. If there are no leaks, inspect the strangler and see that it opens fully. Also verify that the air filter is not choked. This requires to be cleaned occasionally (see page 40).

Adjusting Jet Needle position. If the mixture is correct and the engine is running well, do not tamper with the carburettor setting advised by the makers. This setting is given on page 26, but it should be noted that position No. 3 specified for the jet needle in the needle jet (page 27) gives rather a rich mixture which

OBTAINING GOOD CARBURATION

is suited for running-in. After covering some 200 miles it is generally desirable to weaken the mixture by lowering the taper needle *one notch*. Fit the small spring clip in the second groove, counting from the top. To enrich the mixture, it is necessary to raise the jet needle.

Referring to Fig. 14, to adjust the position of the jet needle (19), unscrew the knurled cap (11) from the mixing chamber and withdraw the throttle valve (15) and jet needle (19) together. Next shut the twist-grip and push the throttle valve upwards in order to disconnect valve from the throttle cable and cable nipple $K1$. Now lift the jet needle (19) and the jet needle clip (14) out of the throttle valve; then spring the clip (14) off the jet needle and replace it one groove lower or higher, as required.

When assembling the jet needle (19) and the clip (14), make sure that the throttle cable K lies in the Vee in the clip and also that the throttle return spring (12) lies squarely on top of the clip in the throttle valve recess.

Tuning Single-lever Needle-jet Amal. Normally it should *not* be necessary to make any alteration to the carburettor setting other than to raise or lower the jet needle as described above, but should it be necessary for some reason to retune the instrument, do this in the following manner and sequence after first warming up the engine.

1. Main Jet Size. This takes effect from three-quarter to full throttle. Use the *smallest* size main jet which provides full power when running under load on the level. Each main jet is numbered (e.g. 90) and the bigger the number, the bigger is the jet. If the engine runs slightly better when the throttle is not quite fully open, the jet is all right for economy, but is slightly on the small side in other respects.

2. Needle Position. This affects mixture strength from one-quarter to three-quarter throttle, as used for general running. When the clip is in the extreme end groove (No. 1) of the jet needle, this provides the lowest needle position, giving the weakest mixture. Adjust the needle position as low as possible while maintaining good acceleration and running at half throttle. If "spitting" at the carburettor occurs when accelerating, try the effect of raising the needle one groove (see earlier paragraph).

3. Throttle Valve Cut-away. The slope or cut-away on the throttle valve takes effect when the engine is idling or running light, i.e. up to about a quarter throttle. The number of the cut-away (No. 5 is standard) is stamped on the base of the throttle valve. The bigger the cut-away (and its number), the weaker is the mixture for idling. If the engine tends to "spit" and fade out when idling and when running light, fit a throttle valve with a smaller cut-away. A larger cut-away is required if the engine runs heavily on a rich mixture.

If the throttle valve cut-away is altered, it may be necessary to alter the needle position once more. Where a smaller cut-away is used, the jet needle may require to be lowered one groove. Similarly if a larger cut-away is employed, raising of the needle one groove may subsequently be needed.

The Needle Jet. The standard size needle jet is not marked, but jets with other size bores are obtainable. These jets are appropriately marked for size. If the mixture is over-rich and this cannot be cured by using a larger cut-away or by lowering the jet needle, it is advisable to renew the needle jet, as the old one may have become worn.

If weakness of the mixture prevents good idling and this cannot be remedied by raising the needle position and using a smaller cut-away throttle valve, it is advisable to try the effect of fitting a larger bore needle jet.

Should the mixture become over-rich at *half* throttle on a machine which has done a big mileage, it is very probable that the diametrical size of the needle jet bore has increased. The remedy is, of course, to fit a new needle jet.

Note. On no account attempt to ream *any* Amal jet oversize or to clean it by inserting a wire through the bore. Always use suitable bristles or blow the jet clear. Jets are of comparatively soft metal, and can be very easily ruined.

Maintenance of Single-lever Needle-jet Amal. The following hints should be observed. Occasionally dismantle the carburettor and clean it thoroughly internally and externally. The float chamber should be given special attention. See that any impurities, liable to cause "flooding" are eradicated. Scrutinize the float and its needle. Make certain that the float is undamaged and has not been punctured. Shaking it will reveal by sound any fuel inside. See that the needle is not bent. The needle seating must be perfect and if it is not, rub the needle taper lightly on its seat by twisting the needle between the thumb and forefinger. On no account use any grinding paste. If close inspection of the needle taper reveals a deep circular groove, it may be necessary to renew the float and needle.

Verify that the float chamber tickler operates freely and springs back, also that the air vent hole in the float chamber cover is unobstructed. If elusive "flooding" has occured, detach the fuel pipe connection from the float chamber cover and thoroughly

OBTAINING GOOD CARBURATION

clean out all passages. Visually inspect the needle-jet for wear and bear in mind any tendency for excessive fuel consumption, also the mileage covered by the machine (see paragraph dealing with the needle-jet). Inspect the throttle valve for surface wear and slackness in the mixing chamber. Remember that a slack throttle valve is apt to cause wear of the needle-jet bore through needle movement. Clean the air filter (see page 40), and see that there are no obstructions anywhere in the air-intake.

When refitting the float chamber cover, check that the blunt end of the float needle is located in the guide hole at the base of the float chamber. Then guide the float chamber cover over the tapered end of the needle before screwing down the cover. Finally make quite sure that the carburettor is a good *push fit* on the induction stub. Push it home *fully* and quite true, using a screwing motion after smearing a little oil or vaseline on the induction stub. An air-tight fit is essential to prevent air leaks and a weak mixture. Tighten the carburettor securing clip firmly.

SINGLE-LEVER NEEDLE-JET VILLIERS

The carburettor fitted to Model WD/RE (supplied to the Airborne Forces during the war and subsequently resold in some numbers to the public) is a single-lever needle-jet type 3/2 Villiers. Constructional features of the carburettor and the air filter and strangler are clearly indicated in the exploded view of the complete carburettor shown in Fig. 15.

Is Mixture Correct? The advice given on page 34 for the single-lever needle-jet Amal carburettor applies also to the Villiers instrument, and should be carefully observed.

How to Adjust the Mixture. A carburettor adjustment is normally seldom required, but the mixture strength can if necessary be readily adjusted by altering the position of the taper needle shown at (4) in Fig. 15. Where an adjustment is necessary to correct an unsatisfactory mixture, the best needle position should be found by trial. In most instances a good mixture for all normal purposes is obtained by adjusting the needle position so that $2\frac{7}{16}$ in. of the needle protrudes from the bottom of the throttle valve. For the correct jet size, see table on page 26.

To adjust the needle position, first unscrew the knurled top ring (1) from the top of the mixing chamber (9). Next remove the throttle valve (6) and detach the top disc (2) from the throttle valve. Then to weaken or enrich the mixture, lower or raise respectively the position of the needle (4) in the throttle valve. Do this by adjusting the small screw (3) which screws into the throttle valve. It is best to turn the adjusting screw approximately *half a turn* clockwise or anti-clockwise to weaken or enrich the mixture and then to make a trial run to observe the effect. Repeat the adjustment if necessary until a good performance is obtained.

When Replacing the Throttle Valve. Referring to Fig. 15, when replacing the throttle valve, it is important to make absolutely sure that the tapered end of the needle enters the upper orifice of the centre piece (8) and that the tongue on the top disc (2) mates with the slot in the top edge of the mixing chamber.

Dismantling the Carburettor. Occasionally it is desirable to dismantle the carburettor in order to clean it and inspect the component parts. Referring to Fig. 15, the float (14) and the cup (15) must be removed to clean out any deposits from the bottom of the float chamber. On removing the float, the fuel needle (12) will remain in position and will not fall out.

To remove the fuel needle, remove the centre-piece and jet (8) by unscrewing the two compensating tubes (30), and withdraw the throttle valve (6). The centre-piece (8) can now be pushed upwards into the mixing chamber. Then by swinging the float lever (24) to one side, the fuel needle itself can be removed. Do not try and detach the needle-jet from the centre-piece.

Remove the tickler if the vent hole in the base of the body is obstructed. To do this, remove the split cotter pin at the end of the tickler. This releases the tickler and its spring. Observe that one vent is at the base of the hole in which the tickler fits. The second vent is in the side of the tickler cap.

To remove the strangler, loosen the clip screw (31) and unscrew the body (33) of the strangler from the carburettor air-intake. To remove the strangler lever (26), loosen the grub-screw (25) and

KEY TO FIG. 15

 1 = Top ring
 2 = Top disc (with guide peg)
 3 = Adjusting screw for jet needle
 4 = Jet needle
 5 = Spring for jet needle
 6 = Throttle valve
 7 = Fibre washer for centre-piece
 8 = Centre piece and jet
 9 = Mixing chamber
10 = Clip securing screw (carburettor)
11 = Securing clip
12 = Fuel needle
13 = Fibre washer for cup
14 = Float
15 = Cup
16 = Fibre washer for bottom nut
17 = Bottom nut
18 = Bowden cable
19 = Bowden cable adjuster
20 = Cable lock-nut
21 = Throttle-valve return spring
22 = Inner cable
23 = Cable nipple
24 = Float lever
25 = Screw for strangler lever
26 = Strangler lever
27 = Spring for strangler lever
28 = Ball for strangler lever
29 = Tickler
30 = Compensating tube
31 = Screw for securing clip (strangler
32 = Strangler securing clip
33 = Strangler body
34 = Strangler spindle
35 = Air filter

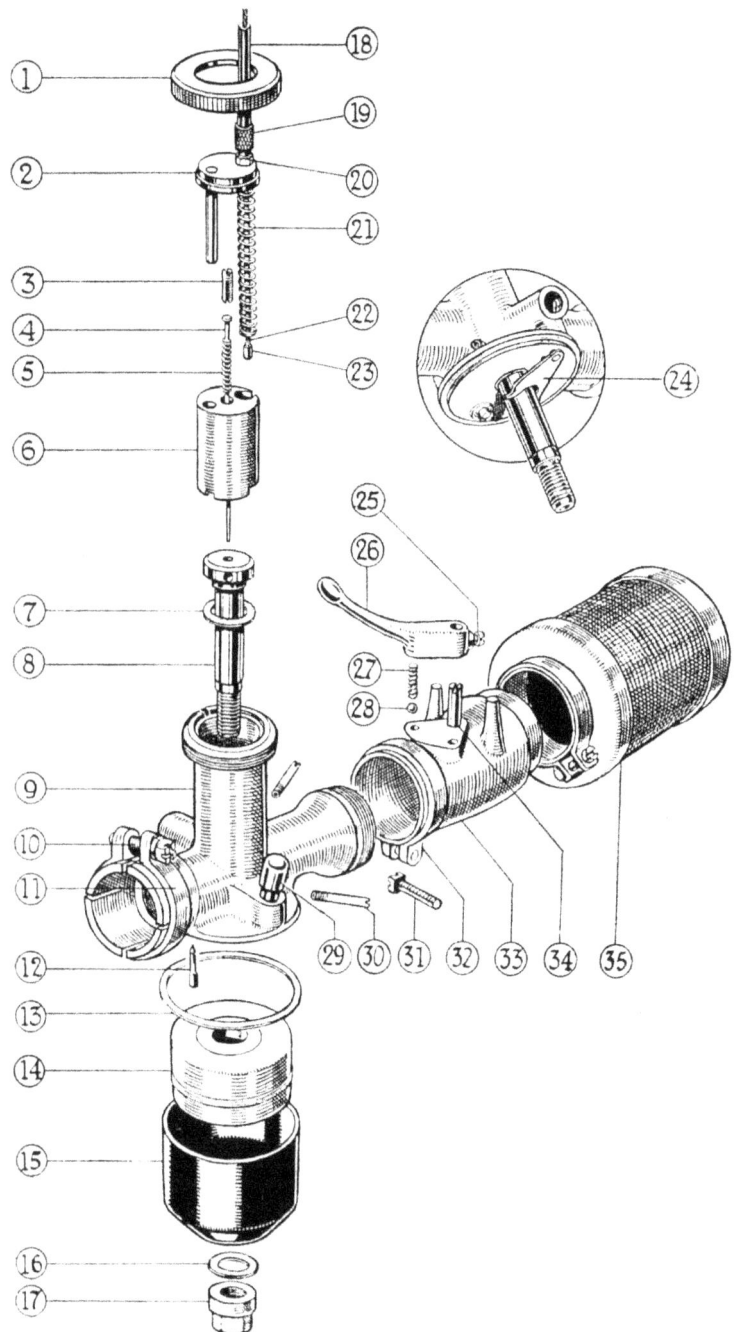

Fig. 15 Exploded View of Single-lever Needle-jet Villiers Type 3/2 Carburettor
(*The Enfield Cycle Co., Ltd.*)

slide the lever off its spindle (34). Be careful not to lose the lever spring and ball shown at (27) and (28) respectively.

Assembling the Carburettor. Referring to Fig. 15, remember when assembling the Villiers carburettor to fit: (*a*) the fibre washer (7) below the head of the centre-piece (8); (*b*) the fibre washer (13) between the cup (15) and the mixing chamber (9); (*c*) the fibre washer (16) between the cup (15) and the bottom nut (17). When refitting the strangler lever (26), place the strangler plate full open and fit the lever in a downward position with the ball in the dimple. Note the following important points—
 1. The compensating tubes (30) are vital, and must not be replaced by solid type screws.
 2. The length of the throttle-valve guide peg (2) is such that the valve never fully uncovers the choke of the carburettor.
 3. The needle jet and jet needle are *not* interchangeable with those in the similar carburettor fitted to the Villiers two-stroke engine.

AIR FILTERS

On Two-stroke Engines. An air filter is fitted to the Amal and Villiers carburettors provided on the 125 c.c. two-stroke engines of Models WD/RE and RE. Occasionally remove the air filter and clean it with some petrol.

In the case of Model WD/RE the filter is someway behind the carburettor and there is an intervening choke unit. In consequence little or no blow-back from the carburettor reaches the filter, and it is necessary to oil the filter when new and after cleaning.

In the case of the civilian Model RE the filter is immediately behind the carburettor and the choke is on the atmospheric side of the filter. In consequence the carburettor is always kept wet from the blow-back from the engine and there is no need to oil it.

On Four-stroke Engines. On the 1939 Model G "350 Bullet" and on the 1939 499 c.c. Models L and J2 "500 Bullet" an air filter is fitted as standard equipment, also on the 1946–9 Models G, J, J2.

The fitting of an air filter does not affect speed, provided that the correct size main jet is used, and it does not affect the carburettor setting (see page 26) on the 1939 Model L. Where the air filter is disconnected or removed from the 1939 "Bullet" Models G and J2, however, it is advisable to fit a main jet size 160 and 170 respectively in place of the main jet sizes 140 and 150. Similarly in the case of the 1946–9 346 c.c. Model G and the

OBTAINING GOOD CARBURATION

499 c.c. Models J, J2 the disconnecting or removal of the air filter calls for the fitting of a main jet *two sizes larger*.

The efficient Royal Enfield air filter (Fig. 16) comprises a large

(*The Enfield Cycle Co., Ltd.*)

FIG. 16. LARGE BOX-TYPE AIR FILTER FITTED TO SOME 1939 AND ALL 1946-9 MODELS

The box contains a pad of oil-wetted steel wool which effectively filters all air entering the engine.

rectangular box secured to the off-side of the machine and connected to the carburettor air-intake. Inside the lower part of this rectangular box steel-wool (oil-wetted) is packed and held between two wire screens. Approximately once every 2000 miles remove the air filter, swill the lower portion out with clean petrol and then dip it in suitable engine oil (see page 60).

CHAPTER III

CARE OF IGNITION SYSTEM

THIS chapter contains all essential information on the care of the ignition equipment provided on 1937 and later Royal Enfields. By following the advice given you can facilitate starting, avoid ignition breakdowns on the road, and obtain maximum performance by ensuring a "fat" spark at the plug.

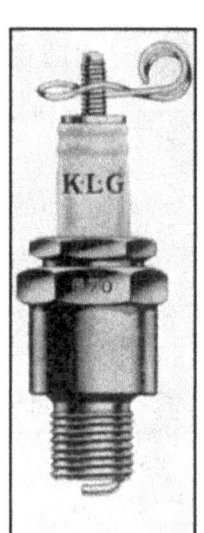  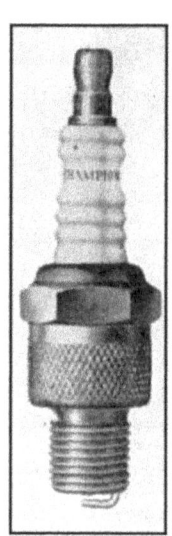

FIG. 17. THREE EXCELLENT 14 MM. PLUGS
SUITABLE FOR O.H.V. ENGINES

Above are shown from left to right the K.L.G. F70, the Lodge H14, and the Champion L-10S

Always Run on a Good Plug. It is important always to fit a reliable make of sparking plug of the correct type and reach for your particular engine. Most 1937 and later Royal Enfield models require a plug with 14 mm. thread and ½ in. reach, but some of the earlier side-valve and two-stroke models (including the S.V. Big Twins and Model A two-stroke) require an 18 mm. sparking plug.

Three reliable makes of sparking plugs (see Fig. 17) are the Lodge, K.L.G., and Champion. Lodge and K.L.G. plugs are of the detachable type, and have "Sintox" and "Corundite" insulation,

CARE OF IGNITION SYSTEM

respectively. Champion plugs are of the non-detachable type and have improved "Ceramic" insulation. The table given below shows the correct types of plugs to fit on Royal Enfield engines.

SUITABLE SPARKING PLUGS (1937 TO 1949)

Engine Type	Plug thread	Lodge	K.L.G.	Champion
Side-valve	18 mm.	C3	M50	7
Side-valve	14 mm.	C14	F50	L-10
Overhead-valve	14 mm.	H14	F70	L-10S
Two-stroke (125 c.c.)	14 mm.	CN,* B14	F20	J-8
Two-stroke (225 c.c.)	18 mm.	C3 or H1†	M50	7

* The Lodge CN plug is a non-detachable single-point type. All other Lodge and K.L.G. plugs specified in the accompanying table are of the detachable type.
† Use the H1 if a harder plug is required.

Check the Plug Gap Occasionally. Occasionally check by means of a feeler gauge, and if necessary adjust, the gap between the insulated centre and earthed outer electrode(s) of the sparking plug. Continuous electrical discharges and high combustion temperatures gradually burn the electrode points and enlarge their gap, even on the very best makes of plugs.

If the gap is permitted to remain excessive, starting up may become difficult and on "Magdyno" ignition models the extra voltage required to make the spark jump the enlarged gap is liable to cause internal damage to the ignition portion of the "Magdyno." Too large a gap must therefore be avoided. If the gap is too small, some misfiring and loss of power may ensue and the plug will quickly oil-up.

The correct gap between the plug electrodes, as measured with a feeler gauge, should be 0·015 in. to 0·020 in. The Enfield Cycle Co., Ltd. recommend a gap of 0·015 in. and 0·020 in. for flywheel magneto and coil ignition models, respectively, and a gap of 0·018 in. for all "Magdyno" ignition machines. A gap of up to 0·020 in. can, of course, be used on all models, provided that easy starting is still obtainable. When adjusting the gap, always bend the *outer* electrode(s) by *pressing* inwards, and on no account attempt to bend the centre (insulated) electrode. For resetting the gap on a Champion sparking plug, a special notched tool is obtainable from the plug manufacturers. This small tool includes feeler gauges for checking the gap.

Cleaning Sparking Plugs. The sparking plug must always be kept in a clean condition internally and externally. It should be removed occasionally and thoroughly cleaned and inspected for cracks in the insulation. All oil, petrol, soot and carbon deposits must be removed. An excellent gadget for cleaning a plug quickly comprises a metal reservoir containing petrol and a number of fine steel wires. To use this gadget, the plug is screwed into the reservoir and then vigorously shaken until clean. A small pen-knife can be used to brighten up the electrode points, or some emery cloth can be used. During the vital running-in period (see page 16) the sparking plug is somewhat liable to oil-up and should be frequently removed for inspection and cleaning.

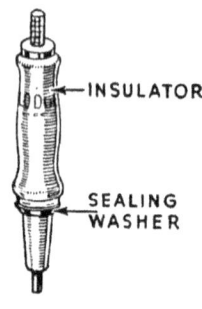
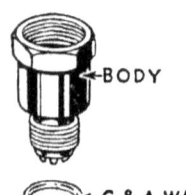

FIG. 18.
LODGE SPARKING PLUG DISMANTLED FOR THOROUGH CLEANING
(*The Enfield Cycle Co., Ltd.*)

Lodge plugs are fitted as standard by the makers on 1948-9 models

At considerable intervals it is desirable to dismantle a detachable type plug such as the Lodge and K.L.G., and then clean it very thoroughly, which is only possible when the plug is stripped down (Fig. 18). To dismantle a detachable type sparking plug, hold the body of the plug by means of the lower hexagon, using a suitable spanner or vice. If a vice is used, be careful not to squeeze the hexagon. Then unscrew the upper gland nut with a suitable box spanner. The insulated centre portion of the plug can now be detached. A suitable tool for dismantling plugs can be obtained from Messrs. Lodge Plugs, Ltd., of Rugby or from Messrs. K.L.G. Sparking Plugs, Ltd., of Cricklewood Works, London, N.W.2.

After a Lodge or K.L.G. sparking plug has been dismantled, clean the "Sintox" or "Corundite" insulation by washing it with petrol or paraffin. Afterwards remove all carbon and soot deposits by using fairly coarse emery cloth or glass-paper. Then again wash the insulation with petrol or paraffin. When the insulation is thoroughly clean, polish it with a soft, dry cloth.

Clean the centre electrode (except platinum pointed plugs) by polishing it with *fine* emery cloth. Then scrape all carbon deposits from the outer (earthed) electrode(s) and from the inside of the plug body. For this purpose use a wire brush or a pocket-knife. Finally rinse the body of the plug in petrol and allow it to dry. Before assembling the plug, make sure that the sealing washer (see Fig. 18) is seating properly and that no grit or dirt has become

CARE OF IGNITION SYSTEM

lodged between the centre insulator and the metal body of the plug. Clean the threads with a wire brush.

With regard to the non-detachable Champion sparking plug, where possible it is best to have this thoroughly cleaned by compressed air at a garage with plug servicing equipment; the plug can be cleaned, regapped and tested in a very short time. The next best method is to pour some petrol between the "Ceramic" insulator and the plug body and set fire to the plug. This will burn off the carbon deposits without harming the plug.

Testing It. The usual method of testing for h.t. current at the plug terminal is to bridge the terminal and the cylinder head with the steel blade of a *wooden-handled* screwdriver, when a spark should be visible on rotating the engine. To test the plug itself, remove it with the h.t. lead attached, clean it, lay it on the cylinder (with the terminal clear of the head) and ascertain whether it sparks satisfactorily with the engine rotated. In daylight the spark is not bright, but it should be distinctly heard. Another way of testing the plug is to use a pencil type neon tube plug tester which can be obtained cheaply from accessory dealers.

Face-cam Contact-breaker (Lucas " Magdyno "). A face-cam type contact-breaker is provided on the Lucas "Magdyno" fitted to most 1937 and later Royal Enfield singles. As regards lubrication, very little attention is needed (see page 72). It is necessary, however, at regular periods (say 1000 miles) to remove the contact-breaker cover and inspect the contacts for cleanliness and adjustment. Provided that the contacts are kept clean and *free from oil*, they will probably require adjustment only at long intervals.

If inspection of the contacts shows them to be dirty or their surfaces irregular and burned (due generally to failure to keep them clean and adjusted), the contacts must immediately be thoroughly cleaned up, otherwise misfiring and probably deterioration of the contacts will occur. To clean pitted or burned contacts, it is best to use fine carborundum stone, or if this is not available, *fine* emery cloth. Polish up the contacts until all pitting is removed and the contacts are bright all over. Be careful to keep the surfaces quite "square." Wipe away any dirt or metal dust with a cloth moistened with petrol. Examine the contact-breaker spring and remove any corrosion. If corrosion is permitted to develop, this will sooner or later cause weakness or a fracture.

To clean the contacts thoroughly and be sure of keeping their surfaces true, it is best to remove the spring arm carrying the moving contact (see Fig. 19) by withdrawing its fixing screw. On replacing the spring arm, be sure that the small backing spring is fitted directly beneath the securing screw and spring washer with the bent portion facing *outwards* as illustrated. After cleaning the contacts and replacing the spring arm, it is necessary to check the gap between the contacts.

The correct gap between the contacts of the contact-breaker is 0·012 in. and can be checked with the 12 "thou" feeler gauge on the magneto spanner. Do not alter the gap unless this varies appreciably from the gauge which should just slide between the contacts without binding. If an adjustment is needed, turn the engine round slowly until the contacts are observed to be *fully* open and then with the magneto spanner slacken the lock-nut securing the inner contact and turn the screw with the magneto spanner applied to its hexagon head until the correct gap is obtained.

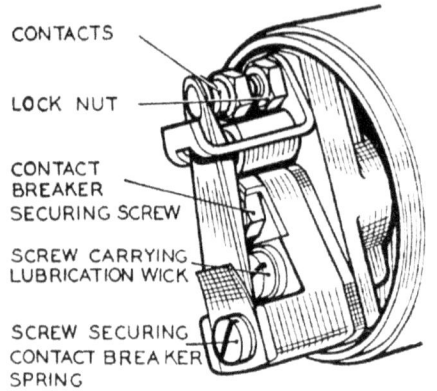

FIG. 19. FACE-CAM CONTACT-BREAKER ON SINGLE-CYLINDER LUCAS "MAG-DYNO" (1937 ONWARDS)
(*Joseph Lucas, Ltd.*)

CONTACTS
LOCK NUT
CONTACT BREAKER SECURING SCREW
SCREW CARRYING LUBRICATION WICK
SCREW SECURING CONTACT BREAKER SPRING

Ring-cam Contact-breaker (Lucas " Magdyno "). A ring-cam type contact-breaker is used on the Lucas "Magdyno" provided on the 1937-9 Big Twins (Models K, KX). Except for occasional lubrication of the cam ring wick (see page 72), no lubrication is necessary. The requirements as regards cleaning and adjustment are the same as for the face-cam type contact-breaker used on the singles (see page 45).

Maintain the gap between the fixed contact and the contact on the rocker arm at approximately 0·012 in. When making a contact-breaker adjustment be careful first to slacken the lock-nut and after an adjustment has been made, make sure that the lock-nut is firmly retightened. Before truing up burned or pitted contacts with a carborundum slip or *fine* emery cloth, it is advisable to remove the rocker arm.

To remove the rocker arm, first withdraw the contact-breaker from its housing. To do this, remove the centre screw with the magneto spanner and pull the contact-breaker off the magneto armature taper. Then push aside the locating spring and with the magneto spanner prise off the rocker arm from its bearing as shown in Fig. 20.

When replacing the contact-breaker, see that the key projecting from the tapered portion of the contact-breaker base engages the key-way cut in the armature spindle, otherwise the ignition

CARE OF IGNITION SYSTEM

timing will be upset. Also be careful not to use excessive force when tightening the centre screw; but it must be firmly tightened. If the rocker arm tends to stick, the trouble can often be remedied by rubbing the inside of the bush with a live safety match.

Occasionally remove the h.t. pick-up (two on 1937-9 Models K, KX) and examine the carbon brush. It should work freely in its guide and not be unduly worn. When examining the brush avoid

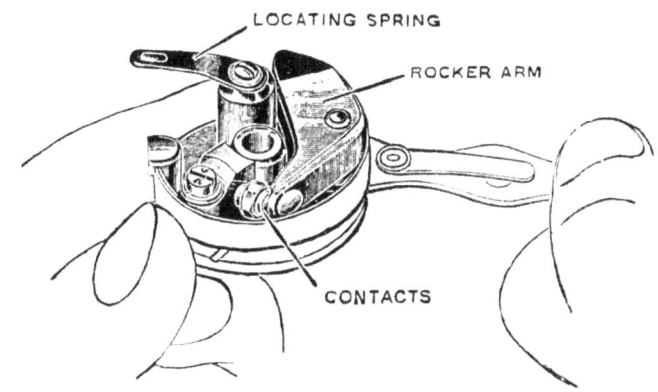

FIG. 20. SHOWING "MAGDYNO" RING-CAM CONTACT-BREAKER AND METHOD OF REMOVING THE ROCKER ARM (1937-9 MODELS K, KX)
(*Joseph Lucas, Ltd.*)

stretching the pick-up brush spring unduly, or a new one will be required. Renew both the brush and spring if they are in questionable condition. Also occasionally clean the slip ring track and flanges by inserting a small rag wrapped round a pencil through the pick-up hole and slowly revolving the engine. Little attention is required in regard to lubrication of the armature bearings, and this is referred to on page 72.

The Lucas Contact-breaker (1937-9 Coil Ignition). Occasionally remove the moulded cover and inspect the contact-breaker (see Fig. 21). The contacts must be kept quite clean and free from grease or oil. If burned or blackened, polish the contacts as in the case of the "Magdyno" with fine carborundum stone or emery cloth and afterwards wipe quite clean with a petrol-moistened rag. If much attention is necessary to the contacts it is best to remove the rocker arm from its housing. After removing the nut and collar securing the rocker arm spring, the rocker arm can be lifted clear of its pin. Finally after polishing and cleaning the contacts refit the rocker arm, replace the collar and nut, and check the gap between the contacts.

The contact-breaker gap should be maintained at 10 to 12 thousandths of an inch, and to test the gap which requires adjustment only at long intervals, slowly revolve the engine by hand until the contacts are wide open. Then insert between the contacts the magneto spanner gauge which should just slide in. If the gap is considerably too large or too small, adjust by opening the contacts fully and then slackening the locking screws until the plate carrying the stationary contact can just be moved. Now adjust the position of the plate until the correct gap at the contacts is obtained. Afterwards the locking screws may be retightened and the gap again checked.

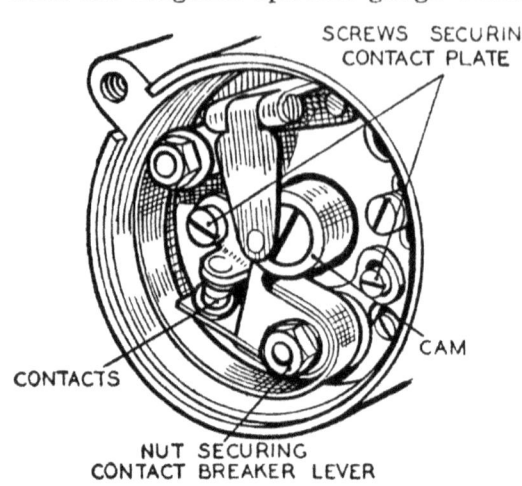

Fig. 21. The Lucas Contact-breaker (1937–9 Coil Ignition Models)

(*Joseph Lucas, Ltd.*)

When refitting the moulded cover it is important to see that the hinged steel blade on the contact-breaker makes good contact with the condenser case within the cover. If the blade fails to press firmly against the case, sparking at the contacts will occur and the contacts will suffer considerably. For advice on lubrication, see page 73.

Miller Contact-breaker (1939 Coil Ignition). On 1939 coil ignition models (with the exception of the 225 c.c. two-stroke Model A and the 148 c.c. O.H.V. Model T) Miller coil ignition equipment is specified. The contact-breaker (see Fig. 22) is gear-driven from the Miller dynamo to which it is attached.

Only a little attention is needed as regards contact-breaker lubrication (see page 73), but the contact-breaker should occasionally be removed (say every 1000 miles) and the contacts inspected and if necessary cleaned and adjusted similarly to the contacts of the Lucas "Magdyno" (see page 45). Always see that the contacts are absolutely free from oil or grease. Should inspection of the contacts show that they are free from oil and grease, but nevertheless excessively pitted and burned, suspect a faulty condenser, but first make sure that the trouble is not due to dirty or insecure battery connections causing excess voltage.

It is best to use a slip of *fine* carborundum stone to clean and

CARE OF IGNITION SYSTEM

true up the contacts. Referring to Fig. 22, although the contacts can be cleaned up without removing them from the contact-breaker assembly (14), it is advisable to remove them. To remove the rocker arm (13), slide off the spring retaining clip, prise off

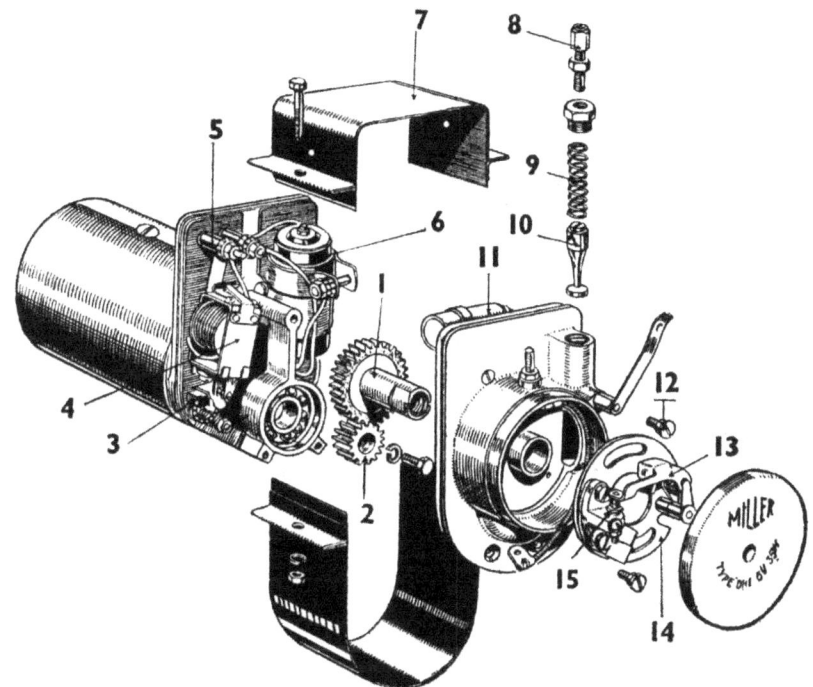

FIG. 22. EXPLODED VIEW SHOWING COMMUTATOR END AND CONTACT-BREAKER DETAILS OF MILLER DHI DYNAMO (1939 COIL IGNITION MODELS)

(*H. Miller & Co., Ltd.*)

KEY TO FIG. 22

1 = Bakelite gear and cam
2 = Steel gear (on armature)
3 = Commutator brushes (two
4 = Cut-out assembly
5 = Terminals B+ and D+
6 = Voltage regulator
7 = Two-piece cover band
8 = Ignition control adjuster
9 = Ignition control spring
10 = Bowden wire holder
11 = Condenser
12 = Contact-breaker securing screw (one of two)
13 = Rocker arm
14 = Contact-breaker assembly
15 = Fixed contact screw

the pressure spring, and then withdraw the arm from its socket. To remove the fixed contact, unscrew the fixed contact screw (15) with the magneto spanner.

The correct gap between the contacts is 0·022 in. and the gap should be checked periodically with a feeler gauge. The gap tends to *decrease* with wear of the contact-breaker rocker arm pad, and this makes it necessary to adjust the points by slackening the lock-nut and turning the fixed contact screw (15) until the correct gap is obtained.

Attention to Coil. No maintenance is necessary as this is an entirely stationary unit and no wear therefore occurs. Be careful not to permit water to reach the terminals, and occasionally wipe the terminal cap and insulated sleeve with a cloth moistened with petrol.

Battery Maintenance. The battery condition is important, especially on 1937–9 coil ignition models where the current is used for both ignition and lighting. Advice on how to keep the battery well charged is given in Chapter V.

How to Test a Condenser. Should a faulty condenser be suspected, remove the condenser and apply a normal lighting mains voltage to its terminals. A lamp should be connected in series. On removing the voltage, pause a few seconds and then short circuit the condenser terminals. If no spark occurs, the condenser is faulty. Quite a snappy spark should be obtained if the condenser is in good condition.

Diagnosing Ignition Trouble (" **Magdyno** " and **Coil Models**). The symptoms of ignition trouble vary. The engine may be hard to start, run irregularly, or cut right out. To diagnose the exact trouble, use a process of elimination. First check that the h.t. lead to the plug is properly connected at *both* ends and that there is no shorting due to its insulation being damaged or burned. Verify that the external insulation of the plug and h.t. lead are not wet. On coil ignition models inspect the connections to the dynamo, battery, contact-breaker, and coil. See that *all* connections are sound.

If you find the above-mentioned points are in order, remove the sparking plug and test it by holding the plug body in contact with the cylinder head and kicking over the engine. A good spark should be observed (and a "click" heard). On coil ignition models do not forget to switch on the ignition before testing the plug. If a good spark is present, the ignition system is in order. If no spark at all, or a poor spark, is obtained, test the h.t. lead (see page 45). If a good spark is obtained from the end of the h.t. lead, the sparking plug *must* be at fault. Inspect it carefully. If the electrodes are burned and red, fit a new plug of the correct type (page 43). If the plug is dirty or oiled-up, dismantle and clean it thoroughly (page 43). See that the gap is correct (page 43).

Where the sparking plug is in sound condition and a poor spark, or no spark at all, is obtained at the plug *and* the end of the

CARE OF IGNITION SYSTEM

h.t. lead, suspect a faulty contact-breaker. See that the points are clean and that their gap is correct (page 45). On "Magdyno" models examine the h.t. pick-up (page 47), and on coil ignition models switch on the lamps and note the intensity of illumination. A badly discharged battery affects the ignition adversely.

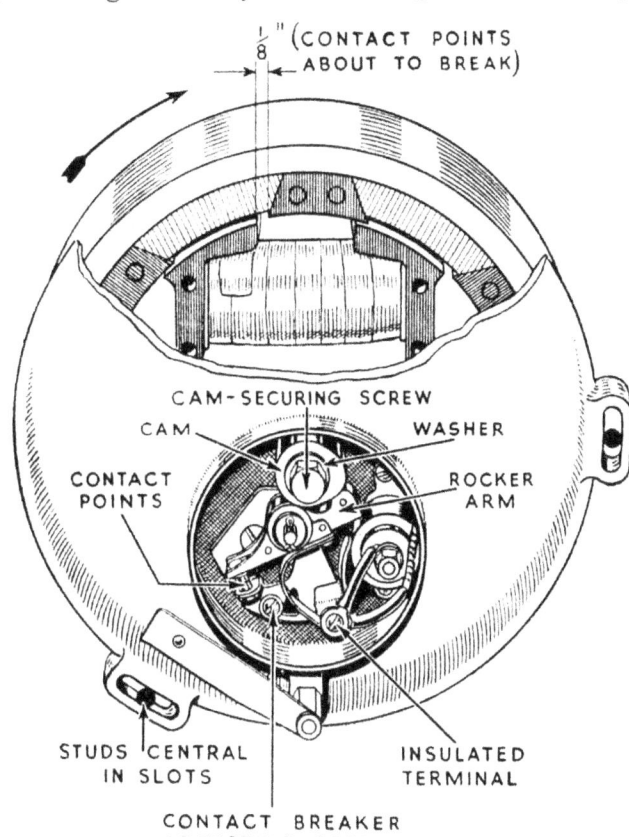

FIG. 23. SHOWING DETAILS OF CONTACT-BREAKER AND MAGNETO POLES ON MILLER FLYWHEEL MAGNETO
(*The Enfield Cycle Co., Ltd.*)
A flywheel magneto is fitted only on 125 c.c. models

Miller Contact-breaker (Flywheel Magneto Models). A Miller type FL/18 flywheel magneto is specified on the war-time 125 c.c. two-stroke Model WD/RE and its post-war successor Model RE. Details of the contact-breaker and magneto pole arrangement are shown in Fig. 23.

Periodically remove the contact-breaker cover and inspect the contacts for cleanliness and adjustment. Also inspect the rocker arm and see that it moves freely on its pivot. If the arm tends to stick, place a spot of thin oil on the rocker arm pivot pin. Apart from the above, no lubrication is necessary. Be careful not to allow any moisture, oil or grease to get on the contacts.

To remove the rocker arm (Fig. 23) so as to place a spot of oil on its pivot pin, or in order to clean up pitted or burned contacts with *fine* carborundum stone or emery cloth, proceed as follows. Detach the split pin and fibre washer and remove the screw securing the spring of the contact-breaker to the insulated terminal. Then withdraw the rocker arm. After cleaning the contacts, be careful to wipe away all traces of dirt or metal dust with a petrol-moistened cloth.

To check the contact-breaker gap, turn the engine over until the contacts are *fully* open and then insert a suitable feeler gauge between the contacts. The correct gap is 0·012 in. to 0·015 in. A slight variation from the correct gap does not call for adjustment, but the spark will be decidedly weak if the gap is permitted to exceed 0·020 in.

It should be noted that an excessive gap increases the period of contact opening, and although the "break" occurs at the right time relatively to pole position, the contacts close at the wrong position relatively to the poles. Furthermore an excessive gap makes it possible for any irregularity in the base circle of the cam to cause the contacts to remain open when they should be closed. An insufficient gap, on the other hand, may not cause a positive break in the primary coil with the result that arcing and a poor spark are likely.

Bedding down of the fibre heel on the rocker arm (particularly on new machines) causes a gradual lessening of the gap, and for this reason it is advisable to regap the contacts at 0·015 in. rather than 0·012 in. when an adjustment is needed. Do not forget that any appreciable alteration in the contact-breaker gap affects both the "electrical timing" and the ignition timing of the flywheel magneto. Therefore always check and if necessary adjust the contact gap *before* checking or adjusting the ignition timing.

To regap the contacts, slacken the contact-breaker adjusting screw (Fig. 23) and move the triangular plate, which carries the fixed contact, as required. After obtaining the correct position of the plate (which pivots about the rocker arm centre), retighten the contact-breaker adjusting screw securely.

Possible Cause of Poor Spark (Flywheel Magneto). Where the sparking plug, contact-breaker are in good order and the ignition timing (see page 53) is correct, a good spark should be obtained. If no spark is obtainable at the end of the h.t. lead, it is possible

CARE OF IGNITION SYSTEM 53

that the flywheel magneto requires expert attention, but before coming to this conclusion, attend to the following—
1. Check for tightness the screw securing the two leads to the fixed end of the contact-breaker spring.
2. See that the nut securing the lead to the centre of the condenser is firmly tightened.
3. Verify that the lead from the end of the contact-breaker spring to the centre of the condenser is unbroken and undamaged.
4. Make sure that the condenser is firmly secured to its bracket and that the two screws holding the bracket to the contact-breaker housing are tight.
5. If the above have been checked and found in order, consider the somewhat remote possibility of the shearing of the key which secures the crankshaft to the magneto flywheel. The effect of such shearing would be to interfere with the "electrical timing" (see page 56). It should be checked as described below.

To Check " Electrical Timing " (Flywheel Magneto). Remove the cam from the contact-breaker and also detach the coil (stator) plate. Next turn the engine until the piston is in the firing position, i.e. $\frac{3}{16}$ in. before T.D.C. It will be noticed that one of the rotor poles is approximately vertical over the engine shaft. Place a suitable straight-edge so that it is in line with the left-hand tip of this pole and the left-hand tip of the pole which is 180 degrees from it. Draw a line passing through these two pole tips and extend the line to the top of the aluminium housing of the flywheel. If the "electrical timing" is correct, this line should be $1\frac{1}{4}$ in. to $1\frac{1}{2}$ in. in front of the centre of the top left-hand attachment stud securing the coil plate.

Renewing H.T. Cable (Flywheel Magneto). Renew the h.t. cable if visual inspection shows the rubber insulation to be brittle, perished, or cracked. 7 mm. cable is required and it should pass right through the removable portion of the h.t. pick-up. See that the cable strands pass through the brass washer and are splayed over and soldered to the washer. Make sure that the h.t. cable is screwed firmly into the suppressor at both ends.

What the Ignition Warning Lamp is For. Its object is to show when the ignition is switched on, as on coil ignition models it is important to disconnect the battery from the coil when the machine is left standing. As soon as the engine revolutions are high enough to cause the dynamo to begin charging, the warning lamp goes out. Should the bulb burn out, the running of the machine is in no way affected, but the bulb should be replaced as soon as possible by a suitable bulb (see page 92), otherwise the ignition may inadvertently be left switched on for a long time with the machine idle and the battery may become exhausted.

Note Concerning Compensated Voltage Control. Most Royal Enfields have compensated voltage control (see page 84) and it is useful to remember that with this equipment it is possible to run with the lights on and the battery disconnected without risk of "blowing" the bulbs. If the battery is disconnected, the positive lead to it should be taped up, not earthed. A coil ignition model may be started with the battery disconnected by running the machine hard in bottom gear. When the engine starts the exhausted battery may be reconnected.

Timing the Ignition. In the event of the "Magdyno" or dynamo (coil ignition models) being removed or the drive disturbed it will be necessary to retime the ignition, which is done as follows.* Turn the engine until the piston is at the top of its stroke, being careful to observe on four-stroke models that it is at the top of the compression stroke, i.e. that no valve has opened during the ascent of the piston. Next set the handlebar ignition lever to the fully advanced position. Then rotate the engine backwards (by means of the rear wheel with top gear engaged) until the piston is exactly a distance from top dead centre position corresponding to the correct ignition or spark advance given in a later paragraph. To measure the distance, which varies on different engines from $\frac{1}{8}$ in. to $\frac{1}{4}$ in., the cylinder head should be removed on side-valve engines, but on the overhead-valve and two-stroke engines it is only necessary to remove the sparking plug and gauge the distance by means of a piece of wire inserted through the plug hole. Two marks must, of course, be scratched on the wire, one indicating top dead centre and the other above it the spark advance.

Some riders prefer to time the ignition by measuring degrees of crankshaft rotation, and in this case a degree disc must be attached to the crankshaft. The author is of the opinion, however, that this method is really "splitting hairs" and quite unnecessary and apt to entail a considerable amount of bother. Measurements taken on the piston stroke are sufficiently accurate as far as ignition timing is concerned for all normal purposes, although in the case of valve timing where extreme accuracy is wanted the degree method of timing is undoubtedly preferable.

Having determined the correct position of the piston when the spark should occur on full advance, it only remains to check that the contact-breaker points are beginning to "break" in this

---

* Before checking the ignition timing or retiming the ignition, always check the contact-breaker gap with the contacts fully open. An incorrect gap affects the timing.

CARE OF IGNITION SYSTEM

position with the spark lever fully advanced. The contacts in this position should not be less or farther apart than will allow a thin piece of tissue paper or cigarette paper to be just freed. If the contacts have not separated or have a wide gap between them, all that is necessary on 1937–9 models with Lucas coil ignition is to remove the contact-breaker cover (held by a single screw) from the end of the dynamo and slacken the large central screw securing the contact-breaker cam to the armature of the dynamo. The contact-breaker cam may then be gently turned until the contacts are beginning to break. Afterwards tighten the central screw and again check the timing.

On 1939 coil ignition models (all except Models A, T) having a Miller DHI dynamo (Fig. 22) it is not possible to rectify the moment of contact opening *at* the contact-breaker. The required adjustment must be effected by means of the dynamo armature driving gear as described below for the Lucas "Magdyno" models.

On the " Magdyno " Models. The contact-breaker is keyed to its shaft and consequently if it is necessary to retime the ignition, the timing cover must be removed and the armature driving slackened on its taper by loosening the fixing nut.

With the 1140 c.c. Big Twins (Models K, KX) either cylinder may be timed, although it is usual to time the rear one. Afterwards the timing for both cylinders should be checked. The cam for the front cylinder is the one following the longer distance between the two cams. On removing the brush holders a brass segment of the slip ring will be seen through one hole and a fibre segment through the other hole. The lead to the rear cylinder should connect with the brass segment. On the Big Twins the ignition may be timed with the cylinder head removed, but if this is in place, timing can be done by removing the small screwed plug from the centre of the head and inserting a wire through the hole. On this machine it is necessary to slacken the "Magdyno" driving sprocket after removing the chain case cover.

Timing (Flywheel Magneto). In the case of the rotating armature type magneto, such as the ignition unit of the Lucas "Magdyno," timing the ignition involves turning the armature *and* the contact-breaker. Hence the position of the armature (rotor) relative to the stator pole pieces when the contacts open is the same for *all* ignition timings, and the "electrical timing" of the instrument is unaffected except in the event of the contact-breaker gap being incorrect or when the contact-breaker cam is moved by the ignition control lever. Correct "electrical timing" *must* be maintained in order to obtain a good spark at the plug.

On the 125 c.c. two-stroke engine (Models RE, WD/RE)

timing the Miller flywheel magneto involves moving the contact-breaker cam on the engine shaft relatively to the rotor (flywheel) poles. Thus the position of the rotor relative to the stator poles when the contacts open is different for different ignition timings, and the "electrical timing" *is* affected by the actual timing, but not by the contact-breaker gap. Nevertheless the gap should be maintained correct for several reasons (see below).

The flywheel (rotor) is keyed to the crankshaft and the keyways in the flywheel centre and crankshaft are disposed such that the electrical timing is correct when the ignition timing is set correctly, i.e. when the contact-breaker points are commencing to open with the piston $\frac{5}{32}$ in. to $\frac{3}{16}$ in. before T.D.C., with the studs securing the magneto coil (stator) plate arranged *centrally* in the lug slots.

Timing the flywheel magneto too early reduces the intensity of the spark at the plug, and if the timing is such that the contacts begin to open with the piston $\frac{1}{4}$ in. before T.D.C., starting the engine may be difficult if not impossible. A late timing also affects the intensity of the spark, but not sufficiently to prevent easy starting. A late timing, however, is liable to accelerate pitting of the contact-breaker points due to sparking across them.

Checking Flywheel Magneto Timing. First check that the contact-breaker gap is correct with the contacts fully open (see page 52). Next verify that the coil plate of the flywheel magneto is set so that the studs are centrally arranged in the lug slots as shown in Fig. 23. Then check that the contacts *do* begin to open with the piston $\frac{5}{32}$ in. to $\frac{3}{16}$ in. before T.D.C. To find the exact piston position a piece of wire can be inserted through the plug hole (see page 54).

KEY TO FIG. 24

1 = Contact-breaker cover
2 = Split-pin for C.B. spindle
3 = C.B.* rocker arm
4 = C.B. insulating washer
5 = C.B. fixed contact assembly
6 = C.B. adjuster screw
7 = Washer for (6)
8 = C.B. fixing screw
9 = C.B. baseplate assembly
10 = Lighting cable socket
11 = Insulating bush for (10)
12 = H.T. pick-up socket and screw (12A)
13 = Coil plate
14 = Ignition coil assembly
15 = Clamp for coil earth wire

16 = Flywheel with magnets, poles
17 = Insulated terminal screw
18 = Condenser and lead
19 = Condenser fixing screw
20 = C.B. cover clip assembly
21 = Spring washer for C.B. screw
22 = Nut for C.B. fixing screw
23 = Ball bearing
24 = Insulating tab for (10)
25 = Bearing plate and fibre washer
26 = Nut for (10)
27 = Bearing plate fixing screw
28 = Spring washer for (27)
29 = R.H. lighting coil
30 = Coil fixing screw
31 = L.H. lighting coil

* C.B. is an abbreviation for contact-breaker

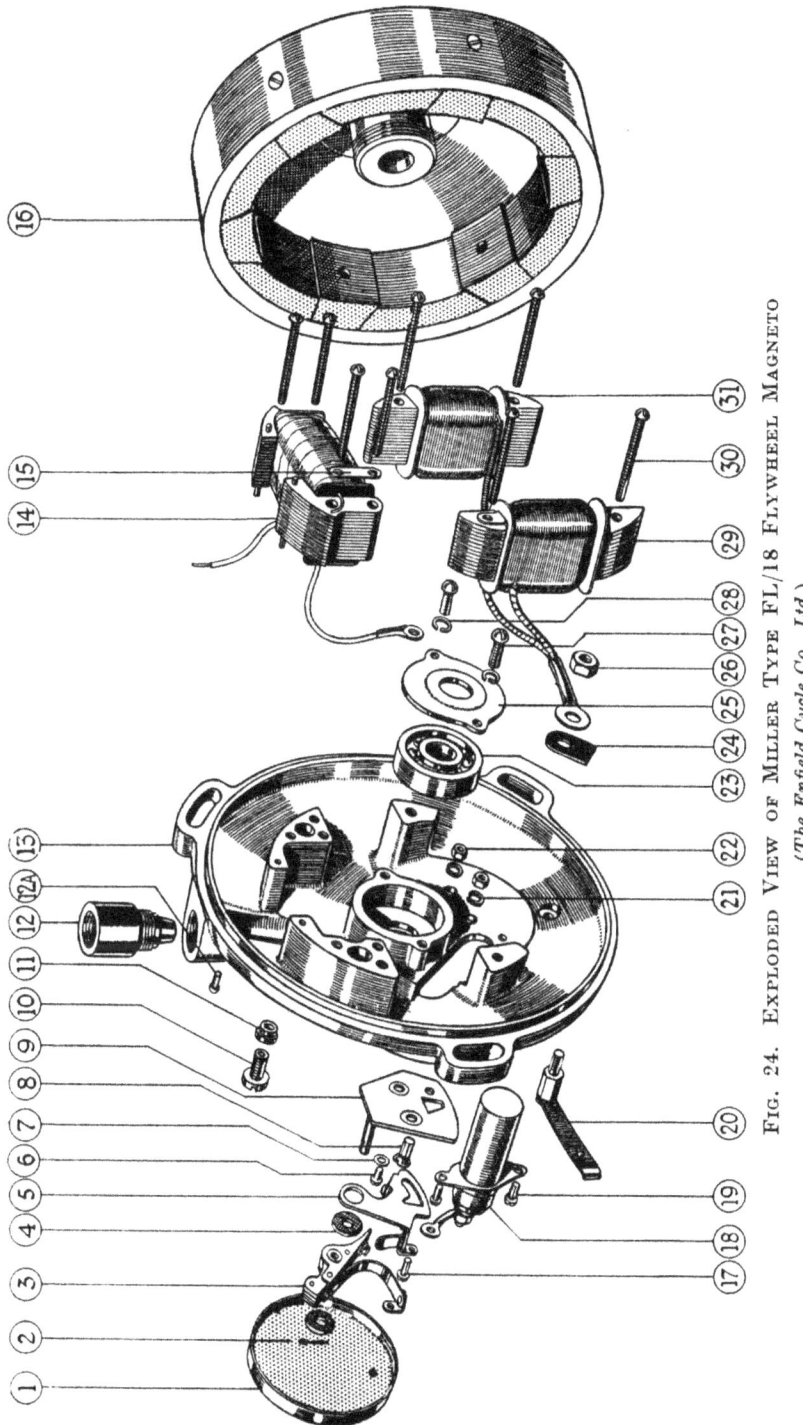

Fig. 24. Exploded View of Miller Type FL/18 Flywheel Magneto
(*The Enfield Cycle Co., Ltd.*)

This magneto is fitted to the 125 c.c. two-stroke Models RE, WD/RE. A key to the numbered parts is given opposite

To Retime Flywheel Magneto. If the magneto timing is found to be incorrect, remove the centre screw securing the cam, and also the plain washer (see Fig. 23). Loosen the cam on its shaft. The cam is tapped to receive a $\frac{5}{16}$ in. B.S.F. bolt which may be conveniently used as an extractor. Next turn the cam (with the piston preferably at $\frac{3}{16}$ in. before T.D.C.) in a clockwise direction until the contacts are just about to separate (this can be felt). Having obtained the correct cam position, tap the end of the cam sharply so as to make it bind on the shaft taper. Finally replace the plain washer and cam securing screw. When tightening the latter, make sure that the cam does not turn on its shaft. Also be careful not to disturb the piston position. It is assumed that the magneto coil plate is in the correct position as shown in Fig. 23.

After correctly retiming the flywheel magneto it is possible without affecting the intensity of the spark to advance or retard the ignition slightly relative to the engine by moving the coil plate anti-clockwise or clockwise respectively about the slot studs.

Ignition Timings (1946 Onwards). When checking the ignition timing or retiming the ignition on all four-stroke models the ignition lever should be placed in the fully *advanced* position. Below are given the correct ignition timings for all post-war Royal Enfields.

On the 346 c.c. O.H.V. Models G and CO (1946 "Export" model) the contacts of the Lucas contact-breaker should commence to separate with the piston $\frac{3}{8}$ in. before top dead centre (T.D.C.). For the 499 c.c. O.H.V. Models J, J2 (two-port) the correct ignition timing is $\frac{5}{16}$ in. before T.D.C. In the case of the 125 c.c. two-stroke Models RE and WD/RE (Service type), the correct ignition timing is $\frac{5}{32}$ in. to $\frac{3}{16}$ in. before T.D.C.

For ignition timings applicable to unused or reconditioned military machines (Models WD, WD/C, WD/CO), see paragraph below dealing with 1937–45 ignition timings.

Ignition Timings (1937–45). All the timings specified below require the ignition lever to be set in the fully *advanced* position. On the 225 c.c. two-stroke Model A the contacts should begin to "break" when the piston is $\frac{1}{8}$ in to $\frac{3}{16}$ in. before top dead centre (T.D.C.). An advance of $\frac{1}{8}$ in. gives superior hill climbing, but for obtaining high speed an advance of $\frac{3}{16}$ in. is somewhat more satisfactory.

On the 148 c.c. O.H.V. Model T the correct ignition timing is $\frac{5}{16}$ in. before T.D.C. On the 346 c.c. Models C, CM, CO, WD/CO, BCO, DC, and the 1140 c.c. S.V. Models K, KX, $\frac{3}{8}$ in. before T.D.C. is the correct setting. On the 570 c.c. S.V. Models H and L give an advance of $\frac{1}{8}$ in. on engines No. 10546 upwards, and $\frac{1}{4}$ in. on earlier type engines. On the 346 c.c. Models G, G2, GM, WD/C and J2 (1938-9 two-valve, two-port) give $\frac{3}{8}$ in before T.D.C.

On the 250, 350 c.c. "Bullets," JF, J2 (four-valve) allow $\frac{1}{2}$ in. before T.D.C. On the 500 c.c. Competition model and Models D, WD, B, BM, J, JM. J2 (1937 single-port) give $\frac{1}{4}$ in. before

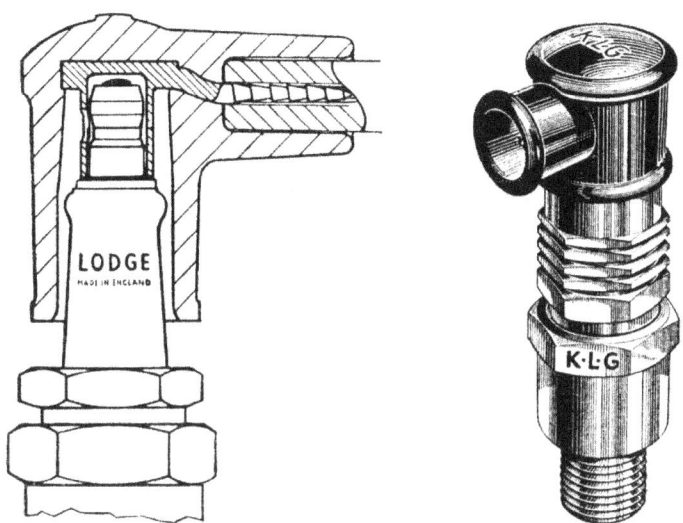

FIG. 25. SHOWING (LEFT) LODGE WEATHERPROOF PLUG TERMINAL COVER, AND (RIGHT) THE K.L.G. WATERTIGHT SPARKING PLUG

T.D.C. On Models S, SM, SF, S2 to obtain the best results, give an advance of $\frac{1}{8}$ in. before T.D.C. for engines up to No. 448, and an advance of $\frac{1}{4}$ in. for engines No. 449 onwards.

Weatherproof Sparking Plugs. Those who do much all-weather riding are advised to fit a weatherproof plug terminal cover or else a watertight sparking plug.

Weatherproof Lodge and K.L.G. terminal covers are obtainable for a few shillings from most accessory firms (see page 107). The Lodge terminal cover is shown in Fig. 25 which also illustrates the K.L.G. watertight plug. This detachable plug has a moulded cap giving protection against oil, dirt, and grit, a steel sleeve protecting the insulator against damage, fins to disperse heat, and a body of non-corrosive steel. It is obtainable with an 18 mm. or 14 mm. thread. Its type number includes the prefix "W" (e.g., WF50, WF70, etc.). Lodge also make a special watertight terminal cover which is a little more expensive than the weatherproof one.

CHAPTER IV

ALL ABOUT LUBRICATION

THIS chapter contains all the information you need concerning the correct lubrication of your Royal Enfield motor-cycle, including the electrical equipment. Not much attention is required, but this attention is *vital* and on it depend continuous good performance and trouble-free running.

On 1937 and later machines two distinct types of lubrication systems are used. The 125 c.c. and 225 c.c. two-stroke models have petroil lubrication. All four-stroke models (148 c.c. to 1140 c.c.) incorporate full dry sump lubrication with plunger type pumps, and an oil tank integral with the crankcase (except some 250 c.c. models).

Suitable Engine Oils. Always replenish the oil tank with a reputable brand of engine oil of the correct grade. The importance of this cannot be over emphasized. Also make a point of buying only from sealed cans or branded cabinets. Suitable engine oils for all four-stroke (summer) and two-stroke (summer and winter) Royal Enfields are as follows—

Castrol Grand Prix.
Shell X-100 SAE 50.
Mobiloil D.
Price's Energol SAE 50.
Essolube Racer.

In the case of all four-strokes during the winter, or if one of the above-mentioned oils is not available during summer, replenish with one of the under-mentioned—

Castrol XXL.
Shell X-100 SAE 40.
Mobiloil BB.
Price's Energol SAE 40 (SAE 50 for pre-1946 models).
Essolube 50.

PETROIL LUBRICATION

This system of engine lubrication used on the two-stroke models A, RE, WD/RE, is extremely simple in principle and application. On the two-stroke engine the cycle of internal operations entails the admission and compression of the petrol vapour in the crankcase and this with a mechanical pump or dry sump system of lubrication would render lubrication of the big-end

ALL ABOUT LUBRICATION 61

and main shaft bearings very hazardous and generally unsatisfactory. The difficulty is overcome in a childishly simple manner with the petroil system by replenishing the tank with a mixture of oil and petrol in certain definite proportions.

The Proportions of Oil and Petrol (Model A). For normal use replenish the tank with a mixture consisting of *one part of oil to sixteen of petrol*, or in other words add half a pint of oil to each gallon of petrol. During the running-in period, however, slightly more oil should be used and the author recommends the mixing of three-quarters of a pint with each gallon of petrol. Always use a good quality oil of a kind suitable for the engine (see page 60).

Correct Proportions (Models RE, WD/RE). On the 125 c.c. machines slightly less engine oil should be mixed with the petrol than on the 225 c.c. Model A referred to above. The correct proportions for the petroil mixture in the tank are *one part of oil to twenty-four of petrol*. This is equivalent to one-third of a pint of oil per gallon of petrol.

Mixing the Petroil. All Royal Enfield two-strokes have a measure attached to the underside of the tank filler cap and on Model A four full measures exactly equals half a pint. It will be noticed that on the Model A measure the rider is instructed to use *five* measures, but this applies only during running-in. Afterwards it is quite sufficient to mix *four* measures of engine oil with each gallon of petrol. In the case of the 125 c.c. Models RE, WD/RE *two* measures of engine oil should be mixed with each gallon of petrol.

The best petrol to use (if available) is a good No. 1 brand. Do not use benzole-mixture, as this is not recommended for two-stroke engines although in the case of high compression overhead-valve engines its use has many advantages and gives good results.

Shake or Stir the Mixture Well. Before pouring the petroil mixture into the tank it should be stirred or shaken well in a separate vessel. Always make a habit of doing this, because if the mixture is poured straight into the tank there is a considerable risk of trouble arising due to the oil settling at the bottom of the tank. If it is impracticable to mix and stir the engine oil and petrol in a separate vessel, turn off the petrol, replenish the tank *first with oil*, then with petrol, and afterwards shake the machine thoroughly.

In Cold Weather. It will facilitate restarting, particularly in cold weather, if the petrol tap is turned off *before* stopping so as to drain the carburettor. This prevents oil collecting in the jets and possibly choking them.

DRY SUMP LUBRICATION

With this type of lubrication system the *whole* of the oil in the oil tank and engine is kept in *constant circulation* by means of plunger type delivery and return pumps housed at the foot of the timing case. A proper understanding of how the oil is circulated is desirable.

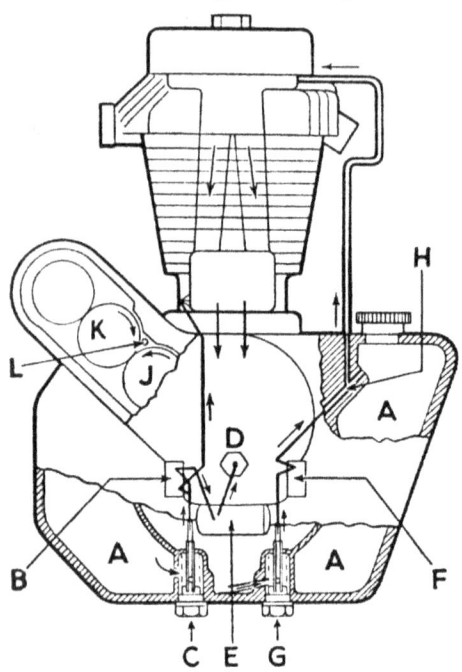

FIG. 26. DIAGRAM SHOWING OIL CIRCULATION ON O.H.V. ENGINES (1946 ONWARDS)
(*The Enfield Cycle Co., Ltd.*)

1946–9 O.H.V. Singles. On Models G, J, J2 engine oil is pressure-fed to the rear of the cylinder, the big-end bearing, the timing gears, and the overhead valve gear. The manner in which the oil circulates throughout the engine is shown diagrammatically in Fig. 26. Referring to this diagram, the engine oil is sucked from the oil tank A, which is integral with the crankcase, by means of the double-acting feed pump B after passing through the gauze filter C.

The primary side of the double-acting feed pump B delivers oil through the filter E, which has a felt element (see Fig. 31), to the feed plug D. The oil is then pressure-fed through the timing side main shaft to the big-end bearing of the connecting-rod. Surplus oil from this bearing splash-lubricates the piston, cylinder, and main bearings. The secondary side of the double-acting feed pump B pressure-feeds additional engine oil to the rear of the cylinder as indicated.

Two wells are provided at the bottom of the crankcase for collecting surplus oil which is sucked up by the double-acting return pump F through the gauze filter G and returned to the oil tank A as indicated in Fig. 26.

A spring-loaded ball valve is incorporated at position H at the

ALL ABOUT LUBRICATION

outlet end of the return passage to the oil tank (see Fig. 26A). The resistance of the ball valve causes some of the returning oil to be forced up into the rocker-box through the external pipe shown diagrammatically in Fig. 26. Surplus oil from the rocker-box finds its way by gravity down the two push-rod cover tubes to the timing gears through grooves cut in the tappet guides. The intermediate gears J and K pick up the oil and return it to the oil tank A via the channel indicated at L.

Action of Double-acting Feed Pump.
Referring to Fig. 27 (left-hand diagram), the pump plunger A is driven by the crank pin B on the end of the worm-driven cross shaft. The plunger is able to reciprocate in a cylinder formed in the disc C which can oscillate in its housing. The disc C is lapped on its seating and is held down by a compression spring located beneath the cover of the pump.

The port T on the lower face of the disc communicates with the pump cylinder. Four ports, W, X, Y, Z are provided on the face at the bottom of the pump housing. Two of these, namely ports Y and Z, are in communication with the feed pipe from the oil tank. As regards the remaining two ports, W communicates with the passage connected to the rear of the cylinder, and X communicates with the felt filter shown at E in Fig. 26 and with the oil feed plug D.

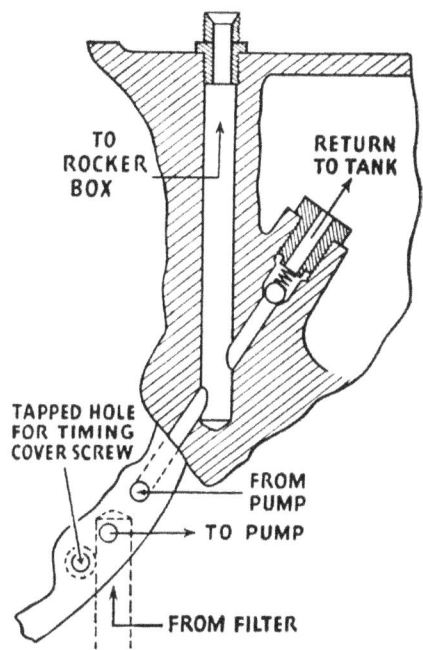

FIG. 26A. SECTIONAL VIEW SHOWING SPRING-LOADED BALL VALVE IN OIL RETURN PASSAGE TO TANK (1946 ONWARDS)

(*The Enfield Cycle Co., Ltd.*)

In Fig. 27 (left-hand diagram) the pump plunger A is shown being withdrawn from its cylinder by the anti-clockwise movement of the crank pin B. Ports T and Y register, and consequently engine oil is sucked in from the oil tank. The withdrawal of the pump plunger A decreases the clearance space in the housing D and oil is therefore displaced through port W to the rear of the cylinder.

When the pump plunger reaches the end of its outward stroke the disc C partially rotates and during the following inward movement of the plunger, the port W is masked by the disc. Simultaneously port Z remains open and ports T and X register, with the result that oil is pressure-fed through port X to the big-end bearing, and is sucked in from the oil tank through port Z.

Action of Oil Return Pump. The general design of the double-acting return pump is similar to that of the feed pump just described, but the ports are somewhat differently arranged. Referring to Fig. 27 (right-hand diagram), the face at the bottom of the pump housing has two ports Y' and Z'. Port Y' is in communication with the suction passage leading from the oil wells at

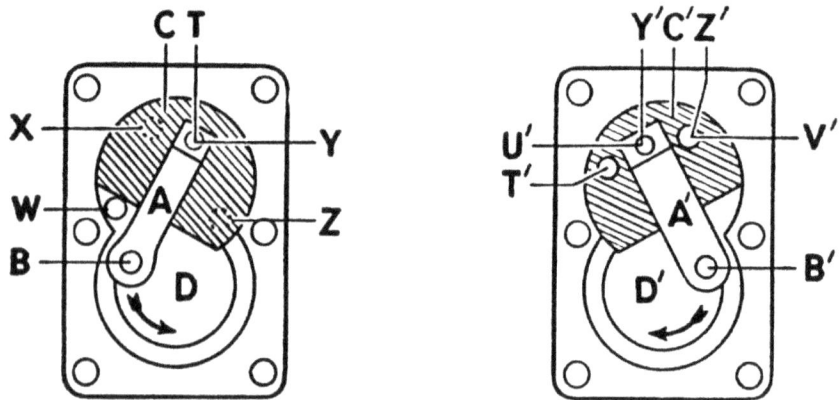

FIG. 27. DIAGRAMS SHOWING ARRANGEMENT OF (LEFT) DOUBLE-ACTING FEED PUMP AND (RIGHT) OIL RETURN PUMP (1946 ONWARDS)

(*The Enfield Cycle Co., Ltd.*)

A similar pump arrangement is used on most 1937–9 four-stroke models

the bottom of the crankcase. Port Z' communicates with the delivery passage to the oil tank.

Three ports T', U', V' are provided on the lower face of the disc. Port U' communicates with the cylinder in which the pump plunger A' reciprocates. Ports T' and V' are drilled right through to the upper face. Fig. 27 (right-hand diagram) shows ports U' and V' registering with ports Y' and Z' respectively, on the outward stroke. Engine oil is being sucked in through ports V' and Z'. During the following inward stroke of the pump plunger ports T' and U' register with ports Y' and Z' respectively. This causes oil to be sucked in through ports T' and Y' and displaced through ports U' and Z'.

1939–46 Models WD/C, WD/CO, CO. On the two 350 c.c. military machines and the 1946 civilian version, Model CO, the engine lubrication system is identical to that used for the 1945–8 O.H.V. singles and already described. On the 350 c.c. S.V. Model WD/C, however, the spring-loaded ball valve in the oil return passage to the tank (see Fig. 26A) diverts some of the returning oil to the valve chest instead of to the rocker-box.

1937–9 Singles. The D.S. lubrication system on all 1937–9 singles is similar to that provided on the later models except for some detail modifications, varying according to engine type and date of manufacture.

On the 250 c.c. engines the port arrangement of the double-acting pumps is slightly different from that shown in Fig. 27, and the engine oil (on engines with a circular shaped crankcase) is

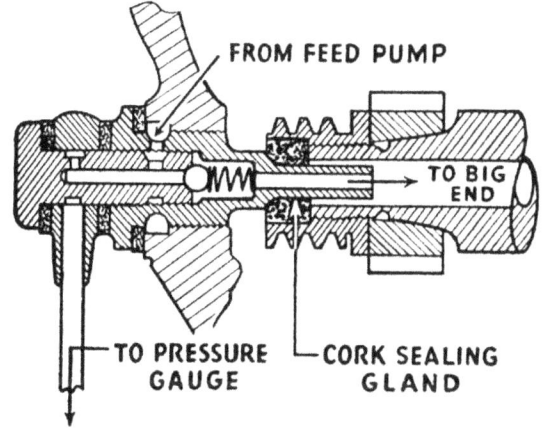

Fig. 28. Sectional View of Oil Feed Plug with Spring-loaded Ball Valve for Oil Pressure Gauge (Some 1939–40 Engines)
(*The Enfield Cycle Co., Ltd.*)

contained in a separate tank mounted between the rear engine plates. The tank has a drain plug and a detachable gauze filter. A second filter protects the entrance to the pipe leading to the feed pump.

On the 1939 engines (except 250 c.c.) the double-acting pumps are identical to those illustrated in Fig. 27, but on 1937–8 engines single-acting feed and oil return pumps are fitted. The single-acting pumps are similar to those shown in Fig. 27 except that the ports *W* and *Z* are omitted from the pump housing.

Where single-acting pumps are provided (1937–8), the oil is sucked from the tank by the feed pump through a filter and is then pressure-fed through the oil feed nozzle into the main shaft on the timing side of the engine. Centrifugal force flings the oil

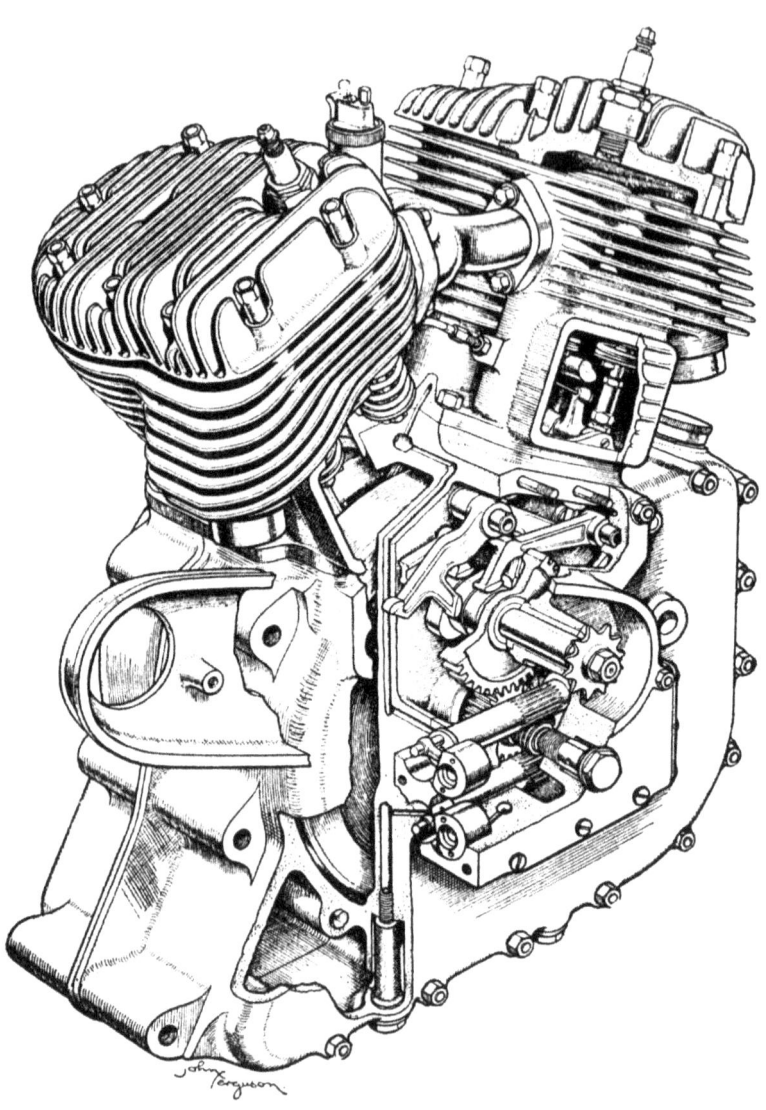

Fig. 29. Showing the Twin Oil Pumps and other Details of the 1140 c.c. Side-valve Engine Fitted to the 1937–9 Models K and KX

(*From "The Motor Cycle"*)

A diagram of the dry sump lubrication system is given on page 69. Prior to 1937 mechanical pump lubrication was used

ALL ABOUT LUBRICATION

through a passage in the flywheel web to the big-end bearing and surplus oil from the big-end splash-lubricates the cylinder. The oil after circulating through the engine collects in the sumps and is drawn through a second filter by the return pump and delivered to the oil tank via the oil return passage. The oil return flow is visible on removing the tank filler cap. The above arrangement applies to the 148 c.c. O.H.V. Model T.

On certain models (H, HM, JF, L, B, BM, C) the oil return passage to the tank contains no spring-loaded ball valve as shown in Fig. 26A but instead the passage is divided, some of the oil flowing direct to the tank, and some to the timing gear.

On the 250 and 350 c.c. "Bullets" a check valve is provided below the union at the foot of the external pipe to the rocker-box. Its object is to stop an excessive amount of oil reaching the semi-enclosed rocker housing.

On a few 1939–40 models (e.g., J2, G3 "350 Bullet") a pressure gauge is fitted. Oil is by-passed to the gauge by a spring-loaded ball valve incorporated at the feed plug (see Fig. 28). The valve resistance build up a pressure of 10–15 lb. per sq. in. which is recorded on the gauge dial.

1937–9 Big Twins. As on the S.V. and O.H.V. singles, a true dry sump lubrication system is provided and it has many features in common with that described above. The oil in the "sump" or crankcase compartment (which has a capacity of over 7 pints) is kept at a level below the flywheels so that they cannot dip. No means of adjusting the oil feed is provided, oil being fed liberally to the big-end, the front cylinder and the timing gears; surplus oil is returned to the "sump" for further circulation.

Referring to Fig. 30, the main oil supply is contained in the oil tank A which constitutes part of the crankcase casting, and is sucked up by the two feed pumps B and C (at the rear end of the timing cover) through the filter D. Oil is delivered by pump B to the big-end and is then splashed over the cylinders and pistons; some of it is also led to the main bearings along special ducts. An auxiliary oil supply is fed by pump C (which is smaller than B) to the front cylinder which on twin-cylinder engines tends to receive less oil than the rear one. Surplus oil accumulates in the sumps E, E at the base of the crankcase and is then sucked up by the first return pump F (which has a capacity greater than the combined capacity of B and C) through a filter G and delivered to the timing case. Oil is drawn from a high level in the timing case by the second return pump H (which is of the same size as F) and returned to the main oil tank or "sump" A. This briefly is the working of the D.S. lubrication system used on Models K and KX.

MAINTENANCE OF D.S. SYSTEM

The following hints apply to all 1937 and later four-stroke Royal Enfields except where otherwise stated.

Engine Oils to Use. The correct grades of five reputable brands of engine oil suitable for all four-strokes are specified on page 60. During the running-in period (see page 16) it is very beneficial to the engine to mix some Acheson's Colloidal Graphite with the engine oil. If you continue to use this compound *after* the running-in period is completed, reduce the amount used by one half, i.e. mix $\frac{1}{2}$ pint with each gallon of fuel.

Lubrication of Overhead Valve Gear. All 1937 and later type models have a positive feed to the rocker-box by means of an external pipe. The oil fed to the rocker-box provides adequate lubrication for the overhead rockers, push-rod ends and valve guides. No adjustment of the supply is necessary or provided. But see that the pipe unions are kept securely tightened.

Replenish Tank Regularly. Bear this in mind. If the tank becomes completely empty, the engine is with the dry sump lubrication system entirely starved of oil and it is only a question of a short time before it "goes west." To be on the safe side, frequently remove the filler cap and with the dip-stick attached to its underside ascertain the oil level and replenish with suitable engine oil (see page 60) if necessary.

The oil level must always be kept well above the end of the dip-stick and the tank should not be replenished beyond the mark near the top end of the dip-stick (2 in. from the top of the tank), otherwise oil may escape from the vent in the filler cap, or from the vent at the rear of the crankcase on earlier models. Always remember that the more oil there is in circulation, the *cooler* will the oil and engine be.

On 250 c.c. engines with a *circular* type crankcase there is no dip-stick provided, the oil being carried in a separate tank. On these machines, maintain the oil level in the tank as high as possible, but do not permit the level to rise above 1 in. from the top of the tank, or leakage from the filler cap vent may occur. Always keep the level well above the bottom of the gauze filter which is situated below the filler cap. This is most important.

To Verify Oil Circulation. Remove the tank filler cap and peer inside when if all is well the oil can be seen issuing from the oil return pipe in a uniform series of drops. It is advisable to check the circulation occasionally.

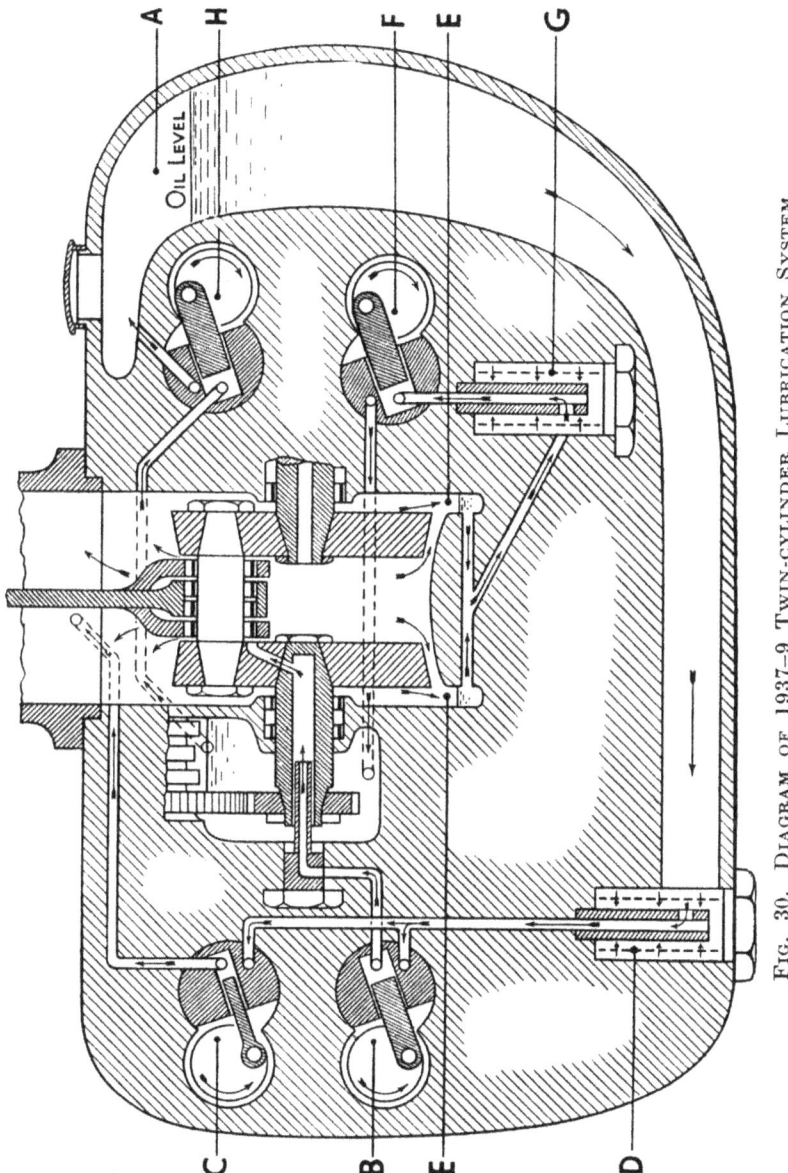

Fig. 30. Diagram of 1937–9 Twin-cylinder Lubrication System

Warm Up Engine Gradually. Some riders as soon as they have started the engine proceed to race it, presumably with the idea of impressing bystanders with the powerful mount they are about to ride. This, apart from the question of ethics, is thoroughly bad practice and is proof of ignorance, for until the engine oil reaches a certain temperature it will not be circulating with maximum efficiency. On the other hand, do not let the engine tick over too slowly when warming up because this reduces the speed of oil circulation, possibly to a dangerous extent when the oil is in a very viscous state. It also tends to cause low-temperature condensation of fuel, which is liable to corrode the cylinder bore.

Pressure Gauge Readings. On certain 1939 models (see page 67) an oil pressure gauge is fitted, and the dial reading should be carefully observed on warming up the engine. On later type 1939 engines with plain big-end bearing (Model J2, engine No. 7413 upwards) the gauge needle will move up to the end of the dial calibrations on starting up from cold. However, as the oil begins to warm up the pressure indicated will decline and eventually remain fairly constant at 10–15 lb per sq in.

On earlier type 1939 engines with a roller big-end bearing, 10–15 lb per sq in. is the normal pressure indicated throughout. Only slight fluctuations occur and these are caused by variations in oil temperature and engine speed.

Drain Oil Tank and Sump Every 2000 Miles. After the first 500 miles and thereafter about every 2000 miles the oil should be drained from the tank and integral sump by removing the two filter plugs shown at *C* and *G* in Fig. 26. The rear plug drains the tank, and the front one the sump. Both filter gauzes should be brushed with paraffin to clean them and the tank and sump swilled through with some clean oil, allowed to drain, and refilled with fresh oil. This procedure is conveniently carried out when the machine is being decarbonized.

The oil will flow more readily if the two plugs are removed at the conclusion of a ride, or the tank and sump may be allowed to drain over-night. Waste of oil is reduced by allowing the oil level in the tank to become *reasonably* low before draining.

Also Drain Timing Case. At the same time as you drain the oil tank and integral sump, you should also drain the old oil accumulated in the timing case (except on engines with circular crankcases). To do this, remove the feed plug, indicated at *D* in Fig. 26, and then tilt the machine over on its off-side.

It should be noted that subsequently to the timing case being drained in the above manner, no oil can be returned from it to the

ALL ABOUT LUBRICATION

tank until the pre-determined level in the timing case has been again built up. Consequently there will be an apparent loss in the oil tank of approximately half a pint. But do not worry; this is only a temporary loss. After changing the oil, allow the engine to tick-over gently for a few minutes.

Clean Felt Filter Every 2000 Miles. A felt-type oil filter is provided on the 350 c.c. military Models WD/C, WD/CO, its

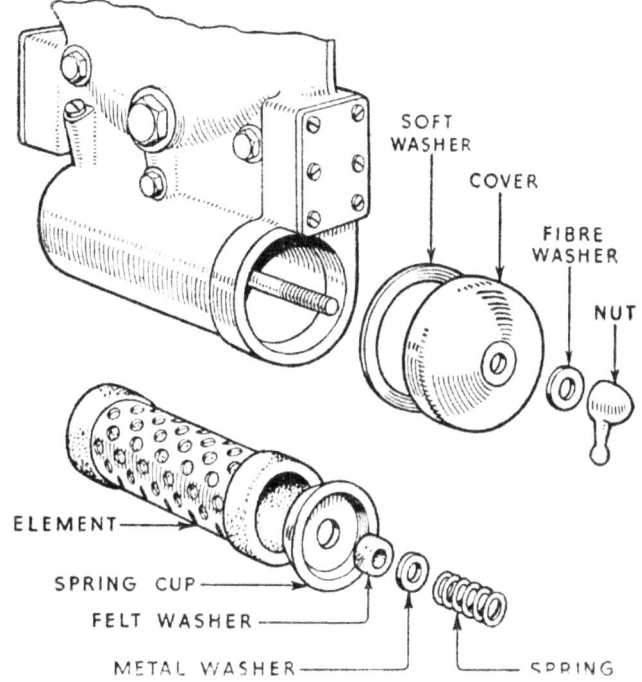

Fig. 31. Exploded View Showing Details of Felt Filter below Timing Case
(*The Enfield Cycle Co., Ltd.*)
This filter is incorporated in the position indicated at *E* in Fig. 26

1946 civilian version Model CO, and the 1946 and later 350 c.c. and 500 c.c. Models G, J, and J2. Details of the felt filter are shown in Fig. 31.

Every 2000 miles (i.e. when draining the oil tank, sump, and timing case), remove and clean the felt element by washing it in petrol. The capacity of the element to filter and pass oil quickly enough deteriorates at about 5000 miles and after this mileage it is advisable to renew the element.

Draining Separate Oil Tank (250 c.c. Models). On 250 c.c. Royal Enfields with circular type crankcases the separate oil tank should be drained and replenished every 1500–2000 miles, for convenience when decarbonizing the engine. Oil wastage is minimized by permitting the level in the tank to fall reasonably low before draining. It is best to drain the tank with the oil *warm* after coming in from a ride. Alternatively the tank can be allowed to drain over-night.

Oil will flow from the tank as soon as the drain plug is removed from its base. Swill the tank through with some petrol and then with some clean oil. When using petrol, the tank should, of course, be disconnected from the engine. After thoroughly draining the tank, replenish it to the correct level (not above 1 in. from the top of the tank) with suitable engine oil (page 60).

When draining the oil tank, also clean the gauze filter below the filler cap by brushing it with paraffin. On no account use a fluffy rag for this purpose.

If the Oil Pumps are Stripped Down, see that they are assembled correctly—the larger plunger goes in the return pump, which is the one in front of the timing cover. Do not omit the spring washer between the pump disc and the cover plate. This is essential to the correct functioning of the pumps (see also page 162).

Lucas " Magdyno " Lubrication. Every "Magdyno" during assembly has the bearings and gears packed with grease, and for this reason no lubricators for the bearings are provided. Further lubrication of the bearings should not be necessary until the time arrives to submit the motor-cycle to a complete overhaul. The "Magdyno" should then be removed and taken to a Lucas service depot or agent for thorough inspection, cleaning, and repacking of the bearings with grease.

On the Big Twins to minimize wear of the fibre heel of the contact-breaker, provision is made for oiling the cam ring. A pocket in the contact-breaker housing contains a length of felt soaked in oil, and in the cam ring there is a hole fitted with a wick to enable the oil to find its way on to the cam ring surface. It is advisable every 5000 miles to withdraw the cam ring and place a few drops of *thin* oil on the felt. At the same time, push aside the locating spring, prise the rocker arm off its bearing (see Fig. 20), and smear the bearing lightly with some petroleum jelly. If the above is done it will be found that the "Magdyno" will run for long periods without it being necessary to adjust the gap between the contacts.

All single-cylinder "Magdyno" models have a face cam type contact-breaker (Fig. 19) and the cam is lubricated by a wick in the base of the contact-breaker. A few drops of thin machine oil should be added about every 5000 miles. By removing the spring arm carrying the moving contact the wick screw can be withdrawn. When replacing the wick screw, see that the small backing spring is fitted directly beneath the securing screw and spring washer, and with the bent portion facing *outwards* as shown in Fig. 19.

On pre-war "Magdynos" a lubricator is provided on the commutator end bracket and a few drops of thin oil should be added every 4000–5000 miles.

Lucas Dynamo Lubrication (1937–9 Coil Ignition). The E3E dynamo armature bearings are packed with grease on assembly as in the case of the "Magdyno" and the preceding remarks apply here also. The contact-breaker, however, requires just a little attention. Every 3000 miles remove the rocker arm and lightly smear some Mobilgrease No. 2 or engine oil on the pivot (Fig. 21) on which the rocker arm works. Also, with a little Mobilgrease No. 2 lightly smear the surface of the steel cam about every 3000 miles. The E3E dynamo has an oil hole at the commutator. Insert a few drops of thin oil every 4000–5000 miles.

Miller Dynamo Lubrication (1939 Coil Ignition). On the Miller DHI dynamo provided on all 1939 coil ignition models except Models A and T, both bearings are generously packed with high-melting point grease on assembly. This should suffice for 10,000–12,000 miles under normal riding conditions. After this mileage has been covered it is advisable to return the dynamo to Messrs. H. Miller & Co., Ltd., or to one of their agents, so that the instrument can be thoroughly inspected, cleaned, and the bearings repacked with H.M.P. grease.

The gears which drive the contact-breaker (see Fig. 22) are packed with graphited grease which is sufficient for 10,000–15,000 miles and can be repacked when the armature bearings are re-greased. A grease nipple is provided in the centre of the contact-breaker cam and you should apply the grease gun to this nipple about every 500 miles. Only a little Mobilgrease No. 4 is required to lubricate the cam shaft, and great care must be taken not to permit any surplus to get on to the contacts of the contact-breaker when applying the grease gun.

Flywheel Magneto Lubrication. On the 125 c.c. Models RE, WD/RE the contact-breaker requires no lubrication whatsoever and the utmost care must be taken to prevent oil or grease getting on the contacts. If, however, the rocker arm tends to stick, it should be removed and a trace of oil applied to its pivot pin.

About every 5000 miles remove the coil plate from the flywheel magneto (see Fig. 24) by withdrawing the contact-breaker cam, unscrewing the three nuts securing the coil plate to the crankcase, and lifting the coil plate away. Remove the two screws (27) securing the bearing plate and fibre washer (25) behind the ball bearing (23). Detach the bearing plate and washer and then repack the ball bearing (23) with some Price's H.M.P. grease. Replace the coil plate, etc. and verify the ignition timing (see page 55).

LUBRICATION OF CYCLE PARTS

Although correct engine lubrication is of vital importance, proper lubrication of the cycle parts, especially the gearbox and transmission, should never be neglected. Neglect will spoil the effective efficiency of a well lubricated and tuned engine, increase fuel consumption, and accelerate wear and tear. Two lubrication charts are provided on pages 75 and 78 for the guidance of Royal Enfield owners.

Four-speed Gearbox Lubrication. On all Royal Enfield (Albion) four-speed gearboxes the correct lubricant to use is engine oil (see page 60). The level of oil in the gearbox should be checked every 500–1000 miles and topped-up, where necessary, to the *level of the filler orifice*. It is desirable always to maintain the oil at this level. If any difficulty is experienced in determining the existing level, it is not a bad plan to insert the dip-stick attached to the oil tank filler cap. On the 148 c.c. O.H.V. Model T keep the gearbox about *half full*.

Do not under *any* circumstances replenish the gearbox with heavy yellow-type grease, or serious under lubrication may occur, with most disastrous results to the highly stressed gears. If occasion is had to strip down the gearbox, it is advisable to pack the box with some *soft* grease on assembly and thereafter to top-up with suitable engine oil. The foot gear-change requires no separate lubrication.

Lubricating Three-speed Gearbox (**Four-strokes**). Follow carefully the instructions given above for the four-speed gearboxes.

Three-speed Gearbox Lubrication (**Two-stroke**). The three-speed gearbox on two-stroke models is packed with soft grease during assembly. On 125 c.c. Models RE, WD/RE remove the filler plug about every 500 miles and top-up the lubricant as required with one of the following greases—

Castrolease Medium.
Mobilgrease No. 2.
Shell Retinax C.D.
Price's Energrease C1.
Esso Grease.

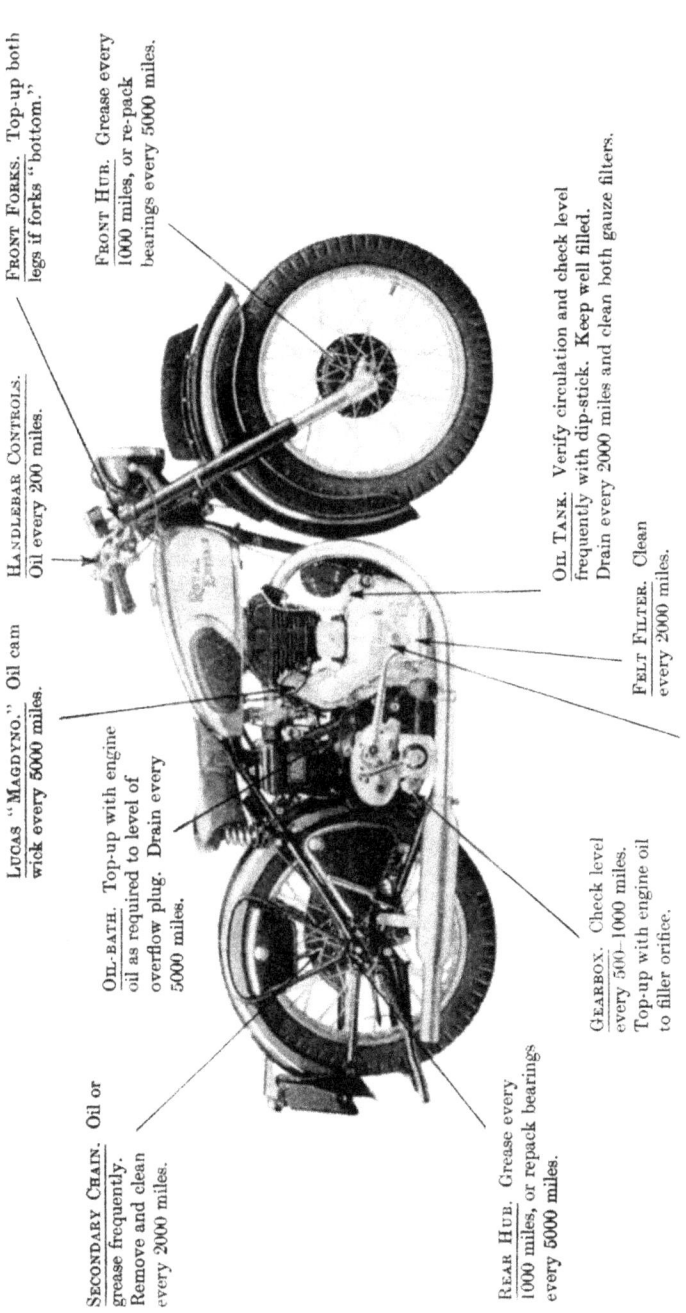

Front Forks. Top-up both legs if forks "bottom."

Front Hub. Grease every 1000 miles, or re-pack bearings every 5000 miles.

Handlebar Controls. Oil every 200 miles.

Lucas "Magdyno." Oil cam wick every 5000 miles.

Oil-bath. Top-up with engine oil as required to level of overflow plug. Drain every 5000 miles.

Oil Tank. Verify circulation and check level frequently with dip-stick. Keep well filled. Drain every 2000 miles and clean both gauze filters.

Felt Filter. Clean every 2000 miles.

Gearbox. Check level every 500–1000 miles. Top-up with engine oil to filler orifice.

Secondary Chain. Oil or grease frequently. Remove and clean every 2000 miles.

Rear Hub. Grease every 1000 miles, or repack bearings every 5000 miles.

Timing Case. Drain every 2000 miles.

Fig. 32. Lubrication Chart for Four-stroke Models (1946 Onwards)

The above chart showing a 1948–9 Model G is also applicable to all 1937–9 four-strokes except for certain differences: the felt filter is fitted only on the 1939 Model CO, and on 250 c.c. machines with circular-shaped crankcases the separate oil tank contains only one gauze filter. On coil ignition models a Lucas or Miller dynamo is fitted instead of a "Magdyno." All 1937–9 models have girder-type front forks and their links require greasing every 200 miles. The same applies to the rear brake pedal and speedometer drive. For steering head and brake cam spindle lubrication, see text

On the 125 c.c. models the gearbox must *not* be replenished with any heavy yellow-type grease, but it is permissible to use some engine oil in addition to one of the above-mentioned greases. Keep the gearbox about half full so that the lay shaft is about covered.

In the case of the 1937–9 225 c.c. Model A two-stroke, it is advisable to remove the filler plug every 500 miles and if necessary top-up to the level of the filler plug orifice with suitable engine oil (see page 60). If preferred, one of the above-mentioned greases may be used in addition to engine oil.

Replenish Oil-bath when Necessary. On four-stroke models having the primary chain enclosed in an oil-bath chain case, top-up the oil-bath when necessary with engine oil (page 60) to the level of the lower edge of the overflow plug. The chain will then be kept clean and efficiently lubricated, giving a sweet-running and quiet transmission. It is advisable to remove the outer half of the oil-bath chain case about every 5000 miles and allow the old oil to drain away. Much of the oil can be drained by removing the oil level plug and tilting the machine over to the near-side. Clean the inside of the case with paraffin, replace the outer half, and afterwards replenish to the correct level with engine oil. See that no sludge remains.

On the 125 c.c. Two-strokes. On Models RE, WD/RE the oil-bath chain case is packed with soft grease on assembly. Occasionally remove the two hexagon-headed plugs from the outer half of the case and pour in engine oil (see page 60) through the upper hole until it begins to trickle from the lower hole. Before replacing both plugs, allow *all* surplus oil to finish oozing out.

It is advisable about every 5000 miles to drain off the used oil by removing the outer half of the oil-bath chain case. Replenish to the correct level with clean engine oil after replacing the outer half of the case. To ensure an oil-tight joint, see that the joint washer is undamaged. It is a good plan to apply some shellac to the rear of this washer.

Where No Oil-bath is Fitted. The primary chain receives a certain amount of lubrication from the breather in the oil tank (except on Model A two-stroke), but this lubrication should frequently be supplemented by applying additional engine oil or grease, especially if the level of oil in the tank is not maintained high. On the two-stroke model mentioned, inspect the chain whenever setting out for a run and lubricate with engine oil or grease if the chain is at all dry.

About every 2000 miles remove the primary chain, wash it thoroughly in paraffin and then allow to soak in melted tallow.

ALL ABOUT LUBRICATION

This treatment ensures every single one of the links and rollers being adequately lubricated. Remember, the primary chain runs very, very fast and must *not* be neglected.

Lubrication of Secondary Chain. Keep this chain well lubricated with engine oil or grease by frequently applying an oil can to the chain run or smearing it with grease applied to the finger. Although a chain guard is provided, this is insufficient to prevent the chain picking up road filth in dirty weather, and the chain should be dealt with about every 2000 miles in the manner described above for the primary chain (no oil-bath fitted).

Grease Wheel Hubs about every 1000 Miles. Inject some thin grease such as "Castrolease Heavy" into the nipples on the front and rear hubs about every 1000 miles. Be careful not to inject excessive grease, otherwise it may find its way gradually on to the brake linings and you may find that your mount is inclined to run away with you in awkward circumstances.

Note. Although grease nipples are provided for hub lubrication, the above method can be improved on. It is infinitely preferable to dismantle the hub bearings about every 5000 miles and repack them with grease. Unless the hubs are nearly full, the addition of further grease through the nipples may not take effect. If the hubs *are* full and further grease is added, brake trouble is in the offing.

Also Grease at 5000 Miles—the brake cam spindle bearings and the steering head bearings. See that the steering is not stiff. If it is, perhaps the bearings need adjusting (see pages 131–132).

Grease nipples are not provided for the steering head bearings on most four-stroke models as they are apt to cut control and lighting cables. Nipples are also omitted for the brake cam spindles, as grease-gun lubrication causes excessive lubrication and brake trouble.

The steering head bearings should be dismantled and repacked with grease about once every 5000 miles, but no harm will result if the bearings are greased somewhat less often; the movement of these bearings is trifling. Remove the brake cam spindles about every 5000 miles and smear them with some grease (see page 79).

Every 200 Miles.—Grease the fork spindles (1937–9, Models RE, WD/RE), rear brake pedal, and speedometer drive; apply a little oil to the handlebar controls, external gear (hand control) and clutch control mechanism, etc., about every 200 miles, or once a week. It is quite surprising how just that little extra attention "makes all the difference."

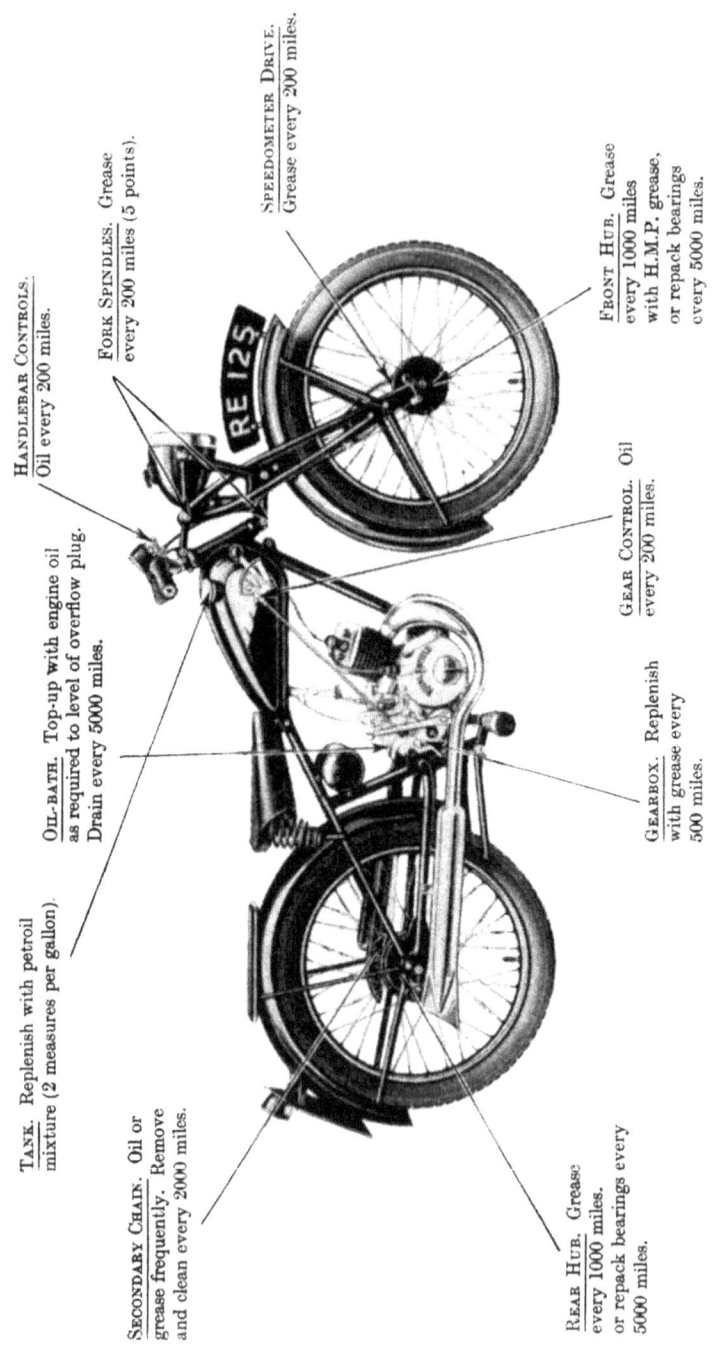

Fig. 33. Lubrication Chart for 125 c.c. Two-stroke Models RE, WD/RE

The two lubrication points for the rear brake pedal are not indicated as the pedal is on the near-side. Apply the grease gun every 200 miles. On the 225 c.c. Model A two-stroke the petroil mixture should comprise ¾ pint of oil per gallon of fuel, and the gearbox should be topped-up with engine oil instead of grease every 500 miles. For steering head and brake cam spindle lubrication, see text

ALL ABOUT LUBRICATION

Topping-up Telescopic Front Forks. The Royal Enfield telescopic type front forks (1945 onwards) are lubricated internally by the hydraulic medium contained within each fork leg. No lubrication is required, but when necessary top-up each leg. Theoretically no leakage of oil should occur, but in practice there is some leakage past the oil seals, especially if a machine is regularly driven over bad roads. The necessity for topping-up is indicated by the onset of sudden damping which gives the effect of "bottoming." The oil used for topping-up *must* be of the correct viscosity and The Enfield Cycle Co., Ltd. recommend the exclusive use of one of the following oils—

Castrolite.
Vacuum Arctic.
Shell X-100 SAE 20/20W.
Price's Energol SAE 20.
Essolube 20.

Prior to topping-up the telescopic front forks, jack the machine up on its rear stand on a level floor. Verify that the forks are in their normal unladen position by pulling upwards on the handlebars and then releasing them.

Referring to Fig. 86, to top-up each fork leg, first remove the small hexagon cap nut A from the top of the leg, also the washer beneath the cap nut. This exposes the gauze filter C. Next unscrew the small drain plug S from the bottom of the fork leg. Place a suitable receptacle below the fork leg to catch surplus oil as it runs out. Then pour in one of the above-mentioned oils through the gauze filter C until the oil reaches the level of the cross-hole V. This is the correct oil level and any surplus oil will run out from the drain plug hole at the foot of the leg. As soon as surplus oil ceases to drip out, replace the washer and drain plug S. Tighten the latter firmly. Deal with each fork leg similarly.

Use the Correct Grease. It is important to charge the grease gun with suitable grease. Greases recommended for insertion through all grease nipples including those on the front and rear wheel hubs are those specified below.

Castrolease Heavy.
Mobilgrease No. 4.
Shell Retinax A.
Price's Energrease C3.
Esso Grease.

It is a good plan after applying the grease gun to the various nipples to make a practice of checking over the various external nuts for tightness.

Topping-up Telescopic Front Forks (**1950 Model RE**). When the machine is assembled by the makers one fluid ounce (about 28 c.c.) of hydraulic fluid is inserted into each fork leg, this is the correct amount. This should suffice for an almost indefinite period, but should leakage (causing "bottoming") occur after riding over rough roads, top-up each fork leg with one of the oils mentioned on page 79. Insert the oil through the small lubricator in the cap at the top of each leg.

Dipper Switch Lubrication. About every 5000 miles apply a little thin machine oil to the moving parts of the dipper switch.

Sidecar Chassis. Where a sidecar is fitted, it is wise to grease occasionally with graphited grease the front and rear ball-jointed connections. Also grease periodically the sliding joint at the base of the seat-pillar connection tube.

Lubricate the sidecar hub when the other hubs are being greased, and paint the springs with light engine oil occasionally.

CHAPTER V
CARE OF LIGHTING EQUIPMENT

IN this chapter we are concerned solely with the electrical equipment used for lighting purposes, although in the case of the coil ignition models the battery is used for both lighting and ignition. The various components used for ignition only, such as the magneto portion of the "Magdyno," the contact-breaker, coil, ignition switch and warning lamp have already been dealt with in the appropriate part of Chapter III, and no further reference will be made to them here.

Where coil ignition is not used, the lighting equipment comprises (except on Models RE, WD/RE which have a Villiers set with direct lighting from a flywheel dynamo): the dynamo portion of the Lucas "Magdyno" (which is detachable); a 12 amp.-hr. battery; a Lucas type headlamp with double-filament bulb, the upper bulb giving an anti-dazzle beam controlled by a handlebar operated dimming switch; and an MT110 tail light. The lighting switch and ammeter are on the tank panel or headlamp.

On 1937-8 coil ignition models the lighting equipment is the same except that a Lucas type dynamo is used in conjunction with a large headlamp and MT210 tail light. On 1939 coil ignition models a Miller DH1 dynamo is used in conjunction with a Miller 73 CV headlamp.

The following instructions apply to the dynamo portion of the Lucas MO1 "Magdyno" or the separate Lucas E3E dynamo provided on 1937-8 coil ignition models and the 1939 Models A, T.

An Important Precaution. It is advisable when making any alterations or connections to the wiring to disconnect the positive lead at the battery. This will prevent the risk of a short-circuit. This precaution, however, is not necessary when removing the dynamo cover to inspect the commutator and brushes, as the cut-out is open when the engine is stationary and no current can pass from the battery.

THE LUCAS DYNAMO

A brass connector connects the lead from the positive terminal of the battery to the switch lead and to disconnect, first push back the rubber shield and then unscrew the cable connector, taking care that it does not touch any metal part of the frame. If it does touch, a spark will show that the battery has been well and truly shorted. Pull the rubber shield well over the connector when again reconnecting.

Do Commutator Brushes Make Good Contact? About every six months remove the dynamo cover, hold the brush spring levers aside and withdraw the commutator brushes from their holders. Note whether the brushes slide freely in their holders and make good contact with the commutator. If they have been in use for a long time, they may have become so worn that they do not bed down properly on the commutator, and the only remedy is to replace the brushes by new ones of Lucas manufacture. To obtain the most satisfactory result new brushes should be "bedded" to the commutator at a Lucas service depot.

—Are They Clean? It is vitally important to keep the commutator brushes clean and after removing them they should be cleaned with a rag moistened with petrol. When refitting, see that the brushes are replaced in their correct positions. The commutator itself should also be kept clean and free from oil and carbon dust.

To Clean the Commutator. Undoubtedly the easiest and best method is without disconnecting any leads to remove one of the main brushes from its holder and insert through the aperture a dry duster held by a suitably shaped piece of wood against the commutator surface while slowly revolving the engine by hand. If the commutator is very dirty, moisten the cloth or duster with petrol.

What the Ammeter is For. This centre-zero instrument which shows a charge on one side and a discharge on the other is provided to give a reading of the amount of current flowing to and from the battery. It indicates whether or not the electrical equipment is functioning satisfactorily.

Lubrication of Lucas Dynamo. The lubrication of the armature bearings of the dynamo portion of the "Magdyno" and the Lucas E3E dynamo (coil ignition) is covered on pages 72–73. Some dynamos (see Fig. 34) have a lubricator provided on the commutator end bracket. Where such a lubricator is fitted, insert a few drops of high-grade thin machine oil every 4000–5000 miles.

Do Not Tamper with Compensated Voltage Control Unit. This ingenious device, comprising the cut-out and compensated voltage control neatly housed in a box separate from the dynamo, sees to it that the battery is always kept properly charged by varying the dynamo output according to the load and state of charge of the battery. When the battery is run down, the dynamo gives a big output to recharge it as quickly as possible. The regulator effects an increased output when the lights are switched on, so as to balance the current consumed by them. The unit is sealed and should not be tampered with, the only likely trouble, and a

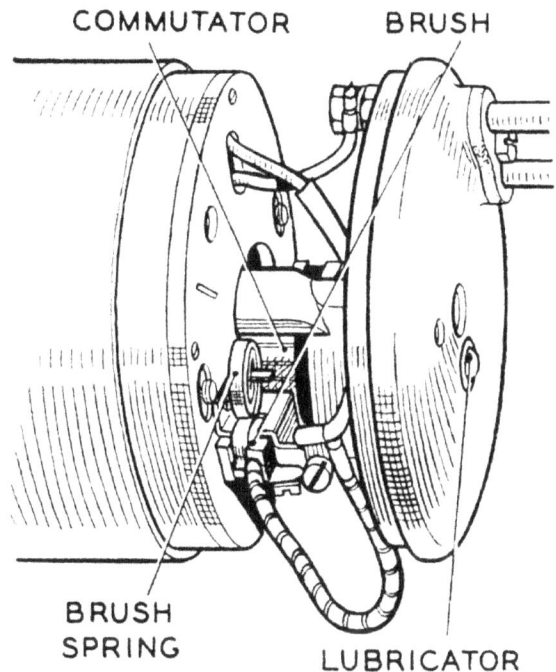

Fig. 34. Commutator End of 1937–49 Lucas Dynamo
(*Joseph Lucas, Ltd.*)

remote one, being oxidization, or possibly welding together, of the points due to accidental crossing of the dynamo field and positive leads. Therefore be careful with the leads at the dynamo end. See also notes on page 84 *re* running with battery disconnected.

The compensated voltage control prevents boiling away of the distilled water in the battery because with the battery well charged the dynamo gives only a trickle charge (1 or 2 amperes at the ammeter) during daylight running. Nevertheless the level and S.G. of the electrolyte should occasionally be checked. Follow the hints given on pages 87–88. It should be noted that immediately after the headlamp is switched on a discharge reading may be observed at the ammeter. This generally occurs when the voltage is high after a long run. After a brief interval the voltage drops and the C.V.C. regulator responds, thus causing the output of the dynamo to balance the load imposed by the lamps. The maximum rate of charge is approximately 7 volts.

Although the C.V.C. unit normally requires no adjustment, if the battery is not kept properly charged, or becomes overcharged, the C.V.C. unit should be examined and readjusted at a Lucas service depot.

If a "Lucas-Nife" battery is substituted for the lead-acid type,

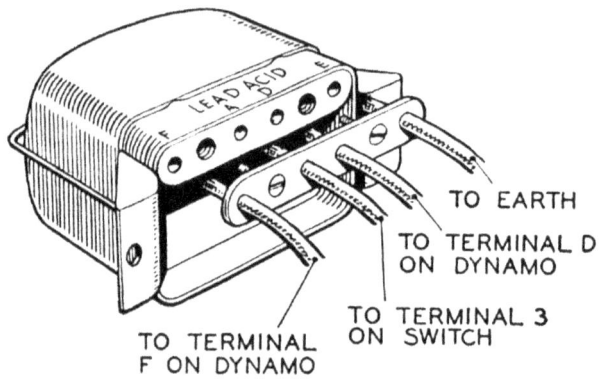

FIG. 35. CONNECTIONS FOR COMPENSATED VOLTAGE CONTROL UNIT
(*Joseph Lucas, Ltd.*)

a new regulator should be fitted, otherwise the dynamo charging rate with a run down battery will not be sufficient.

Advantage of C.V.C. System. One advantage of compensated voltage control is that it makes it possible to run the machine with the battery disconnected and the lights switched on without risking burning out the bulbs. A coil ignition model can be started up with a completely discharged battery by disconnecting the latter, and pushing the machine off in bottom gear. As soon as the engine starts, the battery can be reconnected.

Examine Wiring Occasionally. The various leads in the wiring system should be examined occasionally for chafing or bad contact at the terminals. This is particularly important in the case of the two battery leads and the leads from the voltage control unit to the dynamo and earth. Should the dynamo cease to charge (indicated by a heavy discharge at the ammeter), disconnect the field circuit lead (marked green) from the dynamo; this may save the dynamo from damage, though it will not cause it to charge.

CARE OF LIGHTING EQUIPMENT

The electrical leads connected to the "D" and "F" terminals of the dynamo or C.V.C. unit (see Fig. 35) must on no account be reversed. To prevent accidental reversal, the screw in the dynamo terminal block is slightly off-centre and the screws which secure the regulator terminal clamping plate are of different size.

Identification of Cables. Coloured sleevings are provided on the ends of all cables to assist identification. Lucas wiring diagrams showing the connections and colour schemes employed are given on pages 96 to 99.

Making Connections. To make a connection to the switch, it is necessary first to remove the three screws which secure the head-lamp panel containing the ammeter and lighting switch. Then bare about ¾ in. of the cable, twist the strands together and turn back about ⅛ in. so as to form a small ball. Next remove the grub-screw from the appropriate terminal and insert the wire so that the ball fits in the terminal post. Finally replace the grub-screw and tighten it until a good electrical connection is obtained.

Prior to making a connection to the regulator or dynamo terminals, loosen the fixing screw on the terminal block and detach the clamping plate. Then remove the metal sleeves from each terminal. Thread about 1 in. of cable through the clamping plate holes and bare the ends for ⅜ in. Fit the metal sleeves over the cables, bend back the wire over the sleeves and push the sleeves right home into their terminals. Afterwards tighten down the clamping plate.

THE MILLER DYNAMO

The following instructions apply to the Miller DHI dynamo (see Fig. 22) fitted to all 1939 coil ignition models except Models A and T. A wiring diagram for the Miller equipment provided on Model WD/RE is given on page 99.

Dynamo Lubrication. For advice on lubrication, see page 73.

Commutator and Brushes. The maintenance required is similar to that described on page 82 for the corresponding Lucas components. See that the brushes are kept clean and move freely in their holders. If a brush is "sticky," remove it and clean its sides with a cloth moistened with petrol. Clean a dirty or blackened commutator by pressing a *fine* duster in contact with it while slowly rotating the engine.

New commutator brushes require to be bedded-down. This is conveniently done by a Miller service agent. If, however, you decide to bed a brush down yourself, pass a thin strip of very fine glass-paper between the commutator and brush. Verify that the smooth side of the glass-paper rubs on the commutator. Then pull the glass-paper backwards and forwards a few times and remove the paper. After using glass-paper, be most careful to wipe away all traces of carbon and glass-paper dust.

The Regulator Unit (C.V.C.). This provides completely automatic control and normally should not require any adjustment. The C.V.C. unit sees to it that the dynamo output varies according to the load on the battery and its state of charge. During daylight running with the battery in good condition, the ammeter charge reading will seldom exceed 1 or 2 amperes.

MILLER FLYWHEEL GENERATOR

The Miller (type FL/18) flywheel generator (Fig. 24) used on Models RE, WD/RE supplies current for the lamps only while the engine is running. It provides the correct voltage at 20–25 m.p.h. when riding with top gear engaged. If illumination proves to be insufficient when riding below this speed, change down to a lower gear. For parking purposes, the headlamp on Model RE includes provision for fitting a dry battery. As the flywheel generator has no commutator or brush-gear, it should continue to function for long periods with almost no attention.

Lubrication. About every 5000 miles the ball bearing behind the coil plate requires to be re-greased (see page 73).

Testing Lighting Circuit. If there is no response to switching on the lamps with the engine running and the L.T. connection plugged into its socket, remove the L.T. connection from the flywheel generator and connect it to one terminal of a 6-volt battery. Earth the other terminal of the battery. If it is now found that the lamps respond, the fault is in the lighting coils of the flywheel generator. If, on the other hand, the lamps do not light up, the fault lies in the wiring circuit, the lighting switch, or the bulbs. Should one or more bulbs light up, it is probable that the remainder have burned out filaments.

When a fault is suspected in the wiring circuit (see Fig. 44), it is advisable to follow each lead through from end to end and to verify that the circulation is sound and that the wire makes good contact with the terminals.

LUCAS BATTERY MAINTENANCE

The following hints and tips on how to look after the "juice box" apply only to Lucas 12 amp.-hr. lead-acid batteries, which are fitted as standard on most Royal Enfields.

CARE OF LIGHTING EQUIPMENT

Examine Acid Level Once a Month. The filler caps in the top of the battery should be removed at least once a month and the level of the acid solution inspected. The solution should just reach to the top of the plate separators (i.e. to about $\frac{1}{4}$ in. above the top of the plates themselves), with the battery level. If it does not do so, top-up with *distilled* water to the correct level with a Lucas battery filler.

If acid has been spilled, it must be replaced by a diluted sulphuric acid (H_2SO_4) solution of the same specific gravity as the electrolyte in the cell to which it is to be added (about 1·285).

Do not Hold a Lighted Match near the Vents. If you do, you may cause the gas escaping from the vents to ignite and "blow up" the battery. Also remember that the battery contains diluted vitriol, a devilish substance should it get in the eye.

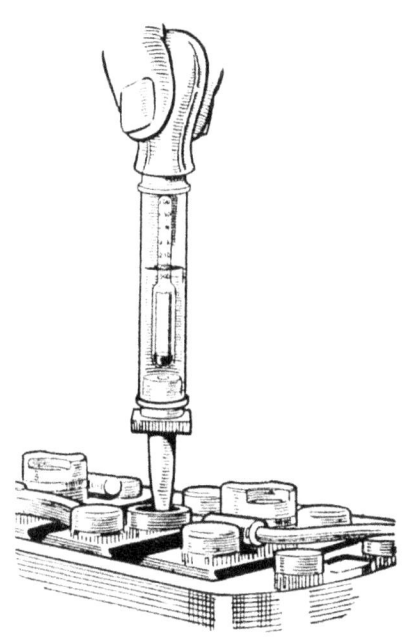

FIG. 36. CHECKING SPECIFIC GRAVITY OF ELECTROLYTE WITH HYDROMETER
(*Joseph Lucas, Ltd.*)

When Laying the Equipment By. Some riders do not use their machines during some months of the year, and although the tyres will not suffer if the machine is jacked right up and kept in a dark, dry place, the battery will not tolerate being forgotten. Forgotten batteries are apt to remind one of their lonesomeness by subsequently refusing duty or failing to work efficiently. To prevent permanent sulphation of the plates when the equipment is laid by for several months, the battery* should be given a small charge about once a fortnight from an independent source of electrical energy (a wireless dealer or garage will do this for a reasonable charge). Under no circumstances must the electrolyte be removed and the plates allowed to remain dry. This form of abuse causes a serious and permanent loss of capacity.

To Test Specific Gravity. If any loss of acid has occurred or the battery is misbehaving itself it is advisable to check the

* Whenever the battery is disconnected, the positive lead to it should be taped up. It must never be earthed.

specific gravity with a Lucas hydrometer. The specific gravity provides a good indication of the state of charge of the battery. Readings should be taken in each cell and should be approximately the same. If one cell shows a reading differing from that of the others, probably some acid has been spilled or there may be a short between the plates. The correct S.G. figures at a temperature of about 60 degrees Fahrenheit are: fully discharged, below 1·150; about half discharged, about 1·210; fully charged, 1·280–1·300.

"Export" Batteries Uncharged. On "Export" Royal Enfields the batteries are sent out dry and uncharged, and it is necessary to fill them with a diluted sulphuric acid solution of 1·285 S.G. and charge for 32 hours at 0·8 amps. Subsequently careful dynamo charging should suffice to keep them in good condition.

EXIDE BATTERY MAINTENANCE

The foregoing instructions concerning the maintenance of Lucas lead-acid batteries also apply to Exide batteries (fitted to 1939 coil ignition machines, except Models A, T), but the following variations should be noted.

Topping-up. When topping-up the battery, add distilled water to bring the level ⅛ in. above the tops of the separators, but well short of the bottom of the vent plugs. Topping-up is best undertaken prior to a run, as the ensuing agitation and "gassing" (due to charging) will ensure the thorough mixing of the electrolyte. This applies to all batteries.

Specific Gravity Readings. With Exide batteries the normal S.G. readings indicated by a hydrometer (at about 60 degrees F.) are as follows: fully discharged, about 1·150; about half discharged, about 1·210; fully charged, about 1·285 to 1·300.

Are Battery Connections O.K.? Whether an Exide or a Lucas battery is concerned, it is essential always to keep the battery connections tight and clean. Burned out bulbs are often caused through neglect in this matter. The occasional application of a little petroleum jelly will prevent or reduce corrosion.

LAMPS (LUCAS AND MILLER)

On most 1937–49 models Lucas lamps are fitted, the headlamp having a double-filament main bulb. The out-of-focus filament is controlled by a handlebar dip switch. A pilot bulb is, of course, also included. On 1937 models the ammeter and lighting switch

CARE OF LIGHTING EQUIPMENT

are mounted on the instrument panel, but on all 1938 models they are embodied in the headlamp. The 1939 coil ignition machines (except Models A, T) have Miller lamps. Miller equipment is also provided on the 125 c.c. Models RE, WD/RE.

Switch Positions ("**Magdyno**" **Models**). The lighting switch which is mounted on the instrument panel or else on the headlamp behind the ammeter (Fig. 37) has the following three positions—
"Off"—Lamps off.

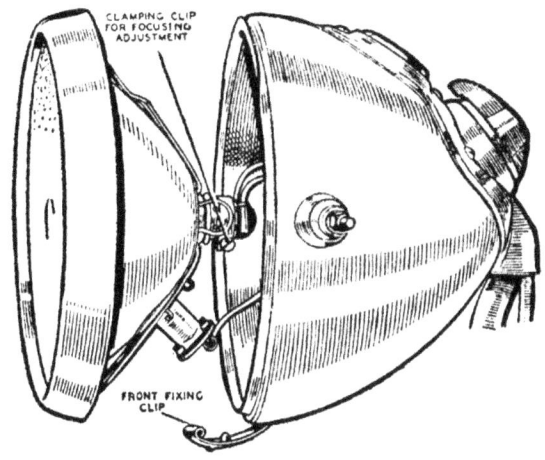

FIG. 37. THE LUCAS DU42 HEADLAMP USED ON MOST MODELS
(*Joseph Lucas, Ltd.*)
The slightly larger DU142 headlamp fitted to some pre-war models is similar. The latest type MU42 headlamp is somewhat different and has a domed and fluted front glass

"L"—Headlamp (pilot bulb), tail light and sidecar light (where fitted).
"H"—Headlamp (main bulb), tail light and sidecar light (where fitted).
It should be noted that the dynamo *in all switch positions* charges according to the load on the battery and its state of charge. The speedometer is illuminated with the switch in the "L" or "H" position.

Switch Positions (Lucas Coil Ignition). The switch on the tank panel (1937) or headlamp (1938) has the same positions as on the "Magdyno" models, but instead of being marked "Off," "L," "H" they are marked "Off," "Low," and "High." In the centre of the switch is the ignition key and a warning lamp (see page 53) is included.

Lucas Switch Positions (Models CO, WD/CO). On the 1946 346 c.c. Model CO the lighting switch has the same three positions as for the "Magdyno" models (page 89), and a dipper switch is provided. The 1941-5 Model WD/CO, however, has a four-position switch and no dipper switch. In addition to the usual "OFF," "L" and "H" positions, the lighting switch has a "T" position which lights the tail lamp only.

On the later Model WD/CO a "repeater" type lighting switch is

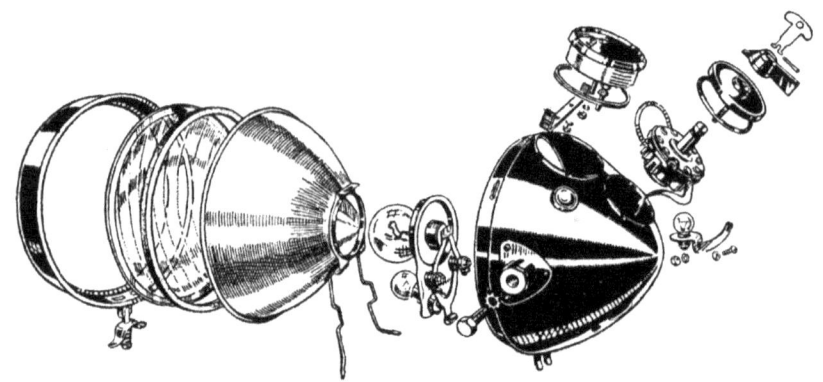

FIG. 38. EXPLODED VIEW OF MILLER HEADLAMP FITTED TO 1939 COIL IGNITION MODELS

(*H. Miller & Co., Ltd.*)

On the 1939 coil ignition Models A, T, and on all 1937-8 coil ignition models, Lucas lighting equipment is provided

situated beneath the saddle and no ammeter is fitted. The three positions are as follows—

"Off"—All lamps off.

"T"—Tail lamp on.

"H"—Tail lamp and headlamp main bulb or pilot bulb on, according to the position of the push switch at the rear of the headlamp.

Switch Positions (1939 Miller Coil Ignition). The switch positions on 1939 coil-ignition models (except A, T) are as follows: "PK" (pilot and tail with ignition off); "OFF" (ignition and lights off); "IG & CH" (ignition on, lights off; "H" (main bulb, tail and ignition on); "L" (pilot, tail and ignition on).

Miller Switch Positions (Model RE). On the 125 c.c. Model RE two-stroke the Miller flywheel generator supplies current for the lamps only while the engine is running, but for parking purposes the headlamp (type 62ED) has a dry battery. It is important not

CARE OF LIGHTING EQUIPMENT

to leave the dry battery in the lamp after it has become completely run down, otherwise the contacts will become corroded.

The lighting/ignition switch is at the rear of the headlamp. It has three positions. In the centre position all lamps are switched off. In the left-hand position the dry battery (where fitted) illuminates the headlamp pilot bulb and also the tail lamp. When the switch is in the right-hand position the flywheel generator illuminates the headlamp main bulb and the tail lamp. The main driving light can be dipped if desired by means of the dipping switch on the left-hand side of the handlebars. With the switch in the right-hand position the speedometer is also illuminated.

Miller Switch Positions (Model WD/RE). On the 125 c.c. Model WD/RE issued to the Forces during World War II the headlamp does not include provision for a dry battery and lights are available only while the engine is running. The general design of the headlamp and the internal switching arrangement are quite different from that employed on Model RE, and no dipping switch is included. The lighting switch at the back of the headlamp has the following four positions—

"CH"—All lamps off.
"H"—Headlamp main bulb and tail lamp on.
"T"—Tail lamp on only.
"P"—Headlamp pilot bulb and tail lamp on.

To prevent burning out of the pilot and tail lamp bulbs with the switch in the "T" and "P" positions, a resistance is incorporated in the headlamp. Being switched in parallel with the bulbs, it absorbs surplus generator output.

Correct Bulb Replacements. The life of the lamp bulbs depends to some extent on how the bulbs are treated, but all bulbs gradually deteriorate under the influence of heat and vibration. It is advisable to renew a bulb before it actually burns out because a sagging filament is never in true focus. When bulb replacement is called for, see that a new bulb of the correct type is fitted to the Lucas or Miller lamp. Also make sure that the headlamp main bulb is fitted such that the dipped beam filament is *above* the centre filament. All Lucas bulbs have their identification number stamped on their metal caps, and this number should always be verified.

With the Lucas headlamp provided on all "Magdyno" models fit a Lucas No. 70, 6-volt, 24/24 watt, double-filament main bulb; fit a No. 200, 6-volt, 3 watt centre-contact bulb for the pilot, tail, and sidecar lamp (where fitted).

In the case of the Lucas headlamp fitted to 1937–8 coil ignition machines and 1939 Models A, T, insert a No. 180, 6-volt, 18/18 watt double-filament main bulb; use a No. 200 6-volt, 3 watt bulb for the pilot and tail lamp. On some Lucas coil ignition models the warning lamp (see page 53) does not go out as the engine is accelerated, but on other machines it does. In the former instance a 3·5-volt, 0·3 amp. bulb is required; in the latter case fit a 2·5-volt, 0·2 amp. bulb. Bulbs of lower amperage than those

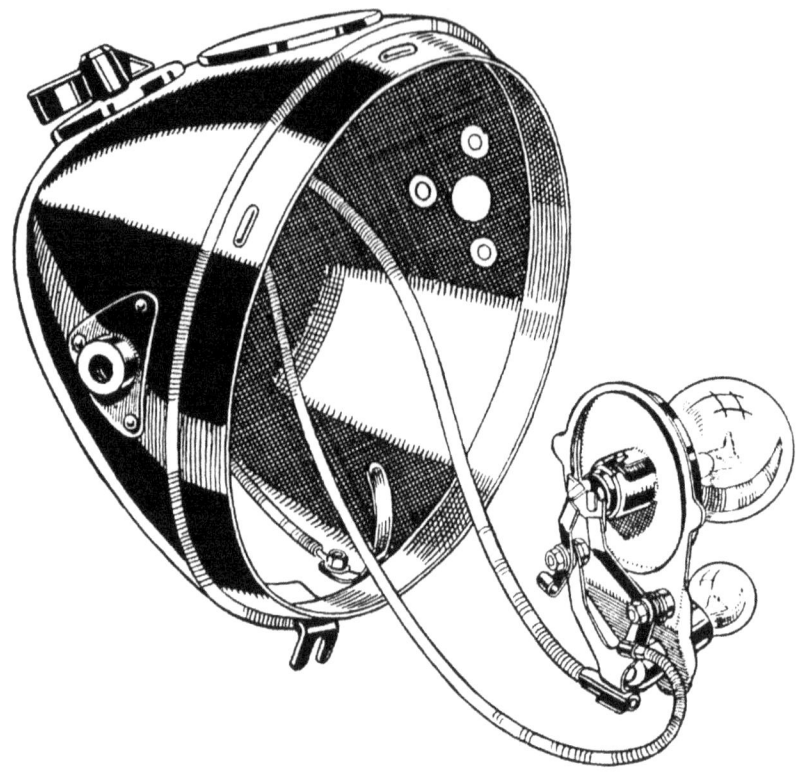

FIG. 39. MILLER HEADLAMP (MODEL WD/RE) WITH BULB HOLDER AND FRONT REMOVED

(*The Enfield Cycle Co., Ltd.*)

The Miller headlamp on Model RE is similar, but on this civilian machine the internal switch design is different and provision for a dry battery is included

specified above will rapidly burn out and should not be used. On Models D, S, SF, fit an 8-volt, 0·1 amp. bulb.

The correct bulb replacements for 1939 machines with Miller coil ignition (i.e., all except Models A, T) are: headlamp, 6-volt, 18/18 watt double-filament main bulb; 6-volt, 3 watt pilot bulb; and 6-volt, 3 watt tail lamp bulb.

In the case of the 125 c.c. Models RE, WD/RE the Miller

CARE OF LIGHTING EQUIPMENT

headlamp requires a 6-volt, 24 watt, double-filament main bulb (small bayonet cap). On Model WD/RE (which has no provision for a dry battery) if the filament in service burns out, reverse the bulb in its holder.* Alternatively change the lead from the headlamp terminal of the switch (see Fig. 44) over to the alternative connection on the bulb holder. The correct pilot bulb for Model RE is 2·5-volt, 0·2 amp., screw-fitting. Do not use a larger capacity pilot bulb, otherwise the dry battery will quickly become run down. The pilot bulb required for Model WD/RE is 6-volt, 3 watt, S.B.C. On Model RE fit a 6-volt, 3 watt, single-contact bulb (small bayonet cap) for the tail lamp. On Model WD/RE the correct type of bulb for the tail lamp is 6-volt, 3 watt, S.B.C., but a 12-volt, 6 watt, S.B.C. bulb can also be fitted.

Speedometer Light. If the speedometer light fails due to the bulb burning out, replace the bulb with a 6-volt, 1·8 watt (0·3 amp.) bulb with miniature bayonet cap. This applies to the speedometer light on all Royal Enfield machines.

Is Headlamp Alignment Correct? If in doubt, take your machine to a level, straight stretch of road and inspect the beam with the main driving light on. The beam should be straight ahead and parallel with the road surface. If it is not, slacken the headlamp fixing screws and depress the lamp or raise it as required. Be sure the fixing screws are firmly retightened.

Fitting Bulbs and Focusing. On all Lucas lamps it is a simple matter to fit new bulbs and the appropriate instructions are given hereafter. After renewing a Lucas headlamp double-filament main bulb, it is advisable to check that it is correctly focused, otherwise maximum illumination may not be obtained. On Miller headlamps no focusing adjustment is necessary or provided. With few exceptions Lucas and Miller bulbs have a bayonet type fixing and the headlamp bulbs can be instantly detached when the bracket holding them to the reflector is removed by pushing aside the securing clips or springs.

Lucas Headlamps. To remove the lamp front and reflector it is only necessary to press back the fixing clip at the bottom and then withdraw them together. To focus the headlamp, slacken the main bulb holder by loosening the clamping clip at the rear of the reflector. Then move the bulb holder backwards or forwards as required until the correct focus is obtained. A long range beam having no dark centre indicates that the focus is correct. Having

* This applies also to the double-filament main bulb on Model WD/CO.

focused the main bulb, tighten the clamping clip screw firmly so as to lock the adjustment. When replacing the lamp front and reflector, locate the top of the rim first, next press it on at the bottom, and finally secure the front by means of the fixing clip. Fig. 37 shows the Lucas headlamp with the front removed and bulb holder in position. If it is desired to remove the bulb holder, release it by pressing back the two securing springs.

Miller Headlamps. On Miller headlamps (see Figs. 38, 39) the double-filament main bulb is located permanently in focus and there is *no adjustment*. To detach the lamp front and reflector, release the spring-loaded catch at the base of the lamp. On replacing the lamp front, first locate the top of the rim, then press it on at the bottom, and secure with the catch.

The bulb holder can be removed from the reflector by releasing the securing springs and pressing them apart until the bulb holder can be withdrawn. To detach the reflector from the lamp front, release the securing spring clips inside the rim of the lamp, and then lift away the reflector and bulb holder. Be careful when replacing the reflector to see that it is the right way up, with the pilot lamp at the *bottom*.

Cleaning Lamps. Use a good car polish to clean the black body of a lamp. To clean the plated rim, first wash off any dirt with water and then polish the rim with a chamois leather or a soft dry cloth. On no account use metal polish to clean the reflector. If its transparent and colourless covering becomes marked with the fingers, remove such marks by polishing with a chamois leather or a very soft dry cloth.

Lucas Tail Lamp (" Magdyno " Models). A Lucas type MT110 tail lamp is fitted to the 1937 and later "Magdyno" models made for civilian use. The front portion of the lamp is let into a circular hole in the rear number plate and the bulb holder is mounted on a rubber diaphragm to prevent vibration. The bulb also has a cushioning device. To remove the portion of the lamp carrying the bulb holder (see Fig. 40), turn it *anti-clockwise* so as to release the bayonet fixing. To replace it, engage the bayonet fixing and then turn the portion carrying the bulb holder clockwise until it clips into position.

Lucas Tail Lamp (Coil Ignition). The rear part of the Lucas MT210 tail lamp fitted to 1937–9 coil ignition models can be detached for bulb replacement by giving it a half turn to the left. This depresses the spring catch and permits of the rear portion being withdrawn. When replacing, engage the slots in the body

CARE OF LIGHTING EQUIPMENT

with the two spring clips on the base and push home to secure the body.

Miller Tail Lamps (Models RE, WD/RE). The tail lamps fitted to Models RE, WD/RE are type 31WD and 36E respectively. On Model WD/RE to remove the cover carrying the red glass in order to gain access to the bulb, first remove the small screw from the top side of the lamp. Then pull away the cover. When replacing it, push it home over the base of the lamp and turn the cover until the small screw can be inserted.

On Model RE the tail lamp is entirely different to that fitted to Model WD/RE. It also has a much larger aperture containing a red celluloid disc, secured by a wire circlip. To gain access to the tail lamp bulb, remove the wire circlip, then the plated "fret," and finally the red celluloid disc.

Lucas Sidecar Lamp. Slacken the bottom screw in order to remove the lamp front and reflector. For bulb replacement, withdraw the bulb holder from the back of the reflector. Alternative positions for the bulb are provided, and each position

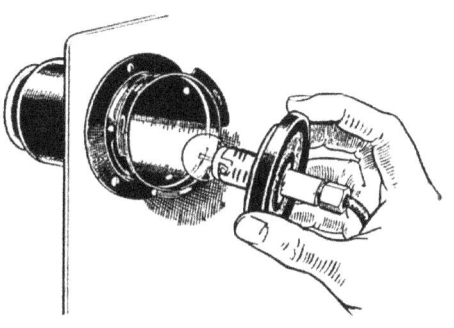

FIG. 40. LUCAS TAIL LAMP (TYPE MT110)
(*Joseph Lucas, Ltd.*)

can be experimented with until the best position is obtained. When replacing the lamp front, locate the top of the rim first, next press on at the bottom, and finally secure by tightening the fixing screw.

Trouble with Electric Horn. If the Lucas horn fails to vibrate or gives only a choking sound, do not assume that a breakdown has occurred. Check that no external trouble is the cause. Verify the connections, see that there is no short-circuit in the wiring, make sure the battery is charged, and last but not least check that the horn push bracket makes good electrical contact with the handlebars. Do not dismantle the horn. If it really is at fault, have it inspected at a Lucas service depot.

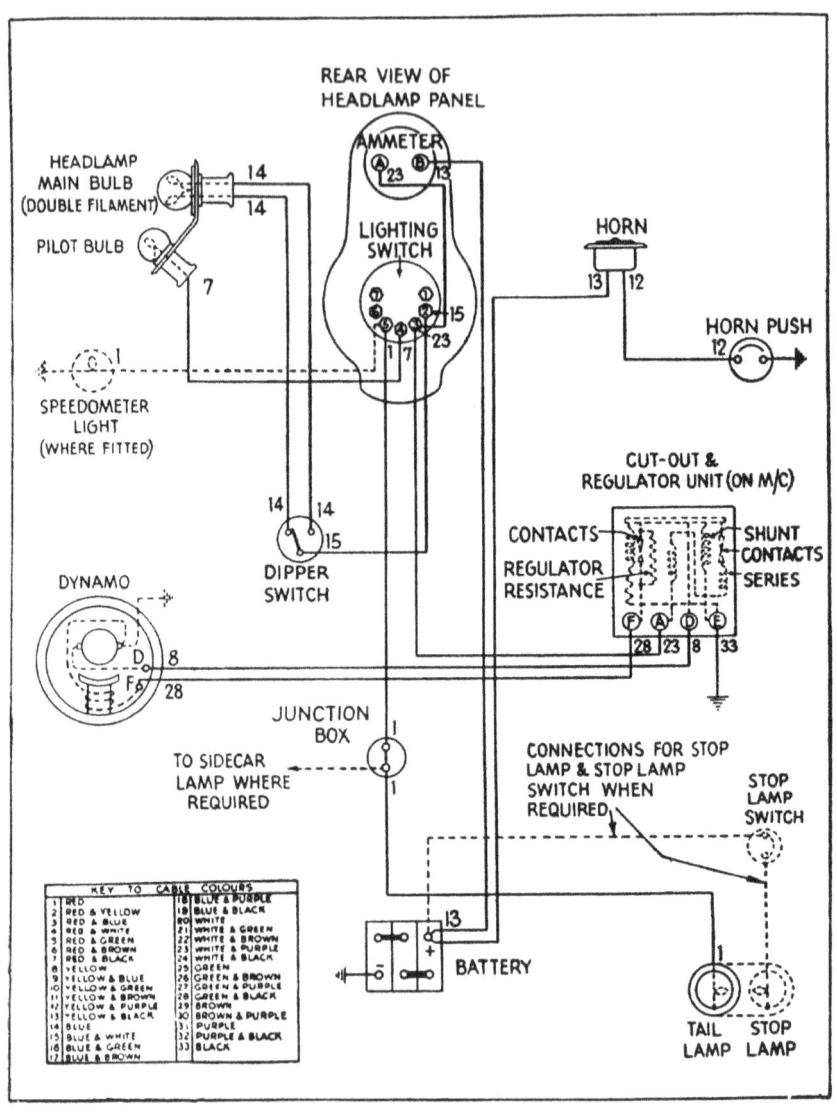

Fig. 41. Wiring Diagram for Lucas "Magdyno" Lighting Equipment with Compensated Voltage Control
(Applicable to all 1937 and later models without Instrument Panel)
(Joseph Lucas, Ltd.)

All internal connections and optional wiring are shown dotted and the cable ends are identified by coloured sleevings. The panel light is not shown

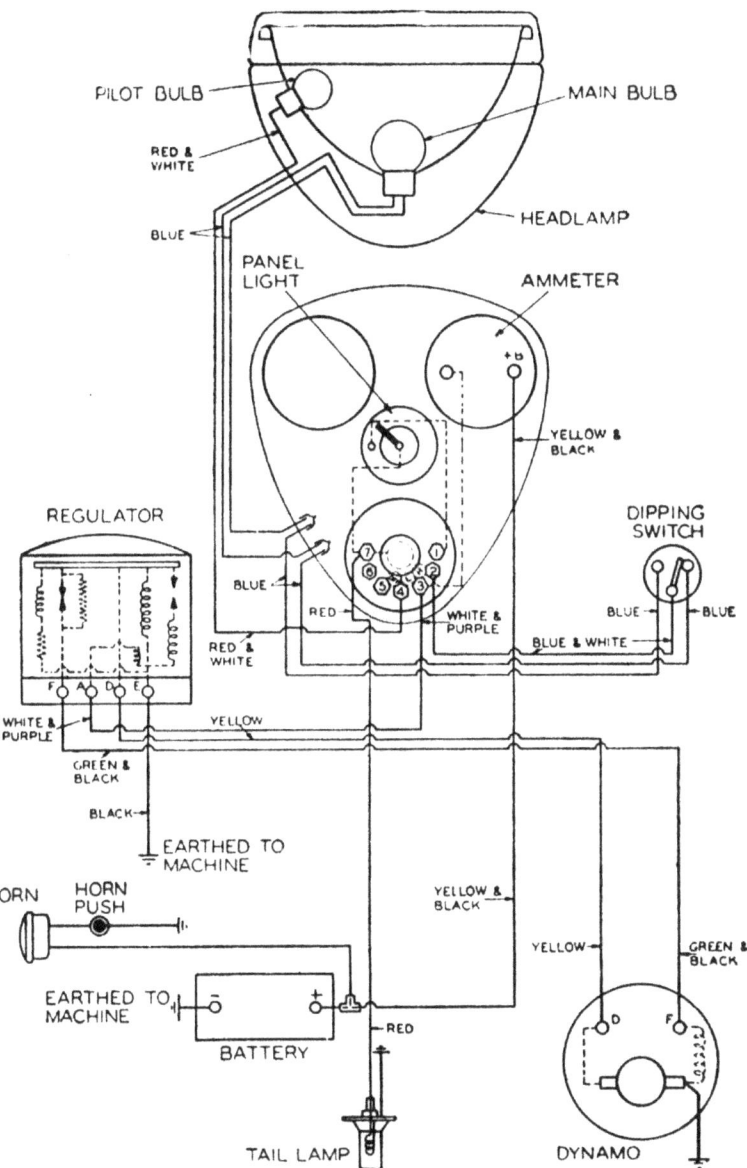

Fig. 42. Wiring Diagram for Lucas "Magdyno" Lighting Equipment with Compensated Voltage Control (Earlier Models with Instrument Panel)

(*Joseph Lucas, Ltd.*)

All internal connections are shown dotted and the cable ends are identified by coloured sleevings

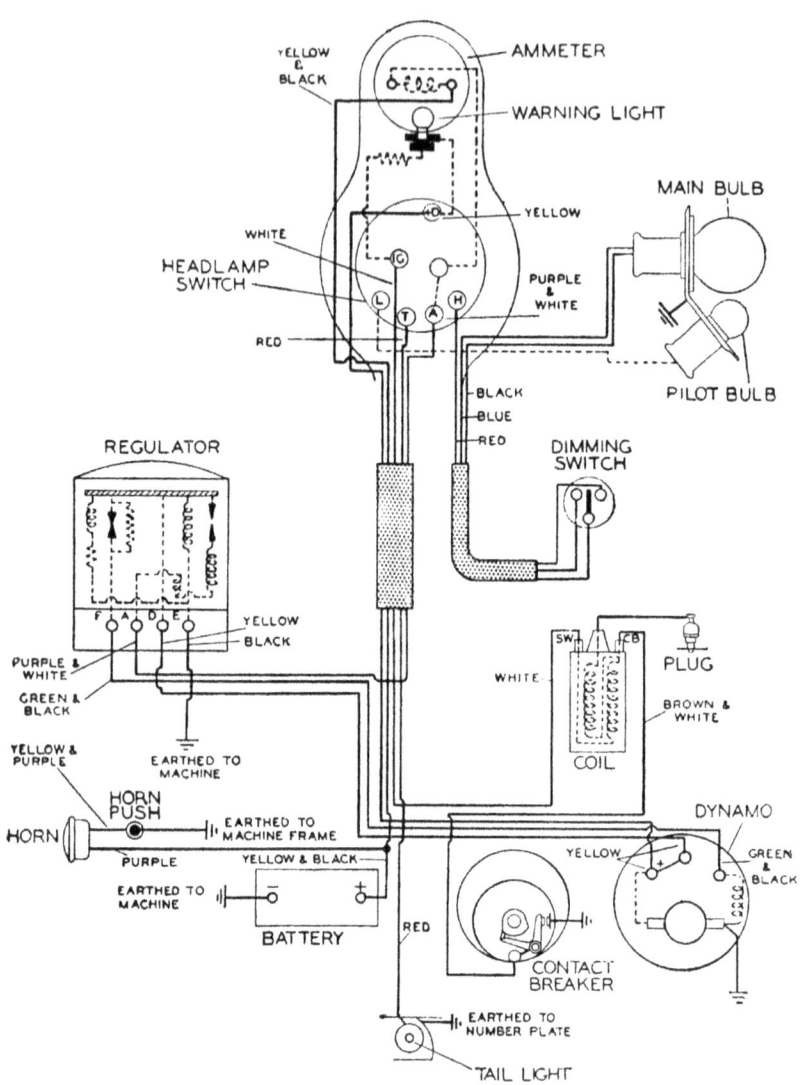

Fig. 43. Wiring Diagram for Lucas Dynamo Lighting and Coil Ignition Equipment with Compensated Voltage Control

(*Joseph Lucas, Ltd.*)

This diagram is applicable to all 1938 coil ignition models and 1939 Models A, T. On the 1937 models a tank panel housing the ammeter and lighting switch was provided. All internal connections are shown dotted

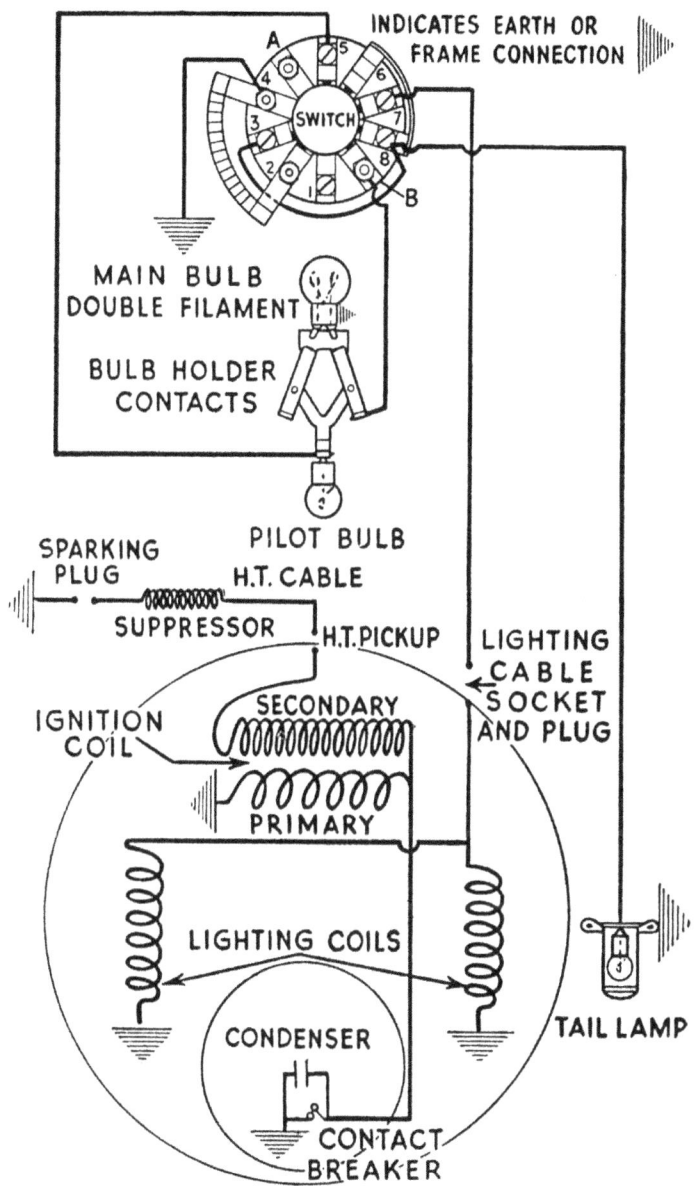

Fig. 44. Wiring Diagram for Miller Lighting and Ignition Flywheel Generator Set on Model WD/RE

(H. Miller & Co., Ltd.)

On Model RE (125 c.c. two-stroke) the internal switch arrangement is different and the pilot bulb is supplied with current from a dry battery in the 62ED headlamp

CHAPTER VI

GOOD TYRE MILEAGE

THE Dunlop cord tyres fitted as standard on all Royal Enfield models are made of the very finest material by a firm which has the world's land speed record to its credit, and with proper attention these tyres will give a very big trouble-free mileage. To obtain the best result from your tyres you should—

Always Maintain Correct Tyre Pressures. All Dunlop tyres now have the valve shown in Fig. 45 and, with the aid of a pressure

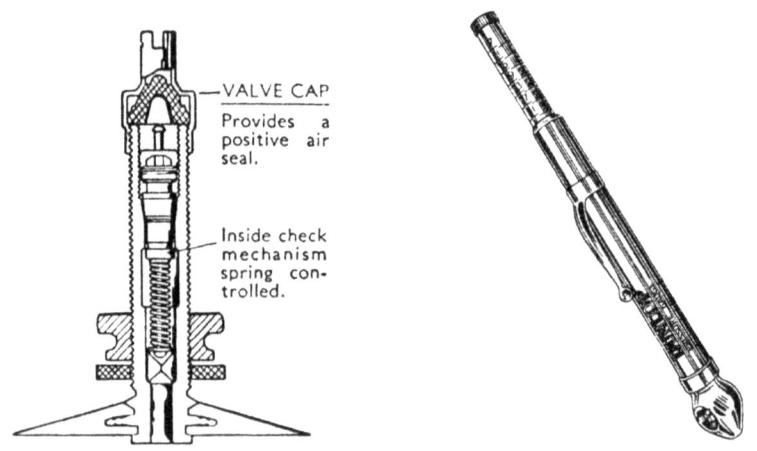

FIGS. 45, 46. SHOWING (*Left*) DUNLOP VALVE AND (*Right*) POCKET PRESSURE GAUGE

Check both tyre pressures frequently, and keep the valve caps firmly screwed down. Tighten with hand pressure only

gauge, the pressure can be measured accurately. Convenient types are the Dunlop Pencil Type No. 6 gauge, illustrated in Fig. 46, the Schrader 7750 gauge, the Holdtite gauge, and the Romac pressure gauge. To use these gauges, the valve dust cap (Fig. 45) is taken off, and the end of the pressure gauge is pressed on to the open end of the valve. It depresses the pin and allows air to enter the gauge and push up the piston calibrated in pounds per square inch. It is always wise to keep the dust caps screwed on, though some riders throw them away! Dust or grit getting into the valve stem is liable to interfere with the valve action of the little spring-controlled plunger (Fig. 45) and cause leakage. About once a year valve "insides" (check mechanism) should be

GOOD TYRE MILEAGE

replaced. They can be removed by taking off the valve cap and using the slotted end as a screwdriver. The recommended inflation pressures for the Dunlop cord tyres (standard size) fitted on 1937–49 Royal Enfields are tabulated below, and you should observe them as far as possible. About once a week, certainly not less than once a fortnight, test the pressures in the tyres with the pressure gauge and pump up until the gauge registers the correct pressures.

It must be borne in mind that under-inflation causes severe strain to be set up in the casing of the tyre. If run at too low a pressure the casings will crack and the tyres will be rendered useless when there are still many miles of wear left in the tread. The pressures recommended are, incidentally, for machines which are fully equipped, and if the driver and passenger are very

INFLATION PRESSURES FOR 1946–9 MODELS
(LBS PER SQ. IN.)

Royal Enfield Machine	Front	Rear
Model RE (125 c.c.)	16	20
Model CO (346 c.c.)	16	22
Model G (346 c.c.)	18	22
Models J, J2 (346 c.c.)	18	18

heavy, or if a pillion passenger is habitually carried, higher pressure in the rear tyre, at any rate, is advisable. For a pillion passenger or heavy luggage at least an extra 5–10 lb per sq in. should be allowed for the rear tyre.

INFLATION PRESSURES FOR 1937–45 MODELS
(LBS PER SQ. IN.)

Royal Enfield Model	Front	Rear	Sidecar
A, D, DC, SF, T, TM (solo)	16	24	—
B, BM, C, CM, CO, BCO, S, SM, S2 (solo)	18	26	—
G, G2, J, JM, H, HM (solo)	16	22	—
G, G2, J, JM, H, HM (sidecar)	20	24	16
J2, J2 "500 Bullet", JF, L (solo)	16	18	—
J2, J2 "500 Bullet," JF, L (sidecar)	20	20	16
250, 350 "Bullet" (solo)	18	22	—
"500 Competition" (solo)	18	16	—
K, KX (solo)	16	18	—
K, KX (single-seater sidecar)	16	22	16
WD, WD/C, WD/RE (solo)	16	20	—
WD/CO (solo)	16	22	—

Examine the Tyres Occasionally. If you wish to cut down the risk of roadside hold-ups to the minimum and avoid preventable deterioration of the covers, you should occasionally jack the machine up and carefully examine the treads over the whole of their circumference. Any sharp little flints embedded in the rubber should be gently eased out with a pocket knife and if the flints are of appreciable size, the holes should afterwards be stopped. In time it is inevitable that the tyres will become cut by the glass and sharp flints which are to be found on all our roads.

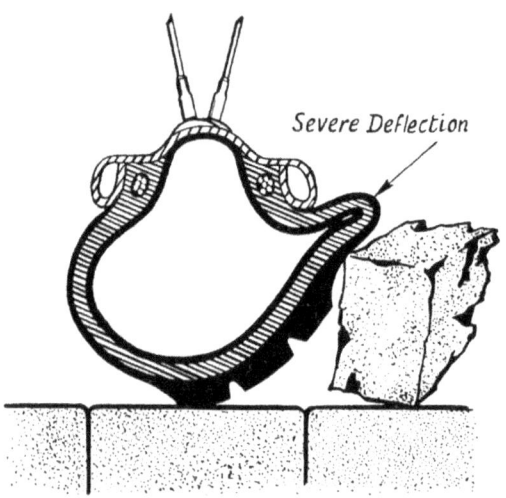

Fig. 47. Diagram Showing how Under Inflation can Cause a Concussion Burst
(Dunlop Rubber Co., Ltd.)
The severe deflection of the cover caused by impact with the edge of a stone when the tyre is under inflated may cause some cover strands to snap, with the result that a concussion burst follows

A superficial cut in the rubber is of little account, but it may spread, and it should therefore be filled with a suitable tyre stopping. If, however, this cut extends to the fabric of the tyre, wet will penetrate into the latter and, in due course, will rot it. Any cut of this nature should therefore be repaired efficiently. The only way to get this done is to remove the tyre and have it vulcanized. Vulcanizing is now much cheaper than it used to be.

Things You Should Avoid. Freak hills and extremely rough surfaces should be avoided. Wheel spin in particular is extremely detrimental to the rear tyre. The majority of riders never subject their tyres to these exceptional conditions, but many of

GOOD TYRE MILEAGE

them do not appreciate the strain which they impose on their tyres by bad driving. Fierce braking, rapid acceleration and fast cornering (particularly on a sidecar machine) should be avoided as far as possible, the same applying to quick engagement of the clutch with a wide throttle opening. This latter procedure, incidentally, is also detrimental to the transmission system. Three important points not yet mentioned are: (a) avoid crossing upraised tram lines or running in the lines; (b) do not allow the tyres to stand in patches of oil or paraffin; (c) when pulling up by the kerb do not allow the side of the tyre to scrape it.

Do You Know This? In recent years tyres became so well-made and reliable that it was customary for many riders to get the last pennyworth out of their tyres by riding until the fabric almost showed through (fast riders, of course, would never do this). This practice now invites trouble—for it is actually illegal to-day to run with smooth tyres (i.e. when all effective tread has disappeared), and it is better to buy a new cover than to waste the money on a fine.

How to Remove a Tyre Without Struggling With It. It is a frequent sight for the author to see a motor-cyclist *struggling* to remove a tyre, and through faulty refitting the tube is sometimes pinched and a second repair becomes necessary. Tyre removal and replacement need offer no difficulty whatever if a few simple precautions are taken. All Enfield motor-cycles are now fitted with Dunlop cord tyres, which have inextensible wired edges fitting into well-base rims. To remove this type of tyre, first completely deflate it by removing all the valve parts, including the check mechanism (Fig. 45). For this purpose use the slotted end of the valve cap. Next remove the knurled lock-nut which secures the valve to the rim. Then push both beads diametrically opposite the valve down into the rim well as far as possible in both directions.

Lever the cover off with two tyre levers used in the manner shown in Fig. 48. Start near the valve and lever the cover off in both directions. The tyre levers should be spaced 2-3 in. apart. Continue with one tyre lever while holding the removed portion of the bead with the other one. No difficulty should be experienced so long as you do not forget the cover beads are inextensible, and keep the beads opposite the valve down in the well of the rim. Work round the whole of the tyre progressively until the bead leaves the rim, enabling the tube to be withdrawn. Do not employ large tyre levers. The detachable mudguard and on many machines the knock-out rear spindle (see page 127) greatly simplifies repairs. With this type of spindle the tube can be completely removed with the rear wheel in position.

Refitting Same. Assuming one edge of the tyre is already in position, slightly inflate the inner tube, insert it inside the cover, and push the valve stem through the hole in the rim. Do not tighten up the lock-nut securing the valve to the rim, and also see that the tube is not twisted. Then start to fit the second edge of the cover at a point diametrically opposite the valve, by placing it over the rim and pushing it down into the rim base. Push on the rest of the cover and, with a pair of small tyre levers, work round each side in such a way that the part near the valve is refitted last. On no account use excessive force. Inflate the tyre slightly and verify that the wired beads are correctly positioned and not down in the rim well. A convenient method of doing this is to inspect the fine line which is moulded on the tyre wall close to the rim. This line should be approximately $\tfrac{1}{4}$ in. from the rim right round the tyre. Finally, replace the valve lock-nut and pump up the tyre to the recommended pressure. After a puncture has been repaired do not immediately pump up to full pressure, but give the patch a chance to stick on hard.

FIG. 48. DO NOT FORGET THE COVER BEADS ARE INEXTENSIBLE

(*Dunlop Rubber Co., Ltd.*)

With a wired type cover it is impossible to ease the cover bead at *A* over the flange of the rim until the cover bead at *B* is pushed off the rim shoulder *C* down into the well *D*

Hints on Repairing a Tube (Non-Synthetic). If a nail or similar sharp object has caused a puncture and its position is definitely known, it is *not* essential to remove the wheel. By removing the mudguard with the wheel in position, one side of the cover can be removed and the tube exposed sufficiently to enable the puncture to be repaired. If the position of the puncture is not known, it is necessary to remove the rear wheel, except where a knock-out spindle is provided. Then determine the exact location of the puncture by partially inflating the tube and immersing it in cold water. Watch carefully for air bubbles. Then clean the vicinity of the puncture with sandpaper after allowing the tube to dry, and rub off all dust. Next select a repair patch of suitable size. Modern repair patches are of the auto-vulcanizing type, such as the Dunlop "Vulcafix" which comprises a cured piece of rubber

GOOD TYRE MILEAGE

faced with an unvulcanized layer. To affix this type of patch, remove the linen backing by stretching the rubber. Then, if fixing without solution, rub the prepared face of the patch with a cloth damped with petrol and transfer the brown deposit on the cloth to the tube. Again repeat this procedure and allow one minute for the patch and transferred deposit to dry. If fixing with solution, apply the solution to the tube only, and allow it to become thoroughly "tacky." The patch should now be applied, using slight pressure, particularly at the edges. After fixing the patch, never attempt to lift it in order to find out whether it has adhered properly. Finally, dust with french chalk and fit the tube. It will automatically become vulcanized.

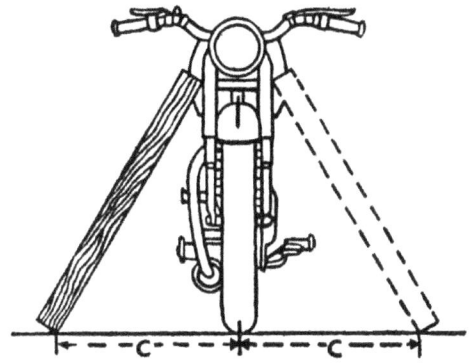

FIG. 49. CHECK VERTICAL ALIGNMENT
(*Dunlop Rubber Co., Ltd.*)
It is necessary to compare the distances C on a sidecar outfit. They should be equal

Keep Wheels in Alignment.
Rapid tyre wear can often be traced to bad alignment of the wheels and when retensioning the secondary chain (see page 123) you should be careful to adjust the set pins in the rear fork ends an equal amount either side. Should an examination of the tyre treads reveal uneven wear or should you suspect misalignment of the wheels, check the alignment.

On a solo Royal Enfield one straight edge or a plain board about 6 ft long, 4 in. wide, and 1 in. thick is needed. Place your machine upright on its stand and turn the handlebars until the front and rear wheels are parallel. Then check the alignment of the two wheels by holding the board or straight edge in contact with the front and rear tyres as shown on the right-hand side of Fig. 50. It should contact each tyre at the front and rear if alignment is correct. Should different section tyres be fitted to the front and rear wheels, the straight edge or board will *not* make contact with the front tyre. In this instance measure the clearance between the front tyre and the edge of the board or straight edge on *both* sides. With true alignment, the clearance should be the same.

Alignment of Sidecar Wheels.
To prevent excessive tyre wear and a tendency for skidding, wheel alignment on a sidecar outfit is even more important than on a solo machine. In this case

two plain boards, about 6 ft long, about 1 in. thick, are needed. Both boards must have one true edge. A third similar type board, about 4 ft long, is also required. A steel measuring tape and a pencil should be available when checking the alignment of the three wheels. When not using the above-mentioned boards, these should be kept quite flat to prevent warping, and care must be taken not to damage their planed faces.

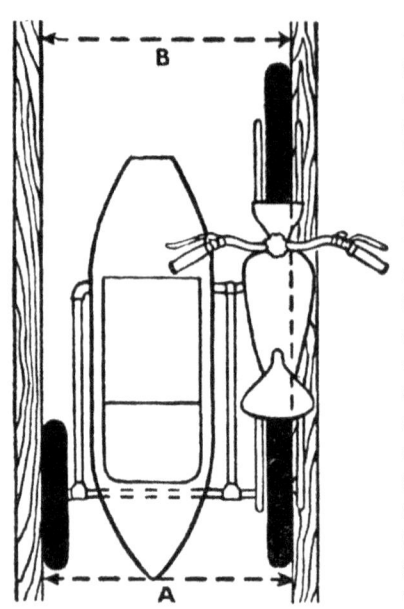

Fig. 50. Checking Motor-cycle and Sidecar Wheel Alignment
(*Dunlop Rubber Co., Ltd.*)

To verify whether all three wheels of a sidecar outfit are running in track, place the outfit on a smooth floor, preferably concrete. Then place one of the long boards alongside the front and rear tyres of the motor-cycle. Adjust the position of the front wheel to obtain the best contact, and note whether the board touches each tyre at two points, as already mentioned in the case of a solo machine. Now without disturbing anything, position the other long board with its true edge contacting the sidecar tyre, as shown in Fig. 50. Then measure dimension A and also dimension B, taking the measurements with the steel measuring tape as close to the tyres as possible. The sidecar wheel should not run absolutely parallel to the wheels of the motor-cycle, or there would be a tendency for the outfit to pull towards the left. To obtain the best results, distance B should be $\frac{1}{8}$-$\frac{3}{16}$ in. smaller than distance A.

Besides checking the wheels for track, it is necessary to check that the motor-cycle itself is quite *vertical*. Usually it is possible to verify this point by visual inspection, but a dimensional check should be made while undertaking a wheel alignment check. Referring to Fig. 49, take the smaller board and rest it at a given point against the upper portion of the front forks. Where the board touches, mark the floor. Now transfer the board to the other side of the machine in a position so that it touches the front forks in an exactly corresponding manner. Again mark the floor where the board touches. The dimensions C should both be exactly the same if the machine is vertical.

CHAPTER VII
ADJUSTMENTS AND OVERHAULING

THERE are a number of minor adjustments which it is desirable that the Enfield rider should attend to every few hundred miles, or when circumstances necessitate these adjustments being made. If the rider values his machine, however, he will not wait till adjustment *has* to be made, but will carefully inspect his machine as a matter of routine and make the necessary adjustments before they become absolutely essential.

Five Large Accessory Firms. The author would draw your attention to five large firms (with branches throughout the U.K.)

FIG. 51. FOR WORKING IN COMFORT—THE A.G.1 "EASILIFT" REPAIR STAND

which are able to supply a big variety of engine spares, motor-cycle spares, carburettor spares, lighting equipment, tools, accessories, clothing, and equipment of all kinds. These five firms are: Marble Arch Motor Supplies, Ltd.; The Halford Cycle Co., Ltd.; George Grose, Ltd.; Turners Stores; and James Grose, Ltd. Spare parts can, of course, be obtained direct from The Enfield Cycle Co., Ltd., of Redditch. When applying for spares it is important to state the Model, year of manufacture, and the engine or frame No. (see page 3).

An Excellent Repair Stand. The motor-cycle repair stand illustrated in Fig. 51 is recommended for those who wish to work on their machines in maximum comfort. It is reasonably priced and can be obtained through motor-cycle dealers only. This hand-operated stand occupies a floor space of 7 ft 6 in. × 18 in.

Cleaning. It requires a considerable amount of time to keep a motor-cycle in anything approaching "showroom" condition, but it is the author's opinion that, unless a machine be kept reasonably clean, the fullest pleasure and maximum efficiency cannot be obtained from it. Apart from the question of pride of ownership (and the present range is very handsome indeed with the enamel and chromium plating unsoiled), it is an undoubted fact that dirt covers a multitude of defects and greatly accelerates depreciation in respect of market value. This is, of course, obvious. If neglected, a motor-cycle rapidly becomes shabby and an eyesore. After a ride in dirty weather, cleaning may take at least an hour. It entails the use of stiff bristle brushes and paraffin for removing the filth from the lower extremities, together with cloths, leather, wax polish for the enamelled parts. On no account should a machine be left soaking wet overnight. A serious amount of rusting may ensue. If the rider is so preoccupied that he cannot spare the necessary time for cleaning, the machine should be thoroughly greased all over before use.

Where facilities exist, it is best to clean the enamelled parts with a hose, but sponging down with cold water from pails is quite satisfactory. A brush should be used for cleaning the wheels. To prevent a "smeary" finish, it is a good plan to swill several pails of cold water over the enamelled parts after washing them. Be careful not to let any water get on to vulnerable parts such as the contact-breaker.

Wash fabric-covered sidecars with soap and lukewarm water, or if very dirty clean first with paraffin. Sidecar upholstery and windscreen aprons should be wiped over with a damp cloth and polished with furniture cream. Use metal polish such as "Brasso" for cleaning celluloid.

Cleaning the Chromium. Tarnish (salt deposits) on the chromium-plated surfaces can be removed by rubbing them with a damp chamois leather. On *no account* use metal polish. To obtain a gleaming finish, polish the chromium with a soft duster such as the "Selvyt" type. To prevent any possibility of rusting during the damp winter months, it is advisable to smear some "Tekall" rust preventive on the chromium, using a soft rag or cloth to apply it.

Lubrication. This is comprehensively dealt with in Chapter IV and no further reference is made in this chapter.

Adjustments to Carburettor and Ignition System. These are fully dealt with in Chapters II and III respectively.

VALVE CLEARANCES

For the Sake of the Valves, Maintain Correct Clearances. The exhaust valve operates in a place where the temperature is often in the region of 1000 degrees centigrade. Just imagine what the valve face and its seat are subjected to if the valve fails to close completely during the firing stroke! Unless a sufficient clearance exists when the engine is running between the end of the valve stem and its tappet, rocker or rocker screw, there is a grave danger of the exhaust valve burning, distorting, or even fracturing. If the latter happens on an O.H.V. engine, a well-wrecked engine may be thrown into the bargain. Insufficient clearances at the inlet and exhaust valves also cause considerable loss of compression and power and general efficiency. Excessive clearances create valve clatter and also put excessive strain on the valves.

How to Check Them. On all Royal Enfield four-stroke engines the valve clearances should occasionally be checked with a feeler gauge (except in the case of some O.H.V. engines where no inlet clearance is recommended) and if necessary adjusted as described below. In the case of *new* engines, owing to the initial bedding down of the contacting surfaces, the valve clearances should be checked and if necessary adjusted after the first 250 miles' running. Subsequently they require attention at less frequent intervals. Usually the expert rider can tell instinctively by the "feel" and exhaust note of his engine whether the valve clearances are O.K. To obtain access to the tappets or rockers as the case may be, it is only necessary to remove the quickly-detachable cover which encloses them.

CORRECT VALVE CLEARANCES (1937–45 FOUR-STROKES)

Royal Enfield Model	Inlet (in.)	Exhaust (in.)
S.V. (B, BM, C, D, DC, H, HM, L, K, KX, WD, WD/C)	0·004	0·006
O.H.V. (BCO, CO, CM, S, SM, S2, SF)	nil	0·004
O.H.V. (G "350 Bullet")	nil	nil
O.H.V. (250, 350 "Bullets")	nil	0·002
O.H.V. (J2, JF "500 Bullets")	nil	0·002
O.H.V. (T)	nil	0·005
O.H.V. (G, G2, J, JM, J2, WD/CO)	0·002	0·004

On 1937–49 Royal Enfields the valve clearances should be checked with the piston on top of the compression stroke and the engine *cold*, and a feeler gauge of the correct thickness (see table) should just slide without binding between the end of the valve stem and the adjustable tappet head on the side-valve engines, and between the end of the valve stem and the overhead rocker or rocker screw in the case of the overhead-valve engines. Where no clearance is recommended for the inlet valve on the O.H.V. engines, the adjustment should be such that the inlet push-rod is just free to be turned without any perceptible up and down play. Where adjustable rocker screws are provided it should be possible to pass a single thickness of tissue paper between the end of the adjusting screw and the valve stem. Before checking the exhaust valve clearance, see that the exhaust valve lifter (page 114) is adjusted correctly and is not keeping the valve off its seat.

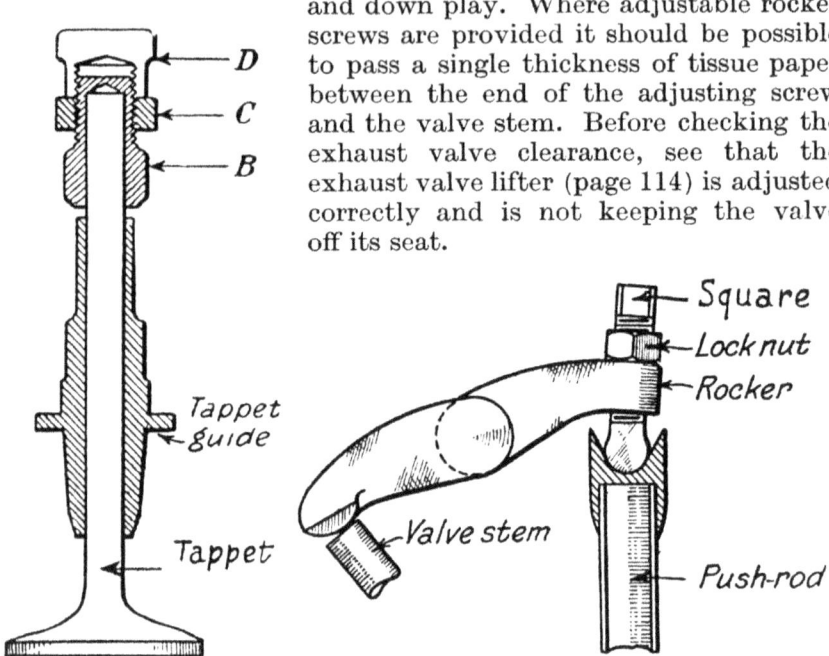

FIG. 52. S.V. TAPPET ADJUSTMENT
(All 1937-9 S.V. Models)

FIG. 53. O.H. ROCKER ADJUSTMENT
(Fitted to 1937-9 Model T only)

Tappet Adjustment (All 1937-9 S.V. Royal Enfields). After removing the valve chest cover (two on K, KX) and putting the piston at the top of the compression stroke, deal with each flat-base tappet as follows.

Referring to Fig. 52 which shows a tappet and its guide, hold the tappet with a spanner applied to the lock-nut *C* (middle hexagon) and apply another spanner to the adjustable tappet head *D* (top hexagon). Then unlock the head by turning it to the right and the lock-nut to the left. The tappet clearance can then be adjusted (see table on page 109) by holding the bottom hexagon *B* on the tappet body with one spanner and then rotating the head and lock-nut to the right or left so as to lengthen or shorten the tappet as required. See that the lock-nut is securely

ADJUSTMENTS AND OVERHAULING 111

retightened and check the valve clearance afterwards in case the tappet head has shifted. Finally replace the valve chest cover.

On Models C, CM, K, KX the position of the exhaust valve lifter prevents a spanner being applied to the adjustable head D of the exhaust tappet, and therefore in this case the second spanner should be applied to the tappet body (bottom hexagon B)

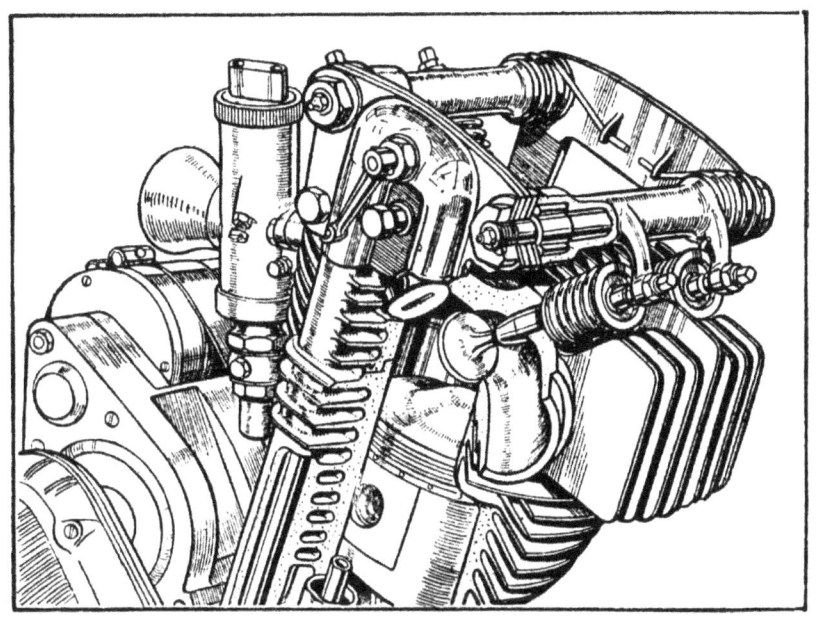

FIG. 54. SHOWING O.H. ROCKER ADJUSTMENT ON EARLIER FOUR-VALVE ENGINES
(*From "The Motor Cycle"*)
This arrangement applies to the 1937-8 Model JF and the 1938-9 J2 "500 Bullets"

when tightening or loosening the lock-nut C. The exhaust tappet adjustment must be made by turning the tappet body to the left or right in order to lengthen or shorten the tappet respectively.

On Model WD/C the exhaust valve lifter arrangement prevents a spanner being applied to the bottom hexagon B on the exhaust tappet body. It is therefore necessary when holding the tappet body while adjusting the exhaust tappet head D to wedge a screwdriver between the hexagon B on the tappet body and the exhaust valve lifter. Alternatively, rotate the engine until the exhaust valve is wide open and then apply a spanner direct to the exhaust tappet head D.

O.H. Rocker Adjustment (1937-9 Model T). On this engine the valve clearances are adjusted by means of the ball-ended adjuster screws at the push-rod ends of the rockers (see Fig. 53). To make an adjustment, all that is necessary is to remove the rocker inspection cover, hold with a spanner the upper squared end of the adjuster screw, slacken the lock-nut and then turn the adjuster screw to the left or right until the correct valve clearance (see page 109) is obtained.

O.H. Rocker Adjustment (1937–9 O.H.V. Four-valve). The four overhead rockers each have a separate adjustment for the valve clearances, but whereas two-valve engines have their adjusting screws situated at the push-rod ends of the rockers, the four-valve engine has the square-ended adjuster screws provided at the valve ends of the rockers. The arrangement is clearly shown in Fig. 54. The adjustment itself is made in exactly the same way as on the two-valve engines (see preceding paragraph), the lock-nut being unscrewed and a spanner applied to the squared end until the correct valve clearance (page 109) is obtained.

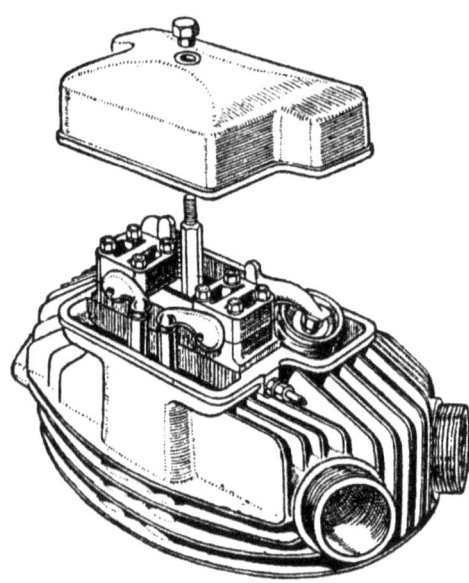

FIG. 55. SHOWING TWIN-PORT CYLINDER HEAD AND OVERHEAD VALVE GEAR ON THE 1937–9 J2 500 C.C. "BULLET"

(*From "The Motor Cycle"*)

Push-rod Adjustment (1937–9 O.H.V. Models BCO, CO, CM, 1937–8 Models S, SM, S2). As is seen from the table on page 109, each of these O.H.V. engines requires an inlet and exhaust valve clearance of *nil* and 0·004 in. respectively, with the engine *cold*. Where a clearance of *nil* is recommended, the push-rod should be just free to rotate. With an exhaust valve clearance of 0·004 in., the push-rod should have just appreciable up and down play. Exact clearances can be checked by removing the rocker-box cover and inserting a suitable feeler gauge between the end of the valve stem and the overhead rocker.

The procedure for adjusting the two push-rods is exactly the same as for the 1946–9 O.H.V. Models CO, G, J, J2 (page 113). To make an adjustment of the clearance for each valve, first loosen the lock-nut (middle hexagon), and then screw the push-rod cup (bottom hexagon) to the left or right to decrease or increase the valve clearance as required respectively.

Push-rod Adjustment (1937-8 250, 350 " Bullets," 1939 Models S, SF, G " 350 Bullet "). On these engines also an adjustment for valve clearances is provided at the foot of the push-rods. The correct clearances are given in the table on page 109 and the procedure for adjusting them is the same as for the 1946-9 O.H.V.

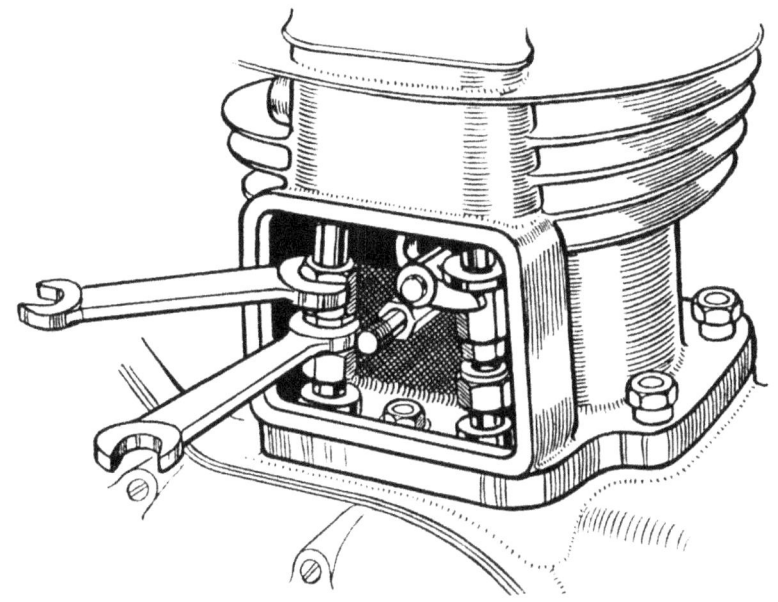

FIG. 56. THE PUSH-ROD ADJUSTMENT ON ALL
1946-9 O.H.V. ENGINES
(*The Enfield Cycle Co., Ltd.*)

engines (see paragraph below). The inlet push-rod should be just binding and the exhaust push-rod just free when the engine is *cold*.

Push-rod Adjustment (1937-9 O.H.V. Models G, G2, J, JM, J2). For appropriate instructions regarding valve clearances and adjustment, see paragraph below dealing with 1946-9 O.H.V. models.

Push-rod Adjustment (1941-5 O.H.V. Model WD/CO). This military machine, many of which are now in civilian use, has valve clearances and a push-rod adjustment identical to those provided for the 1946-9 O.H.V. engines (see below).

Push-rod Adjustment (1946-9 O.H.V. Models CO, G, J, J2). On these models the valve clearance adjustment is provided at the bottom of the push-rods and ready access to the adjustment is obtained by detaching the inspection cover from the off-side of the cylinder. The correct valve clearances are as follows—

        Inlet valve—0·002 in. (engine cold).
        Exhaust valve—0·004 in. (engine cold).

It is not practicable to check the valve clearances at the bottom of the push-rods on account of the ball and socket joints used, and to make a check with a feeler gauge it is necessary to remove the rocker-box cover and insert the feeler gauge between the end of each valve stem and the overhead rocker. It is possible with a little experience to dispense with the feeler gauge check and to rely on the feel of the push-rods. The inlet push-rod should be just free to turn with no up and down play and the exhaust push-rod should have some perceptible up and down clearance. The means of adjustment is shown clearly in Fig. 56.

Referring to Fig. 56, with two spanners hold the push-rod bottom end (top hexagon) and the lock-nut (middle hexagon). Loosen the lock-nut by turning the nut to the left. Then to make an adjustment of the valve clearance, screw the push-rod cup (bottom hexagon) to the left or right to decrease or increase the clearance respectively. When doing this, hold the push-rod bottom end. Having made the required adjustment, lock the lock-nut against the push-rod end. After tightening the lock-nut, again check the valve clearance. Finally replace the inspection cover on the off-side of the cylinder. On new engines the push-rod adjustment should always be checked after the first few hundred miles, as considerable initial bedding-down occurs.

Always Maintain Backlash at Exhaust Valve Lifter. It is important before checking the valve clearances and at all other times always to maintain a small amount ($\frac{1}{16}$ in. to $\frac{1}{8}$ in.) of backlash at the exhaust valve lifter lever with the exhaust valve fully closed, otherwise it is quite impossible for the valve to seat properly and loss of compression, power and burning of the valve (see page 109) will inevitably be occasioned, accompanied probably by a considerable amount of banging in the exhaust system and a very hot exhaust pipe (the author once saw his exhaust pipe actually glowing red due to temporary neglect in this matter!). The necessary adjustment of the exhaust valve lifter can readily be made by means of the adjustable cable stop provided for that purpose. See that the lock-nut is afterwards securely retightened.

The Compression Release Valve (Models RE, WD/RE). Somewhat obscure loss of compression on a 125 c.c. two-stroke engine can be caused by a leaky compression release valve. If leakage is occurring at the valve, it is necessary to regrind it on to its seat.

ADJUSTMENTS AND OVERHAULING

To do this it is not necessary to strip down the release valve completely. The following is the procedure required.

To Remove Compression Release Valve. First remove the screw, nut and washer used to secure its control lever to the handlebars. Next with the aid of a pair of pliers disconnect the control wire from the control lever as shown in Fig. 57. Remove the lever and pull the wire and its ferrule from the clip which is welded to the handlebars. Then unscrew the body of the compression release

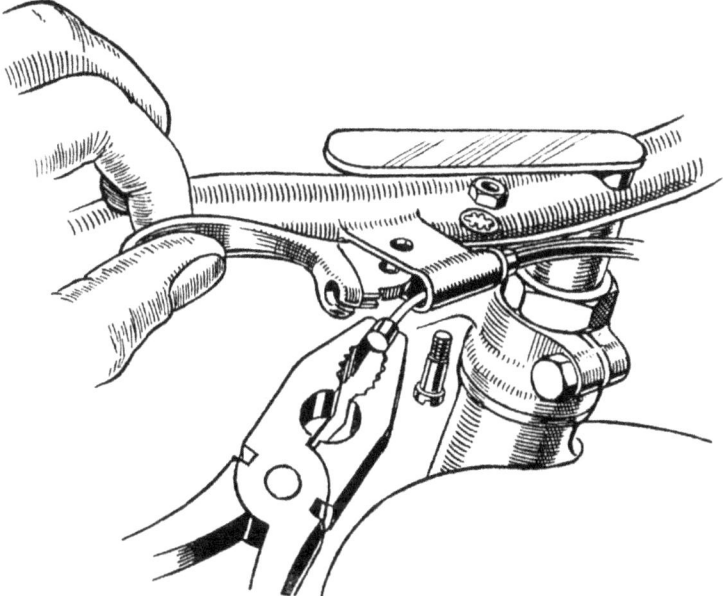

FIG. 57. REMOVING COMPRESSION RELEASE VALVE
CONTROL LEVER
(*The Enfield Cycle Co., Ltd.*)

valve from the cylinder head. This must on no account be done until the control wire has first been disconnected from the control lever on the handlebars.

Grinding-in Compression Release Valve. After removing the compression release valve with control wire attached, as described in the previous paragraph, proceed as follows. Referring to Fig. 58, compress the spring with the fingers and detach the cap. Next unscrew the cable adjusting screw (complete with lock-nut) from the cable block and pull the cable out of the slot in the cable block. Push the spring upwards with the fingers and then pull the cable nipple from the body. The nipple is soldered to the cable, the screw illustrated being provided to give additional security in the event of the solder becoming very hot. Now thread the cable and nipple through the spring. This leaves the compression release valve body (with valve, cable block and spring) discon-

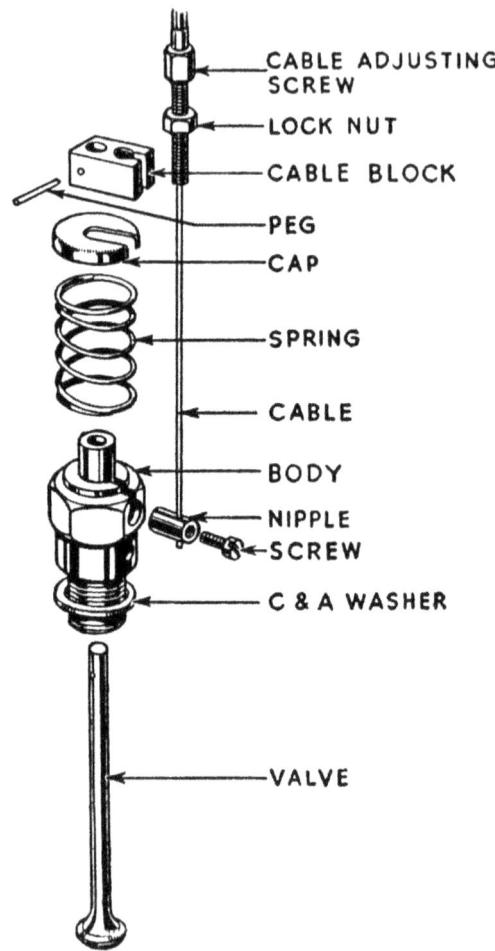

Fig. 58. Exploded View of Compression Release Valve
(*The Enfield Cycle Co., Ltd.*)
(This applies to the 125 c.c. two-stroke engines fitted to Models RE, WD/RE)

nected from the control cable. Replace the cap and carefully inspect the valve and its seat for pitting and damage.

To remove pitting on the valve, grind it in similarly to an ordinary poppet valve. Apply a thin film of fine grinding paste (see page 149) to the valve seat and oscillate the valve by means

ADJUSTMENTS AND OVERHAULING

of the cable block fixed to its upper end. Occasionally lift the valve, and avoid continuous rotation. After grinding-in the valve, wash the assembly thoroughly in petrol while opening and shutting the valve with the fingers. Be quite sure that *no* grinding paste remains.

If the valve is bent or badly burned, or if the stem of the valve is heavily carbonized, causing the valve to stick open, dismantle the compression release valve completely. Knock out the small peg (see Fig. 58) securing the cable block to the valve stem and draw off the cable block. The entire assembly can now be dismantled. Dismantling in this manner is necessary in order to renew the release valve spring. A tendency for the valve to stick open, unaccompanied by burning or bending of the valve stem, can generally be cured by thorough washing in petrol.

GEAR AND CLUTCH CONTROLS

Adjustment of Hand Gear Control (1937-9 Singles). Where hand control is provided it is necessary to check and if necessary adjust the gear control. This is done as follows.

First disconnect the control rod at the quadrant lever, place the gears in second or third gear (second with three-speed gearboxes) and put the control lever in the corresponding notch. Then loosen the lock-nut and screw up or down the vertical rod until the length of the latter is adjusted such that with second or third gear engaged the hand control lever is perfectly free in the *centre* of the corresponding quadrant notch. This adjustment applies to all the gears and should be checked carefully. Do not forget to retighten the lock-nut securely on the forked end.

To Adjust Hand Gear Control (1937-9 Big Twins). Where an adjustment of the control is necessary after adjusting the primary chain, the following procedure is required. Place the machine on its stand and engage second or third gear. Then by means of the two nuts (one on each side of the lever) on the gearbox, adjust the rod for length so that the control lever lies *centrally* in its quadrant notch. Afterwards lock up both nuts and check the adjustment in all gears.

To Adjust Hand Gear Control (Models RE, WD/RE). The quadrant arrangement on the 125 c.c. Royal Enfields is shown in Fig. 59. As may be seen, the quadrant can be pivoted about the fulcrum pin after slackening the adjusting pin securing the quadrant to the tank. If a gear control adjustment is required, pivot the quadrant until the lever is *central* in the middle notch (second gear) of the gate. Having made the required adjustment, firmly retighten the adjusting pin.

Adjustment of Gear Control (Foot). The foot control lever itself or the ratchet mechanism (on Model T) is mounted directly on the gearbox and it is a *sine qua non* that primary chain adjustment has no effect whatever on the gear control. Where the foot lever is mounted independently of the gearbox (i.e. where the ratchet mechanism is fixed to the gearbox) it is possible to vary the position of the foot lever to suit individual requirements by adjusting the length of the connecting rod.

If the Foot-lever Position is Bad. This can happen after primary chain adjustment on models where the lever is fixed

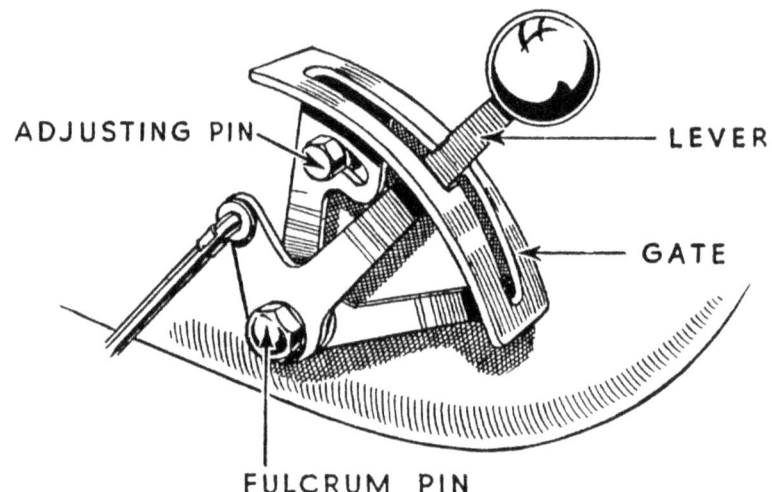

Fig. 59. GEAR CONTROL ADJUSTMENT ON THE 125 C.C. TWO-STROKES
(*The Enfield Cycle Co., Ltd.*)

direct to the gearbox. The remedy is to slacken the pin securing the lever to the operating mechanism on the gearbox, remove the lever, and replace it one serration higher or lower as required.

Neutralizing Lever Adjustment. Where a neutralizing lever is fitted (1946–9 Models G, J, J2), a stop sleeve limits the forward and downward travel of the lever. Should the lever fail to register "neutral" slacken the hexagon-headed screw securing the sleeve and turn the eccentric sleeve as required until the position of the neutralizing lever at the end of its travel is correctly adjusted to obtain "neutral."

Clutch Control Adjustment. It is exceedingly important always to permit a small amount of free movement (about $\frac{1}{16}$ in.) of the

ADJUSTMENTS AND OVERHAULING

clutch operating lever on the gearbox. Unless this free movement exists, some of the spring pressure is taken by the clutch wire

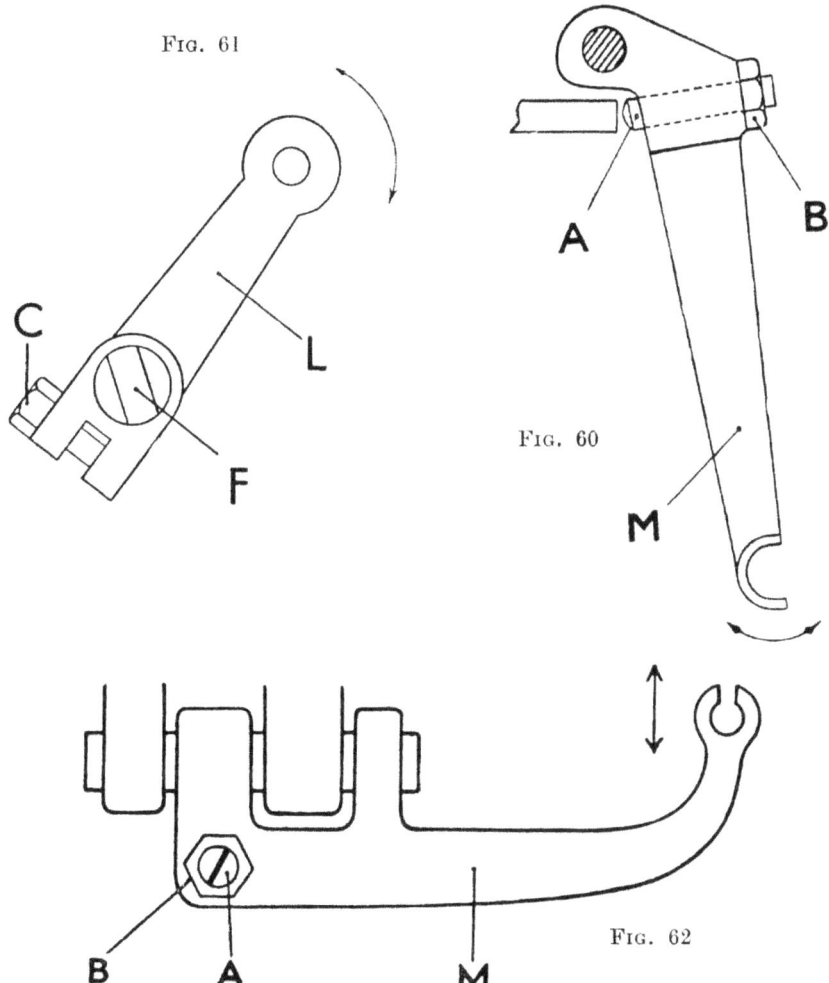

FIGS. 60–62. CLUTCH-CONTROL ADJUSTMENT ON MANY PRE-WAR MODELS
(*The Enfield Cycle Co., Ltd.*)

The multi-plate clutch adjustment shown in Fig. 60 has been provided on many lightweight models, including Model A two-stroke. That shown in Fig. 61 has been used on the Big Twins fitted with foot control of the clutch (and in some cases with hand control). Fig. 62 shows the clutch adjustment provided on a few earlier type lightweights (including Model T). All 1938–49 heavyweight gearboxes incorporate the clutch adjustment shown in Fig. 63

instead of by the friction plates, with the result that the clutch slips, so damaging the friction cork inserts. On new machines these inserts bed down during the first 100 miles or so and the clutch control adjustment should therefore be frequently checked and if necessary adjusted. Five types of clutch operating levers are used on 1937–49 models and these are shown in Figs. 60–64.

Clutch Control Adjustment (Fig. 60). Where the type of clutch operating lever shown in Fig. 60 is fitted to the gearbox, clutch adjustment should be effected in the following manner. First slacken the lock-nut B and then turn the adjuster screw A until the lever M has the required amount of backlash (i.e. about $\frac{1}{16}$ in.). Then tighten the lock-nut B.

To Adjust Clutch Control (Fig. 61). To adjust the quick-thread type of operating lever shown in Fig. 61, first loosen the screw C. Next with a suitable spanner hold the flats F and turn *clockwise* until the clearance between the worm and the clutch push-rod is just eliminated. Then turn the lever L until there is a slight amount of slack in the clutch control ($\frac{1}{16}$ in. approximately). Afterwards retighten the screw C.

Clutch Control Adjustment (Fig. 62). In order to adjust the type of clutch operating lever shown in Fig. 62, loosen the lock-nut B. Then turn the adjuster screw A until the lever M has a slight amount of free motion (about $\frac{1}{16}$ in.). After making the required adjustment, retighten the lock-nut B.

To Adjust Clutch Control (Fig. 63). To adjust the direct type of operating lever shown in Fig. 63, first detach the lever M from the control cable and hinge it back so as to give access to the adjuster screw A and the sleeve B. The correct clearance in the control is about $\frac{1}{16}$ in. To increase the clearance, turn the adjuster screw A anti-clockwise. To reduce the clearance, turn it clockwise. As may be noted from Fig. 63, there is no lock-nut provided in this instance. When the lever M is positioned and the control cable is connected, the screw A and sleeve B are automatically locked by the lever.

Clutch Control Adjustment (Fig. 64). A rather unusual type of adjustment is provided on the 125 c.c. models. As may be seen in Fig. 64, an adjustable nipple is included at the gearbox end of the control cable. As on the other types of clutch control, a clearance of about $\frac{1}{16}$ in. is desirable. To make an adjustment, press on the clutch operating lever B and disconnect the control cable. Then adjust the threaded nipple A as required and reconnect the control cable.

ADJUSTMENTS AND OVERHAULING

Should the threaded nipple *A* not permit of the necessary adjustment being made, alter the position of the operating lever *B* by slackening the lock-nut *C* and unscrewing the set-screw *D* a few turns. If this second adjustment causes excessive clearance in the clutch control, proceed to make another adjustment at the adjustable nipple until the clearance *is* correct.

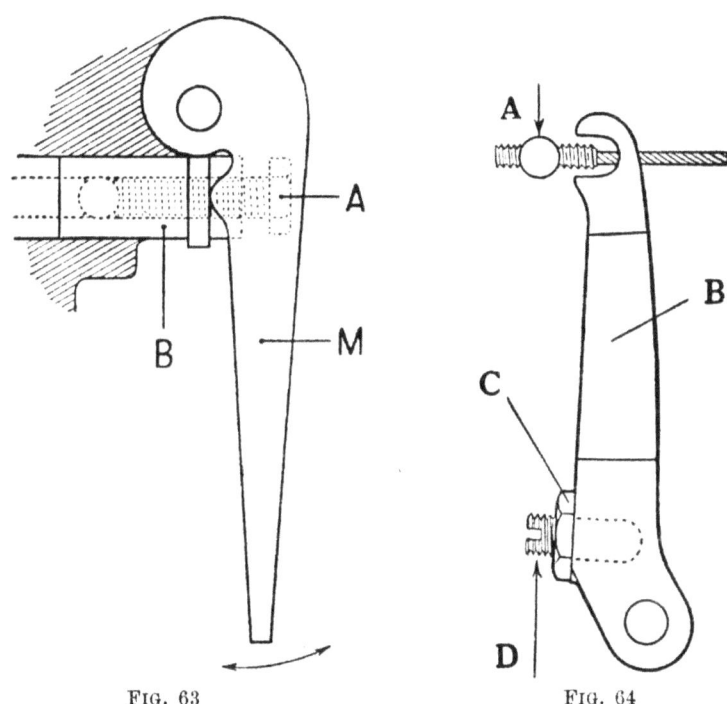

FIG. 63 FIG. 64

FIGS. 63–64 CLUTCH CONTROL ADJUSTMENT ON ALL POST-WAR MODELS
(*The Enfield Cycle Co., Ltd.*)

The adjustment shown in Fig. 63 is provided on 1938-9 models with heavyweight type gearboxes and on all post-war four-strokes. That illustrated in Fig.64 is used on the 125 c.c. Models RE, WD/RE two-stroke

If the Clutch Slips. First of all check the adjustment described on page 120. If this is in order, perhaps the cork inserts are worn flush or burnt. In this case it is necessary to dismantle the clutch and have new inserts fitted. To remove the springs and plates it is only necessary to remove the primary chain cover or chain case (oil-bath models) and unscrew the pins near the clutch centre, when the plates and springs can be lifted out. No adjustment is provided for the spring pressure and the screws should always be kept done up tight. If prolonged clutch slip has occurred, new springs as well as inserts may be required.

Do Not Worry About Oil on It. Cork inserts function equally well whether they run dry or greasy and therefore should oil or grease get on to the clutch, do not spend a sleepless night! As a matter of fact, since oily inserts naturally wear longer than dry ones, it is preferable on oil-bath chain case models to keep the oil-bath well filled.

Clutch Inserts on Models WD/CO and CO (1946). On the military machine, Model WD/CO, Ferodo inserts are fitted. These inserts, though not liable to burning, are apt to slip if excessive oil reaches them. Therefore in the event of clutch slip, wash the plates thoroughly in petrol, dry them, and replace.

The 1946 Model CO has Ferodo discs riveted to the clutch sprocket and this may need occasional washing in petrol. The three loose plates, however, have cork inserts which provide plenty of friction whether dry or oily.

If the Clutch Slips (Models RE, WD/RE). Should clutch slip occur with the engine under load, first check that the clutch operating lever has the required free movement (see page 120). Should nothing be amiss here, detach the outer half of the primary chain case so as to expose the clutch assembly. Then remove the six screws which secure the clutch springs. You will find a packing washer situated behind the head of each screw. Remove all six packing washers and also clean the plates with petrol so as to remove all trace of oil or grease. Then replace the six screws (minus packing washers). By doing this an increase in spring pressure will be obtained. Should clutch slip still persist it will be necessary to renew the clutch plate inserts and/or clutch springs.

CHAIN ADJUSTMENT

Importance of Correct Chain Tension. It is important to keep both the primary and secondary chains correctly tensioned. Chains which are too slack are apt to rattle and jump the sprockets at a critical speed. On the other hand, chains which are too tight cause damage to the chain rollers and wear the chain sprockets quickly, the teeth becoming "hooked."

To Adjust Primary Chain. Pivot-mounted gearboxes are installed except on Models RE, WD/RE, and to adjust the primary chain it is only necessary to slacken the two securing nuts and then to pivot the gearbox about the lower of the two bolts holding the gearbox to the rear engine plates until the centre of the chain run has a free up and down movement of about $\frac{1}{4}$ in. when

ADJUSTMENTS AND OVERHAULING

deflected by the fingers. On the oil-bath chain case models an inspection cover on the chain case gives immediate access to the chain. After retensioning the chain and tightening the gearbox nuts it may be necessary (see page 117) to readjust the gear control.

No Primary Chain Adjustment on Models RE, WD/RE. On the 125 c.c. models the primary chain is well run-in after initial assembly, and if it is kept well lubricated (see page 76) it will stretch very slowly. When new, the chain should have about $\frac{1}{4}$ in. free movement up and down. When the amount of free movement exceeds about $\frac{3}{4}$ in., it is generally advisable to renew the chain. If the chain tension differs at various points, check the tension at the *tautest* point. There is no means provided for adjusting the tension of the chain as on the other models.

Secondary Chain Adjustment. The secondary chain should be kept adjusted so that there is approximately $\frac{1}{2}$ in. of free up and down movement. The chain gradually stretches and requires to be retensioned at certain intervals. To do this, slacken both rear wheel spindle nuts and then (except in the case of Models RE, WD/RE with drawbolt adjusters) adjust the set pins in the fork ends until the correct chain tension is obtained. When adjusting the set pins (or draw bolts) see that the adjustment is carried out an equal amount on both sides of the fork ends, otherwise the wheel alignment (see page 105) will be disturbed. After adjusting the secondary chain it may be found necessary to make an adjustment to the rear brake (described in a later paragraph).

To Adjust Dynamo Chain (Model A). The chain should be kept adjusted so that it has the same free up and down movement as the primary chain, i.e. $\frac{1}{4}$ in. To adjust it, loosen the nut underneath the dynamo (below the engine plates) which holds the fixing strap and then turn the dynamo in its housing until the correct chain tension is arrived at.

Dynamo or " Magdyno " Chain (1939 250 c.c.). To adjust the chain on these models (D, S, S2, SF), loosen the nut on the front bolt securing the platform to the engine plates, and then tilt the platform about the rear securing bolt. When the correct tension is obtained (about $\frac{1}{4}$ in. up and down movement), retighten the nut securely.

" Magdyno " Chain Adjustment (Models, K, KX). On these machines to adjust the dynamo chain so that it has a free up and down movement of ¼ in., loosen the two bolts securing the "Magdyno" mounting to the engine plates and then tilt the mounting the necessary amount, afterwards retightening the two bolts.

When Refitting a Chain. Always see that the spring link is fitted so that the open end faces *away* from the direction of chain movement. This is important because should a chain part at high speed, particularly a secondary chain, there is no knowing what damage, personal and material, it may cause. The author once

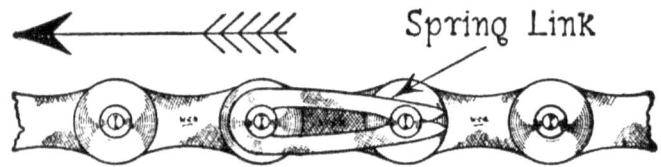

FIG. 65. SHOWING THE CORRECT WAY TO FIT A CHAIN SPRING LINK

It is unsafe to fit the link with the open end facing the direction of chain motion

ran with a chain guard missing, and a chain parting at 30 m.p.h. caused a slap on the back sufficient to cause semi-consciousness!

BRAKES AND WHEELS

Adjust Brakes to Give Maximum Efficiency. The front brake can be adjusted by means of a knurled nut on the cover plate or forks (125 c.c.) and the rear brake by means of a wing nut at the end of the brake operating rod. Always keep both brakes adjusted to give maximum efficiency by adjusting the nuts so that the brake shoes are in close contact with the drums and yet do not bind when the brakes are released. To test for free rotation of the wheels when adjusting the brakes it is advisable to jack up the wheels and spin them by hand.

If Grease gets on the Linings. Remove the brake shoes and scrape and wash their frictional linings in petrol. Also clean the inside of the drums. The usual cause of grease getting on the linings is over-zealous lubrication of the wheel hubs. Greasy linings cause a very marked deterioration in braking efficiency.

The brake linings are of a special woven material and the colour varies from deep yellow to dark brown according to the

ADJUSTMENTS AND OVERHAULING

severity of use. The linings should normally have a polished appearance and should not be roughed up with a file to remove this polish. Dull black streaks on the linings indicate mud or grease which can be scraped off with a knife or a hacksaw blade. After cleaning and reassembling a brake it is a good plan to run the machine in second gear for some distance with the brake hard on. This will burn off any remaining grease without causing any harm. If you fit new linings, see that they are of the correct size and type for the particular machine, and insert the end rivets last to prevent any buckling. The rivets must be flush, and do not forget to grease the brake cam spindles when assembling the brakes (see page 77).

Adjustment of Wheel Bearings. You cannot adjust the wheel bearings on any four-stroke models even if you wish to do so, because there is no adjustment provided! Single-row deep groove journal races designed for dealing with heavy radial and thrust leads are used except on 125 c.c. two-stroke models having frame and engine Nos. lower than 8171. In this case cup-and-cone type ball bearings (nine balls each side) are fitted. On the 1937–9 Model K adjustable taper roller bearings are used.

Where cup and cone ball bearings are provided, it is advisable to remove the wheels prior to adjusting the bearings. To make a bearing adjustment, loosen the lock-nut securing the brake cover plate and turn the notched washer which fits over the end of the adjusting cone outside the cover plate as required. Tighten the lock-nut (securing the cover plate) before making a final check for correct adjustment. This should be such that the wheel can be rotated readily with the finger and thumb. There must be *no* stiffness and a minimum of side play. The former is the more important.

Adjusting Wheel Bearings (1937–9 Model K). Model K has taper roller bearings which are correctly adjusted at the Works, and should never require attention. If, however, the adjustment should accidentally be disturbed they can be readjusted by loosening the lock-nut inside the near-side fork end and turning the adjusting nut. This type of bearing must have a little play, and it should just be possible to feel a trace of side movement at the rim. The best procedure is to remove the wheel and adjust the bearings so that the spindle can be turned freely with the fingers.

Removing Front Wheel. First raise the wheel clear of the ground either by putting the machine on the central stand or both stands (never use a front stand alone), or else by slipping a suitable box underneath the crankcase. Then disconnect the front brake cable by detaching the pin passing through the **stirrup** (after first removing the split pin). Next on machines with **girder** type front forks remove the two spindle nuts. By springing **the** fork girders apart slightly, the front wheel will slide out of **the** slotted fork ends. After removing the front wheel from a 125 **c.c.**

FIG. 66. BY MERELY UNDOING FOUR NUTS THE REAR MUDGUARD CAN BE INSTANTLY DETACHED

On 350 c.c. and 500 c.c. models the provision of a knock-out spindle and distance piece enables tyre repairs to be effected without removing the rear wheel

Model RE or WD/RE it will be found that the machine **rests** securely on the centre stand and the rear wheel.

On machines having telescopic front forks, after disconnecting the front brake cable, remove the two nuts securing the cap to each fork leg end (shown at *T* in Fig. 86). The front wheel will then slide out.

The Detachable Rear Mudguard. On all models rear wheel removal and tyre repairs are very greatly facilitated by the quickly detachable rear mudguard and carrier (where fitted). To remove the mudguard (see Fig. 66), slacken the four nuts securing the

ADJUSTMENTS AND OVERHAULING

mudguard stays to the rear of the frame and lift the mudguard (and carrier) away. Nothing could be simpler.

Puncture Repairs in "Knock-out" Time. On 350 and 500 c.c. Models it is possible to repair a puncture in the rear tyre with amazing speed, thanks to the detachable mudguard (see above) and the knock-out rear wheel spindle which permits of a tube being removed or fitted without *removing* the wheel. To remove a tube in "Brooklands" manner, proceed as follows: After detaching the mudguard remove the off-side spindle nut and push the

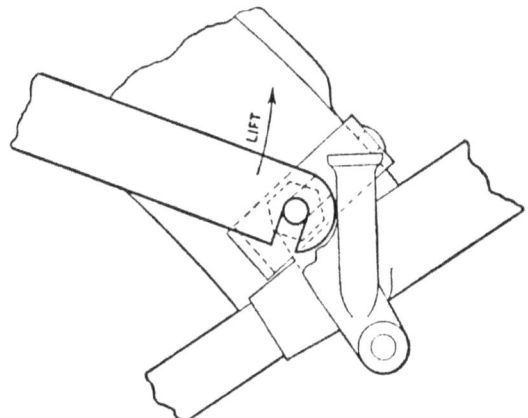

Fig. 67. Before Removing Rear Mudguard, Lift Stays as Indicated (Where Pillion Seat and Pannier Bags Fitted)
(*The Enfield Cycle Co., Ltd.*)

spindle out of the other side. Then slightly spring apart the rear forks and slide out the knurled distance piece between the hub and the off-side fork end. If you now disconnect the brake rod from the slotted operating arm and also one end of the brake anchor arm you can now slip the tube out through the gap left on the off-side. Be careful not to put any strain on the rear wheel when the distance piece and spindle are removed.

To Remove Rear Wheel. After detaching the mudguard as described in a preceding paragraph, remove the pin retaining the brake anchor arm and the wing nut on the brake rod, disconnect the secondary chain at the spring link (see page 124), loosen the spindle nuts and slide the wheel out of the slotted fork ends.

On machines provided with pillion seats and pannier bags (e.g. Models WD/C, WD/CO) it is necessary before attempting to lift off the rear mudguard to lift up the stays (see Fig. 67) which run from the front of the carrier to the rear stays. It is then possible to lift off the entire assembly comprising the mudguard, carrier, pillion seat, and pannier bags.

Removing 1938-9 Model K Rear Wheel. Put your machine on the rear stand and after removing the detachable rear mudguard (Fig. 66) take out the pin securing the brake anchor arm, remove

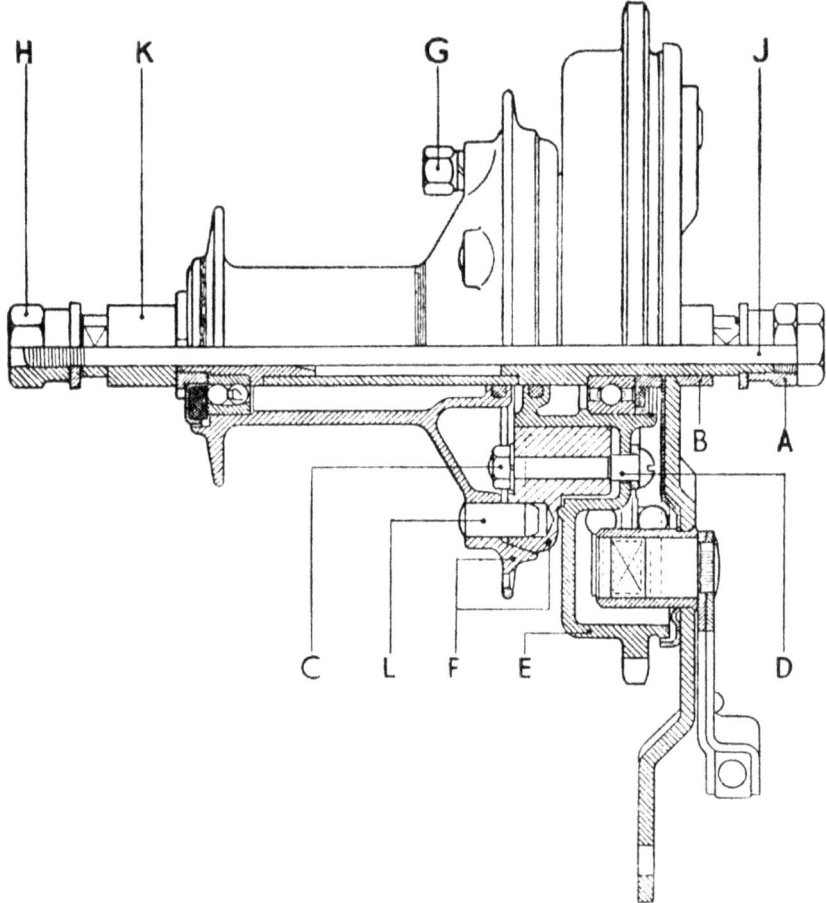

Fig. 68. Sectional View of Detachable Wheel
(1938-9 Model KX Big Twin)
(*The Enfield Cycle Co., Ltd.*)

the wing nut on the rod, disconnect the rear chain, loosen the wheel spindle nuts and allow the wheel to slide out of the fork ends.

Removing 1937-9 Model K Front Wheel. Put the machine on both stands, disconnect the brake control, loosen the spindle nuts, spring out the forks slightly and let the wheel come away.

ADJUSTMENTS AND OVERHAULING

To Remove 1938-9 Model KX Detachable Wheels. Either wheel may be removed as follows. Place the model on the stand(s), unscrew the three pins G and the nut H (see Fig. 68). Then knock out the spindle J and slide the distance piece K out of the fork end. Next pull the wheel over to the side of the machine until the three pegs L are disengaged from the recesses in the cush drive centre F. The wheel can now be removed, leaving the brake in place (also cush drive and sprocket of the rear wheel).

When refitting the wheel, push the spindle J almost into place in order to steady the wheel prior to engaging the pegs C with

FIG. 69. THE CUSH-DRIVE REAR HUB
This vane and rubber block shock-absorber is incorporated in the rear hub of all models to smooth out the transmission

their recesses. Fit distance piece K and tighten nut H *before* tightening the three pins G. Be sure to tighten them evenly so as to pull the wheel squarely on to the conical seating of the cush drive centre F.

The Cush Drive Rear Hub. All 1937 and later Royal Enfields except the 125 c.c. two-strokes have a patent cush drive rear hub. This absorbs all engine shocks, prevents transmission snatch, and reduces wear of the rear tyre to the minimum. As may be seen in Fig. 69, the drum on the driving side of the rear hub (on singles) has three metal vanes. Three similar vanes are provided on the inside of the driving sprocket. Six equal size blocks of solid rubber are placed in the drum, one on each side of each vane, and the three vanes on the inside of the driving sprocket each fit between a pair of the rubber blocks. Thus the assembly comprises a rubber block and a vane alternately. No adjustment is necessary and the only attention required is the renewal of the rubber blocks after a very big mileage has been covered.

On the 1140 c.c. Model KX the rear brake drum is positioned where the cush drive is fitted on the singles, and the cush drive is therefore located between the hub and the back of the brake drum. Referring to Fig. 68, to dismantle the cush drive, first remove the detachable portion of the rear wheel as described in a previous paragraph. Next slacken nut *A* and disconnect the secondary chain, rear brake rod, and the anchor strap. Now slide the brake, sprocket, and cush drive assembly out of the fork end. Remove nut *B*, and lift off the brake cover plate. Then unscrew the three nuts *C*, knock out the shouldered pins *D* and lift the brake drum *E* off the cush drive centre *F*.

FRONT FORKS, STEERING HEAD, ETC.

Adjusting Front Forks (Tubular Type). To take up side play in the front fork links, slacken the nuts on the front fork spindles and adjust the spindles by means of their squared ends. Avoid adjusting the forks so closely as to interfere with their free action. Each spindle has a right- and left-hand thread so that rotation of the spindle in one direction opens the fork links and rotation in the other direction closes them. The L.H. threads are situated on the off-side of the machine and the R.H. threads on the nearside, and the lock-nuts are slackened by rotation in the direction marked by the arrows on the fork links.

On Models WD/C, WD/CO, CO (and some 1939 models) to take up side play in the top swivel pins, unscrew the lock-nut on the *near* side and adjust the pin as required. Afterwards tighten the lock-nut. To obtain access to the lock-nuts on the front bottom swivel pins (later models), it is necessary first to remove the shock absorber adjusting nuts and the star washers on machines with hand-adjusted shock absorbers.

If a sidecar is fitted, the bottom fork links should be removed and the steering stem turned round so that the offset is to the front. On re-fitting the fork links the wheel will be located farther forward, giving delightfully light steering.

Adjusting Front Forks (Pressed Steel Type). The adjustment for the pressed steel forks fitted on the lightweight models is the same as for the tubular type, the adjustment of which is described above, except that the *front upper* spindle has *bushes* screwed on the fork spindle and it is necessary to adjust these bushes after slackening the lock-nuts until the correct adjustment is obtained (i.e. until side play has been eliminated).

To Adjust Front Fork Links (Models RE, WD/RE). The two rear swivel pins (see Fig. 70) are threaded into the links on the

ADJUSTMENTS AND OVERHAULING

off-side of the machine and the adjustment should be made by slackening the lock-nuts and turning the heads of the swivel pins. Tighten the lock-nuts before checking the adjustment. This should be such that side play is eliminated as far as possible without interfering with the free movement of the forks. No adjustment is provided for the front swivel pins.

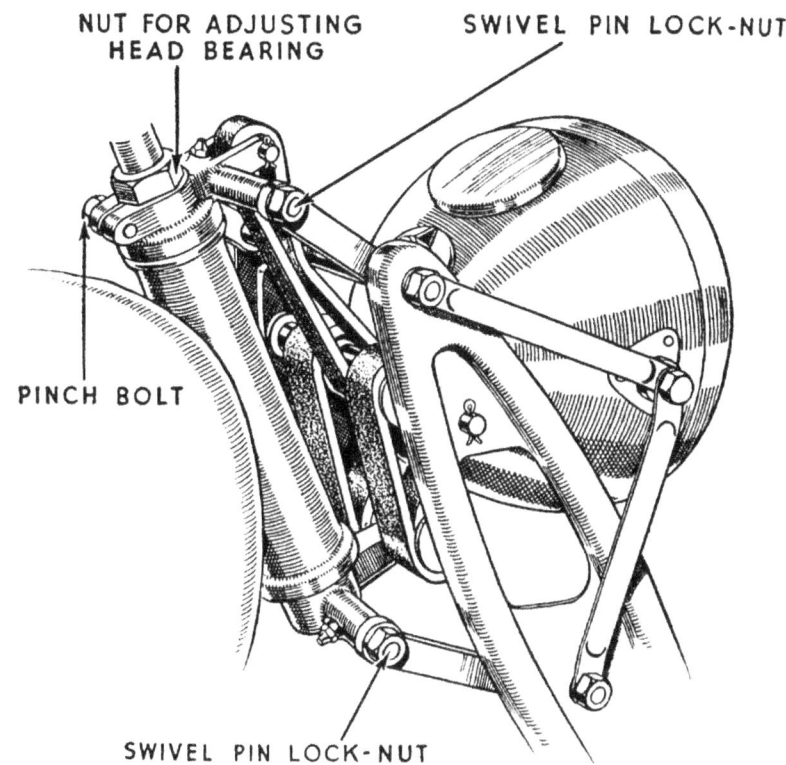

Fig. 70. Front Fork and Steering Head Adjustment on 125 c.c. Two-strokes
(*The Enfield Cycle Co., Ltd.*)

To Adjust Steering Head (Models RE, WD/RE). To check for play in the steering head, remove the weight from the front wheel by placing the machine on the stand and lifting at the lower end of the forks. Any play present can be felt by placing one finger across the head races just beneath the ball head clip. With the weight removed from the front wheel, the handlebars should swing over freely with the very minimum of play in the steering head.

To adjust the steering head, slacken the nut on the pinch bolt (see Fig. 70) through the ball head clip and adjust by means of the large plated nut for adjusting the head bearings. Having made the necessary adjustment, be sure to retighten the pinch bolt nut. Failure to do this may cause the threads of the large plated nut to strip under load.

To Take Up Steering Head Play (Other Models).
All models have ball bearing steering heads of generous proportions and these rarely require any attention. Should it be found, however, on attempting to "shake" the handlebars that some play has developed it should be taken up *at once*, otherwise the balls will come in for a severe hammering, for which they are not designed. To take up play in the steering head, first of all obtain a suitable box and place it under the crankcase so that it takes the weight of the machine off the front wheel. Then on medium- and heavy-weight machines *with girder forks*, slacken the nut on the pinch bolt which passes through the steering head clip and adjust the plated nut on top of the steering column until all up and down play has disappeared. Be careful not to tighten the nut so much that stiffness of steering is caused and do not omit to retighten the nut on the pinch bolt.

On the Models A and T a steering head clip is not fitted and it is only necessary in order to take up play in the steering head to unscrew the large plated nut on top of the steering column and then make the necessary adjustment by means of the lower nut. See that the upper nut is securely retightened after making the adjustment.

Where Telescopic Front Forks are Fitted.
On all post-war four-strokes telescopic type front forks are fitted. These incorporate long flexible internal springs and hydraulic damping. Referring to Fig. 86, the action of each fork leg is hydraulically damped by oil passing through the valve port Q which is restricted by the bottom spring stud O. This has a double taper designed so as to have little effect at the normal laden position, but an increased effect at either end of the travel. Two well spaced bearings inside each fork leg are automatically lubricated and the forks require no attention whatever except for occasional topping-up of both legs with oil (see page 79).

Where telescopic forks are fitted, adjust the steering head in the following manner. First remove the weight from the front wheel by inserting a suitable box below the crankcase. Next slacken the clamp bolt passing through the steering head clip, and also loosen the two clip screws shown at U in Fig. 86. Then eliminate any play in the steering head races by tightening the large plated nut on top of the steering stem. Be careful not to tighten the nut so that the steering is unable to fall over to full lock when given a light tap in either direction. Having made the

ADJUSTMENTS AND OVERHAULING

required adjustment, see that the clamp bolt and the two clip screws are firmly retightened.

Shock Absorber Adjustment. Where finger adjustment is provided it is quite independent of the fork spindle adjustment described on page 130 and can, of course, be made in a few minutes. To obtain comfortable riding on average roads the best use should be made of the hand adjustment provided. It is best to adjust the shock absorbers so that they have little effect when weight is applied to the handlebars, yet exert a marked retarding effect on the fork rebound when the weight is removed. The adjuster on the off-side has a L.H. thread (except on some 1937–8 models with a wing nut) so that when astride the saddle both shock absorbers are tightened by turning the adjusters towards you. The shock absorber adjusters will not slacken off while riding, thanks to the spring-loaded plunger provided.

Where hand adjustment of the shock absorbers is not provided it is necessary to adjust them by tightening the fork links as described on page 130.

The Steering Damper. Intelligent use should be made of this fitment where fitted, and it is quite surprising to those not accustomed to the steering damper how effective it is in steadying the machine at fast speeds. Generally speaking, slacken off at low speeds and tighten at high speeds. The exception to the rule is the sidecar, where to obtain comfortable steering it is best always to have the damper tightened down to some extent.

Are You Comfortable? Although you cannot expect armchair comfort on a motor-cycle you can on Royal Enfields get a very considerable degree of comfort if you adjust the riding position to *your* physical make-up. It is possible to vary considerably the tilt of the handlebars and to adjust the footrests also (except on Models RE, WD/RE). Further, the air lever, front brake, and clutch controls (except on pre-war light-weights and Models RE, WD/RE) can be adjusted on the handlebars to suit your requirements.

HOW TO DECARBONIZE

When Advisable. After the first 2000–2500 miles have been covered (on a new engine) and subsequently at intervals of about 4500–5000 (1500–2000 on two-stroke engines) miles an engine usually exhibits signs indicating that it is advisable to decarbonize it. Gone is that youthful vivacity and power, and probably the machine begins to shy at quite ordinary gradients up which it normally romps in a care-free manner and shows its disapproval in no uncertain way by emitting a knocking or pinking noise. Accompanying these objectionable symptoms is a change from a crisp exhaust note to one which is distinctly "woolly" and tells you that the engine is not in a healthy condition. As soon as the engine behaves (or rather misbehaves) in the above manner, and especially if unprovoked knocking is apt to occur, you should

(*The Enfield Cycle Co., Ltd.*)

FIG. 71. CLOSE-UP VIEW OF 346 C.C. O.H.V. ENGINE ON THE 1948–9 MODEL G

The O.H.V. engines on Models J, J2 are similar except that the bore and stroke are 84 mm. × 90 mm. (instead of 70 mm. × 90 mm.), and the Model J2 engine has a two-port cylinder head

dry-dock the machine, remove the cylinder(s) and/or the cylinder head(s) and decarbonize the engine and grind-in the valves if necessary. The last mentioned usually require attention every alternate decarbonizing. Decarbonizing is a long word, but the actual job is quite a short one and presents no difficulties if the following instructions are carefully observed.

What are Carbon Deposits Due To? Carbon deposits are due to a combination of three things: (*a*) burnt lubricating oil; (*b*)

ADJUSTMENTS AND OVERHAULING

carbonizing of road dust; (c) incomplete fuel combustion. When decarbonizing it is always worth while inspecting the valve seatings and *if necessary*, grinding-in the valves. Removal of the valves incidentally facilitates thorough cleaning of the ports.

In connection with decarbonizing there are three types of engines to consider: (a) the side-valve engines; (b) the overhead-valve

(*From "The Motor Cycle"*)

FIG. 72. CLOSE-UP VIEW OF 125 C.C. ENGINE ON THE 1949 MODEL RE TWO-STROKE

On the Forces Model WD/RE a Villiers carburettor is fitted

engines; (c) the two-stroke engines. The general procedure is much the same in each case, although differences in design make the dismantling work somewhat different.

The Side-Valve Engines. The side-valve engines are perhaps the easiest to decarbonize, and as all 1937–9 Royal Enfield engines have detachable cylinder heads above the level of the valves, it is only necessary to remove the heads in order to decarbonize. When it is desired to inspect the piston rings and piston, the cylinder barrel as well as the head must, of course, be removed. Although the valves can be removed with the cylinder in position, it is much better to remove the cylinder barrel for this purpose.

and the removal of the head and barrel is advised every alternate decarbonizing. Petrol tank removal on Big Twins is not essential.

The Overhead-valve Engines. All O.H.V. engines naturally have detachable heads and hence to decarbonize the engine and grind-in the valves it is only necessary to remove the head complete with valves, unless it is desired to examine the piston and rings, in which case the barrel also must come off. Cylinder head removal on all 1937–49 models except Models S, S2 entails preliminary removal of the petrol tank without disturbing the lighting wiring. On the above mentioned two models it is possible to remove the cylinder head and cylinder barrel *together* with the tank in position, but if it is desired to remove the head only, the tank must first be removed.

The Two-stroke Engines. No detachable head is provided on Model A 225 c.c. two-stroke and to decarbonize it is necessary to remove the entire cylinder without disturbing the petrol tank. On the 125 c.c. two-stroke engines (Models RE, WD/RE) a detachable cylinder head is provided and this can be removed before or after removing the cylinder barrel which is always desirable when decarbonizing. The petrol tank need *not* be disturbed.

To Remove Petrol Tank (O.H.V. Model WD/CO and 1946-9 O.H.V. Models CO, G, J, J2). To remove the petrol tank (necessary prior to decarbonizing), first disconnect the fuel pipe. Next remove from beneath the tank the four bolts which secure it to the mounting brackets. Then lift the tank off. Its removal is facilitated by removing the saddle front attachment bolt.

To Remove Petrol Tank (1937 O.H.V. Models with Tank Panels). On "Magdyno" models with the lighting switch on the tank panel the panel will slide through the slot in the tank after removing the two panel securing screws, and the switch lever. It is not necessary to disturb the lighting wires, but one battery lead should be disconnected to avoid the possibility of a short circuit. After removing the tank panel, take off the tank itself.

On coil ignition models the location of the ignition switch prevents the panel from sliding through the slot in the tank as referred to above. It is unnecessary, however, to disturb the wires to the panel as they are sufficiently long to enable the tank to be lifted back on to the saddle. But it may be necessary to disconnect the leads from the headlamp.

To Remove Petrol Tank (1937-9 O.H.V. Models S, S2). This is required to enable the cylinder head to be removed, leaving the

ADJUSTMENTS AND OVERHAULING

cylinder barrel undisturbed. Get to work as follows: take away the handlebars and clips complete by unscrewing the two pins attaching the handlebar clips to the ball head yoke. Then unscrew the four tank securing pins and lift the tank back on to the saddle. The panel wiring (1937) need not be disconnected; the leads are long enough to enable the tank to be lifted back on to the saddle far enough to permit of the cylinder head being removed.

To Remove Petrol Tank (1937-9 O.H.V. Model T). To prepare Model T for decarbonizing the tank should first be drained. Then remove the balance pipe which connects the two halves, unscrew the four tank support bolts and lift the tank back on to the saddle. The wires leading to the panel switch are made extra long to allow of this being done, and it is quite unnecessary to interfere with the wiring. 1938-9 models have no tank switch.

To Remove Petrol Tank (1937-9 S.V. Models K, KX). Do not interfere with the lighting wires to the tank-mounted panel. Remove the two screws securing the panel to the tank and also remove the switch lever. Disconnect one of the battery wires to prevent a possible short. Then slide the whole panel through the slot in the tank.

To Remove Cylinder Head (1937-9 S.V.). Unscrew the nuts holding the detachable head (or heads in the case of Model K) to the cylinder barrel and then lift directly off the studs. If stiff, give a sharp tap sideways with a mallet or suitable implement (do not use a hammer, or the brittle casting may be damaged). Some models (D, WD) have a cylinder head stay which must first be swung aside.

To Remove Cylinder Head (1946-9 O.H.V.). The following is the procedure to remove the cylinder head on Models CO, G, J, J2 (and Model WD/CO). First remove the petrol tank as described on page 136. Next remove the rocker-box cover, the Amal carburettor, exhaust pipe (two on Model J2) and silencer(s). Now remove the rocker bearing caps and rockers and withdraw the two push-rods from their cover tubes. Should the collar on the exhaust push-rod fail to clear the joint between the cylinder head and barrel, leave this push-rod *in situ* until the cylinder head has been removed. Unscrew the four cylinder head securing nuts and lift the cylinder head off the barrel.

To Remove Cylinder Head (Models RE, WD/RE). To remove the cylinder head with the petrol tank not removed and the cylinder barrel removed or in position (optional), unscrew the four nuts securing the head to the cylinder barrel of the 125 c.c. engine. Then lift the head off. Removal of the head is not essential, but its removal facilitates chipping off carbon deposits without risk of damaging its inside. If the joint is stiff, prise off the head with two screwdrivers very carefully. If the barrel has been removed, tap the inside of the head with a hammer shaft.

To Remove Cylinder Head (1937-8 O.H.V. Model JF). Remove the tank (page 136), plug, carburettor, exhaust pipes, silencer and exhaust valve lifter, disconnect the ends of the rocker return springs (see Fig. 54) and unscrew the four large nuts securing the rocker spindles, and also the five $\frac{3}{8}$ in. pins holding the rocker plates to the four-valve cylinder head. Next remove the plate on the near-side, prising it off gently if necessary with a screwdriver. For safety, it is advisable to replace the near-side rocker spindle nuts and washers. Then remove the front half of the off-side plates (the exhaust valve lifter lever comes away with it), followed by the rear half of the off-side plates, bringing the rockers with it. The push-rods may be lifted out of their tubes. Finally remove the cylinder head by unscrewing the four nuts situated below the second fin from the top and lift the head clear of the cylinder barrel.

To Remove Cylinder Head (1937-9 Models G, G2, J, J2, JM, CO, CM, S, SM, S2, SF). First of all the petrol tank must be removed. The wires to the lighting panel on 1937 and 1939 models need not be disturbed as they are sufficiently long to allow of the tank being lifted back on to the saddle. Disconnect the headlamp wires if necessary from the lamp. Having removed the tank, proceed to remove the valve gear cover, the carburettor and the exhaust system. Next remove the rocker bearing caps and rockers and lift the push-rods from their tubes. It is then possible to lift off the cylinder head gently after unscrewing the four fixing nuts.

In the case of the 1937-8 Model G there are five cylinder base nuts, and cylinder removal is straightforward after disconnecting the exhaust valve lifter (G, J) and putting the piston on B.D.C. On the 1939 Models S, SF the induction pipe and cylinder head stay must be removed prior to removing the rocker bearing cups.

To Remove Cylinder Head (1937-8 250 and 350 c.c. "Bullets"). The petrol tank must first be drained and removed. Since there is not too much room to spare, removal of the rocker housing and cylinder head is greatly facilitated if the five cylinder holding-down nuts (one is placed between the tappet guides) are first removed, the exhaust pipe and carburettor taken off and the cylinder lifted clear of its studs and turned round so that the *push-rods face the front.* The rocker housing may now be removed

ADJUSTMENTS AND OVERHAULING

after taking out the four securing pins. Next detach the push-rods from the tubes cast in the cylinder, remove the four cylinder head nuts and lift the head off the cylinder barrel. Should difficulty be experienced in getting the push-rods past the head joint, lift the rods away with the head.

To Remove Cylinder Head (1939-40 J2 500 C.C. " Bullets ").
An oil pressure gauge is mounted on the tank panel of these models and it is necessary to disconnect the oil pipe to the gauge at the *engine* connection. The centre pin must be replaced so as to prevent any possibility of the spring and ball (see Fig. 28) being lost. Also disconnect the screwed connection for the electric lead to the gauge between the headlamp and tank. If no screwed connection is provided, remove the panel rubber and the metal panel plate and then disconnect the lead from below the gauge. Afterwards proceed to remove the petrol tank and cylinder head as already described for the 1937-8 Models G, G2, J, etc. If a four-valve cylinder head is fitted, follow the earlier instructions for the 1937-8 O.H.V. Model JF.

To Loosen Cylinder Head (1939 Model G " 350 Bullet ").
Remove the petrol tank after disconnecting the pressure gauge oil pipe and electric lead as described in the previous paragraph. Next remove the covers over the valve rockers, and also the rocker bearing caps. Now lift away the rockers and the push-rods. Having done this, detach the Amal carburettor, exhaust pipe and silencer. Also disconnect the exhaust valve lifter at the control end. Then loosen the cylinder head joint after removing the six head securing nuts. The head and barrel must be removed together.

To Remove Cylinder Head (1937-9 O.H.V. Model T).
Firstly it is necessary to lift the petrol tank back on to the saddle as described on page 137. Then unscrew the large knurled nut and remove the cover from the overhead valve gear. Also remove the central stud securing this cover and unscrew the eight pins attaching the rocker housing to the head and lift away the rockers and housing. The push-rods may now be pulled out of their tubes. Remove the exhaust pipe and silencer, the carburettor, sparking plug, and unscrew the four long sleeve nuts and lift the cylinder head off the barrel.

To Remove Cylinder Head and Barrel (1937-9 O.H.V. Models S, S2).
On these, as has been mentioned above, removal of the petrol tank is not essential in order to remove the cylinder head, provided it is taken off together with the barrel, which is done as follows : first remove the cover from the overhead valve gear and

preferably the centre stud securing it. Next remove the small plate from the side of the cylinder, turn the engine round until

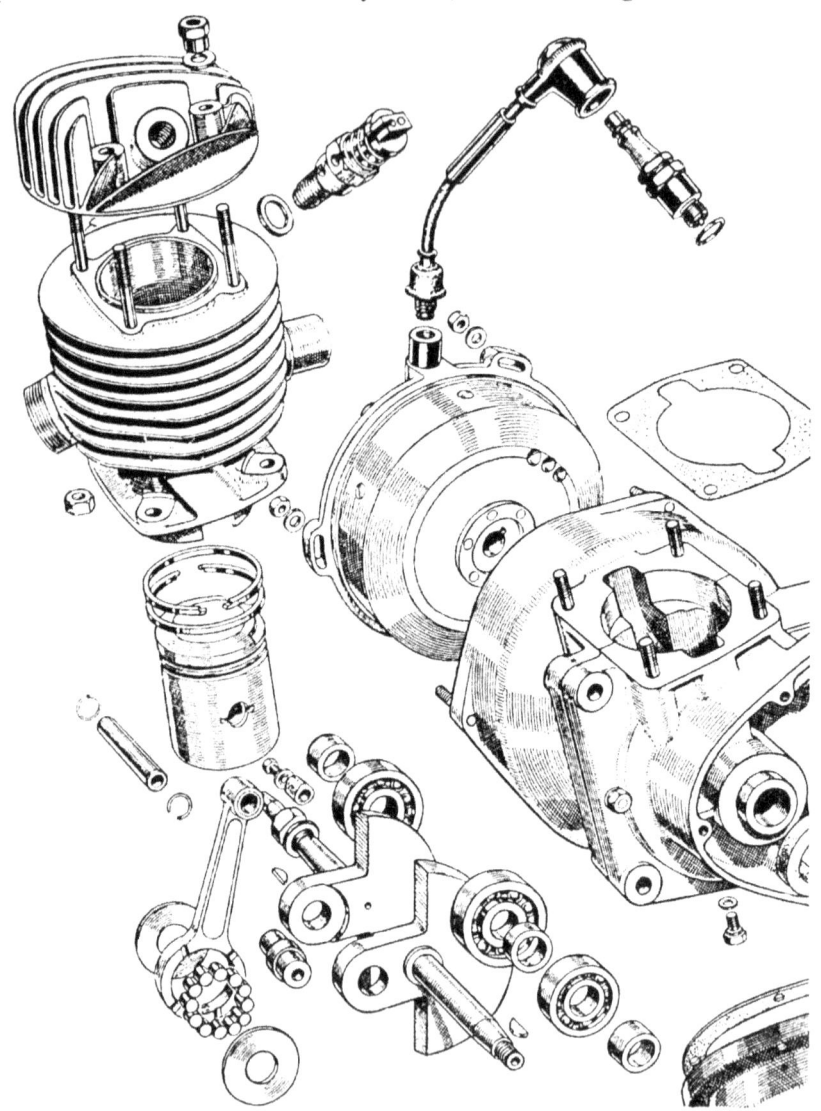

Fig. 73. Exploded View Showing Details of 125 c.c. Two-stroke Engine (Models RE, WD/RE)
(*The Enfield Cycle Co., Ltd.*)

the exhaust valve opens, disconnect the exhaust valve lifter wire, unscrew the adjusting bush and pull the wire and case clear away from the cylinder. Then unscrew the four cylinder base nuts,

ADJUSTMENTS AND OVERHAULING 141

put the piston at B.D.C. and lift off the cylinder barrel and head. The exhaust valve lifter lever will hold the exhaust push-rod in place, but the inlet push-rod will fall out.

As soon as the cylinder base clears the crankcase studs, turn the cylinder slightly until the inlet push-rod can be dropped behind the timing case and lifted away. The cylinder and head should then be carefully drawn off the piston together as described for the cylinder barrel on the S.V. engines. By undoing the cylinder head nuts the barrel and head can then be parted. If it is desired to remove the cylinder head only, leaving the barrel in position, this necessitates removing the tank (page 136) and proceeding as described on page 138.

Removing Cylinder Barrel (1937-9 S.V.). On the single-cylinder engines after removing the detachable head (page 137), remove the silencer and exhaust pipe, the carburettor, disconnect the exhaust valve lifter cable and remove the valve chest cover. Where there is an oil pipe leading to the valve chest (e.g. on Model WD/C), remove this pipe. On the twin-cylinder Models K, KX, after removing both heads, detach the silencer and exhaust pipes and then proceed to remove the induction pipe complete with carburettor.

To remove the cylinder barrel or barrels, unscrew the four cylinder base nuts, place the piston at bottom dead centre and draw the cylinder carefully off the piston (support it), taking care not to put any side strain on the connecting-rod or to allow the piston skirt to strike the connecting-rod or crankcase when the barrel comes away. On the 1937-9 Big Twins (K, KX) it is advisable to unscrew the three back cylinder head *studs* before attempting to withdraw the rear cylinder barrel.

It is the safest course to wrap a rag round the connecting-rod as soon as the piston sees daylight so as to prevent damaging it and to prevent foreign matter entering the crankcase hole.

Removal of Cylinder Barrel (1937-49 O.H.V. Engines). After removing the cylinder head, push-rods, etc. (see appropriate paragraph), disconnect the exhaust valve lifter cable (from the handlebar lever on post-war models). On the 1937-8 250, 350 c.c. "Bullets" and Model JF the exhaust valve lifter will have been disconnected during head removal.

Unscrew the four cylinder base securing nuts. A fifth nut is situated between the inlet and exhaust tappet guides on the 1938-9 Model G, the 250, 350 c.c. "Bullets," and the 1946-9 Models G, J, J2, CO (and WD/CO). This nut is instantly accessible on removing the cover from the tappet chest. Position the piston at or near B.D.C. and then carefully withdraw the cylinder barrel from the piston, supporting the latter with one hand while doing so.

Remove Cylinder Head and Barrel Together on 1939 Model G "350 Bullet." First loosen the cylinder head as described on page 139. Then put the piston at B.D.C. and carefully withdraw the cylinder head and barrel *together*. Simultaneous removal is necessary on this engine due to a small clearance above the cylinder head.

To Remove Cylinder (Models RE, WD/RE Two-stroke). As has been stated on page 136, the cylinder head can be removed before or after the removal of the cylinder barrel. The following is the procedure for removing the cylinder head and barrel together. First disconnect the exhaust pipe by unscrewing the gland nut at the exhaust port. Remove the complete exhaust pipe and silencer. Next disconnect the upper end of the fuel pipe and remove the Amal or Villiers (WD/C) carburettor, complete with air strangler and filter. The throttle slide can be left attached to the control cable. Also disconnect the compression release valve control cable from the handlebar lever. Remove the lever from the lugs on the handlebar and unscrew the release valve from the cylinder head. The appropriate instructions are given on page 115.

Remove the H.T. cable and the sparking plug, unscrew the four nuts securing the cylinder flange to the crankcase. Then place the piston at B.D.C. and together carefully withdraw the cylinder barrel and cylinder head from the piston. If the cylinder head is to be removed proceed now as described on page 137. An exploded view of the engine on the 125 c.c. models is shown in Fig. 73.

To Remove Cylinder (1937-9 Model A Two-stroke). Remove the exhaust pipe and silencer, carburettor (with the induction pipe) and sparking plug. Then unscrew the four cylinder base nuts, place the piston at the bottom of its stroke and lift the cylinder till the end of the gudgeon pin is exposed. Push out the gudgeon pin and lift the cylinder and piston away together.

Piston Removal. The gudgeon pin is of the fully floating type, i.e. free to rotate in the piston and connecting rod bush. The pin is held in position on most engines by means of two spring circlips which fit into grooves machined at each outer end of the gudgeon-pin hole through the piston. One of these circlips can easily be removed with the tang end of a file or a pair of round-nosed pliers. It is advisable not to use again the circlip after removal, but to fit a new one. On no account interchange the pistons on a twin-cylinder model, and mark them on the inside so that they are replaced correctly.

Each piston laps out the cylinder in which it fits in a certain way, depending upon the connecting rod thrust, lubrication, and other

ADJUSTMENTS AND OVERHAULING

factors, and it is *never* advisable to alter its original position on the connecting rod. On twin-cylinder S.V. engines mark the front piston "F," the rear piston "R." If the above two markings are scratched on the inside of the surface which faces the front there will be no doubt as to which is the correct way round to fit the piston on the connecting rod. On all the singles except the two-stroke (see p. 154) scratch the mark "F" as shown in Fig. 74 to indicate which is the front of the piston.

Piston Rings are Easily Broken.

Great care must be taken when removing the piston rings as they are made of cast iron and are exceedingly brittle. It is unsafe to spring them out wider than the diameter of the piston crown, and the best method of removing the rings is shown in Fig. 75. Three strips of sheet tin about 1½ in. long and ⅜ in. wide are inserted under the rings opposite the slots, enabling the rings to be gently eased off one by one. Broken pieces of an old hacksaw blade will answer the same purpose. Be careful on the two-stroke engine not to damage the pegs.

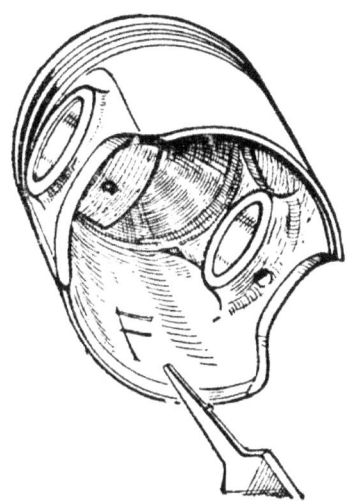

FIG. 74. MARK INSIDE OF PISTON TO ENSURE CORRECT REPLACEMENT
(*From "The Motor Cycle"*)

The Piston Rings.

The rings should be polished round the whole of their surfaces, and if any ring is discoloured or has a black patch on it, it means that gas has been leaking past, and it should therefore be replaced by a new one. With the rings removed the piston should be washed, so that the degree of carbon deposit in the grooves may be readily seen. If any is found here it should be scraped away, but extreme care is necessary in order that the surfaces of the grooves are not damaged by a scraping tool. If so a loss of compression will result, and if a slot is badly cut or dented a new piston will probably have to be fitted for first-class results to be obtained. Any carbon deposit on the inside of the rings should also be scraped away. It is important to note that the rings should be quite free in their grooves, without much up-and-down movement. The piston and rings must again be washed in paraffin, after the carbon deposit has been removed.

Refitting the rings is quite a simple matter. Before this is done a few drops of oil should be placed in the grooves and the top ring may then be pushed over the top of the piston until it is home, followed by the other rings. Alternatively the method shown in Fig. 75 may be used. See that the piston ring gaps are opposite each other. On a two-ring piston they should be spaced at 180 degrees and on a three-ring piston at 120 degrees. When replacing the piston rings it is important on a two-stroke piston to make

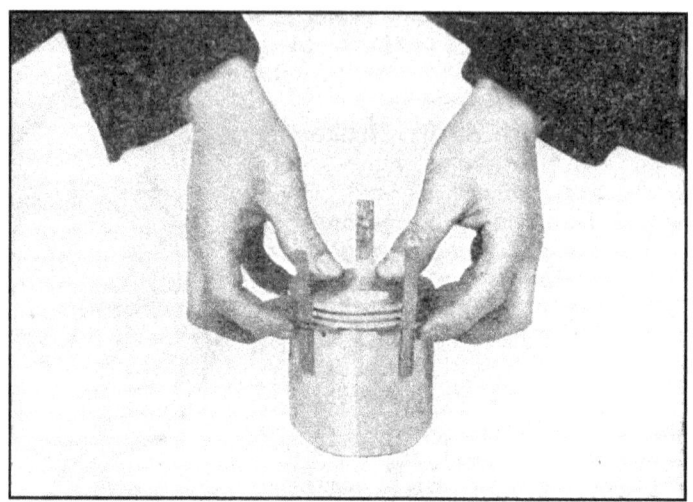

Fig. 75. Safe Method of Removing and Fitting Piston Rings

sure that they fit freely in their grooves and that the pegs engage correctly in the gaps in the rings.

Fig. 76 shows the correct way to fit the two piston rings on the 125 c.c. two-stroke engine of Models RE, WD/RE.

Ring Gap Dimensions. All pre-war and post-war four-stroke engines have two compression rings and one scraper ring. A

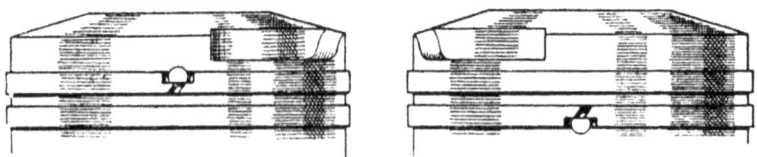

Fig. 76. How to Fit Piston Rings on 125 c.c. Two-stroke Engine
(*The Enfield Cycle Co., Ltd.*)

slotted scraper ring is fitted on all except some pre-war engines which have a stepped scraper ring. Compression and scraper rings require the same gap. The correct gap for new rings in new cylinders is 0·008 in.–0·012 in. for 250 c.c. and 350 c.c.

ADJUSTMENTS AND OVERHAULING

four-stroke engines. In the case of 500 c.c. and 570 c.c. four-stroke engines the correct gaps are 0·010 in.–0·014 in. and 0·016 in.–0·020 in. respectively. The last-mentioned gap is also correct for the S.V. Big Twins. On the 125 c.c. two-stroke engine (Models RE, WD/RE) the correct ring gap (new) is 0·008 in.–0·012 in. Where the 225 c.c. two-stroke engine (Model A) is concerned, the correct gap (new) is 0·010 in.–0·015 in.

A piston ring having a gap of $\frac{1}{16}$ in. can be refitted if the ring is otherwise satisfactory. Where the gap exceeds $\frac{1}{16}$ in. the ring will probably continue to function well, but when the engine is dismantled and the ring gaps are observed on inspection to have reached $\frac{1}{16}$ in. it is advisable to reject the rings and to fit new ones.

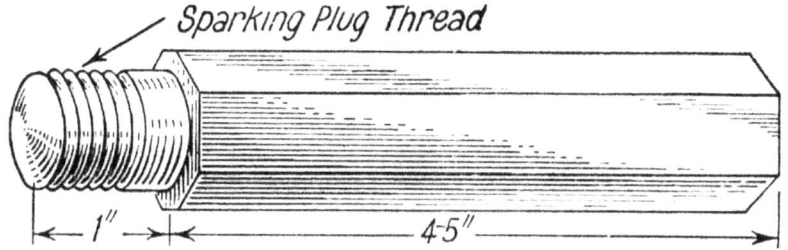

FIG. 77. A HEXAGON STEEL BAR TURNED AND THREADED AT ONE END TO HOLD A CYLINDER HEAD WHEN DECARBONIZING
On O.H.V. engines with integral cylinder head and rocker-box the head can be rested nicely on the top of the rocker-box and the above gadget is not required

Removing the Carbon. Thoroughness in decarbonizing well repays the labour expended. The more completely the carbon is removed the better will the engine performance be, and the longer will it be before decarbonizing again becomes necessary. It is inadvisable, however, to decarbonize the piston ring grooves more than about once every alternate decarbonization, when the cylinder as well as the cylinder head should be removed. When undertaking an ordinary top overhaul, the carbon deposits on the piston crown and on the inside of the cylinder head need alone be scraped off. To do this, a suitable scraper such as the end of a screwdriver should be employed. Be careful, however, not to employ excessive force on the piston, or its comparatively soft aluminium surface will be deeply scratched. When decarbonizing the cylinder head, do not overlook the exhaust ports, which are usually heavily sooted or carbonized, and, as before mentioned, see that the face on the cylinder head is not scratched. A good method of holding the head on some engines when decarbonizing it is to fit a hexagon steel bar screwed at one end into the sparking-plug hole. Such a bar is shown in Fig. 77. The cylinder head may then be held in a vice by means of the bar. If a bar is unavailable, an old sparking plug makes a good substitute. After the deposits have been removed, clean the surfaces with a calico rag damped in paraffin.

If desired, carbon deposits can be removed effectively from the valves, ports and combustion chamber by immersion in a solution containing 4 ounces of commercial potash per gallon of water. But the aluminium alloy piston must on *no* account be permitted to come in contact with this solution.

In the case of Model A two-stroke where the entire cylinder has to be removed, the top of the piston may afterwards be rubbed

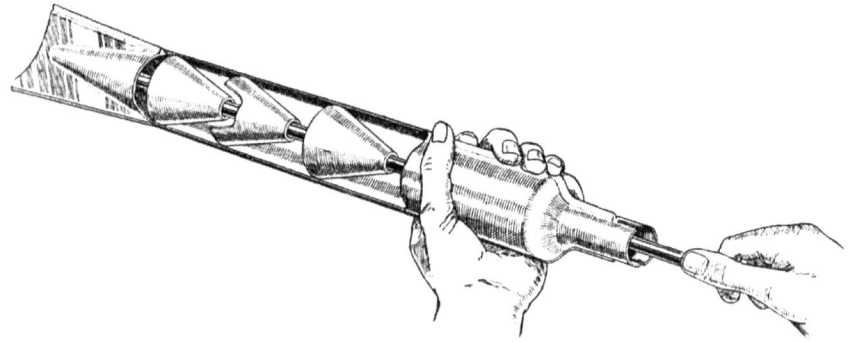

Fig. 78. Cleaning Silencer with a Metal Rod
(*The Enfield Cycle Co., Ltd.*)
This method applies to Models RE, WD/RE

with *very fine* emery cloth until a perfectly smooth surface has been obtained. This method of finishing off may also be used for the detachable heads on all models, but is definitely *not* recommended for aluminium alloy pistons, because some abrasive particles may become embedded in the soft metal. Any such abrasive particles left on the piston and getting down on to the rings may cause bad scoring of the cylinder walls.

On Model A two-stroke the deposits on the integral cylinder head may be reached through the cylinder mouth. Care should be taken not to allow the screwdriver shank to scratch the part of the cylinder included in the piston stroke. See also that all carbon is removed from the exhaust port, the piston ring grooves and the inside of the piston, and clean the silencer.

When occasion is had to remove the piston or pistons, do not attempt to remove carbon from the outside of the skirt. Only the crown, the inside, and the piston ring grooves should be scraped and cleaned. The latter may be cleaned of all deposits after the rings have been removed by running a small, sharp, flat-ended tool round their circumference. Only a tool of the right size should be used, or the shape of the grooves may be spoiled. A piece of broken piston ring can be used, but it is better to use a special tool.

Cleaning Silencer (Models RE, WD/RE). When decarbonizing a 125 c.c. two-stroke model, the silencer must also be thoroughly cleaned. As may be seen in Fig. 78, the silencer contains three conical baffles. The ½ in. diameter holes in these baffles are in line and can be effectively cleaned as shown by means of a long steel rod (about 15 in. long and ⅜ in. diameter). The best method is to hold the rod in a vice, thread the silencer over it, and work the silencer about the rod until the baffle holes are cleared of all adhering carbon. Alternatively the silencer (and exhaust pipe) may be cleaned in a solution consisting of 4 oz. of commercial potash to one gallon of water.

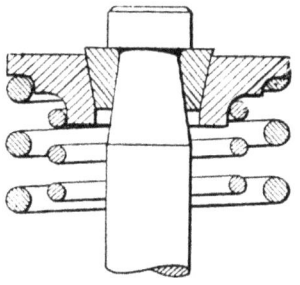

FIG. 79. SPLIT COLLET VALVE SPRING ANCHORAGE (Used on all models except the Big Twins)

To Remove the Valves (1937–9 S.V.). After removing the cylinder and cylinder head, removal of the valves can be readily undertaken for inspection of the valves and seats and subsequent grinding-in if necessary. Place the cylinder barrel upside down on the bench (or on a table or suitable box if you do not possess a bench), place a little soft packing below the valve heads so as to keep them firmly down on their seats, and then depress each valve spring by pressing down on the outer valve spring cap with a large screw-driver or suitable spanner until it is possible to remove the split collet (Fig. 79) from the tapered recess in the valve stem, or in the case of the twin-cylinder engine the flat steel cotter from the slot in the end of the stem. The valve spring, caps and valve may then be withdrawn.

On some engines it may be much more convenient to employ a proprietary valve spring compressor such as the "Terry" illustrated in Fig. 80. The hooked end is rested on the centre of the valve head and the forked end of the lever slipped over the valve spring cap and the lever depressed until the valve spring is compressed sufficiently to enable the split collet or cotter, as the case may be, to be lifted out. If stuck, gently tap it out. With the tool illustrated it is possible to remove the valves with the cylinder barrel in position, but as it is always advisable to grind-in the valves with the cylinder barrel removed, there is no useful purpose served by doing so.

Do Not Interchange the Valves. Even if on some engines the valves are theoretically interchangeable, it is never in practice wise to change them over as each valve is ground into its individual seat and cannot be relied upon to form a gas-tight seal on a strange seat. Further, the highly stressed exhaust valve is usually made of extra special quality steel. If the valves are not marked it is usually possible to identify the exhaust valve by

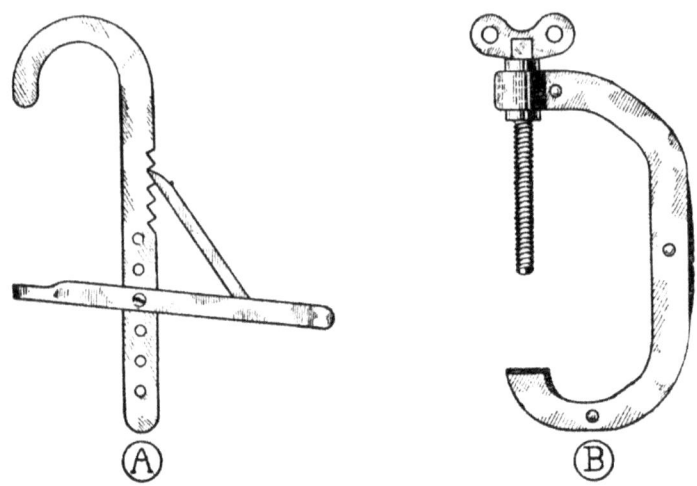

FIG. 80. TWO USEFUL VALVE SPRING COMPRESSORS

Both the above tools are manufactured by H. Terry & Sons, Ltd. That shown at *A* is for S.V. engines and that at *B* for O.H.V. engines

the discoloration of the head due to heat. On the Big Twins it goes without saying that the valves should be marked to ensure correct replacement.

To Remove Valves (1937–49 O.H.V.). Owing to the different arrangement of the cylinder head the type of valve spring compressor shown in Fig. 80A is not suitable for compressing the valve springs on O.H.V. engines and it is necessary to employ a screw type compressor. A tool specially designed for O.H.V. engines (see Fig. 80B) is obtainable for a few shillings from accessory firms (page 107). The method of using this tool after first removing the hardened end caps on the valve stems is to place the forked end on the valve spring collar and the pointed end of the screw on the centre of the valve head and screw up until the valve spring is compressed sufficiently to enable the split collet to be removed. If stuck, gently tap it out. The valve spring collars and valve can then be removed. Deal with each valve similarly. As on the other engines, avoid interchanging the

ADJUSTMENTS AND OVERHAULING

valves after removal and be most careful not to mix up the valves on the four-valve engine of the 1937–8 Model JF.

On most O.H.V. engines the diameter of the inlet and exhaust valve stems differs to the extent of 0·002 in., and on some engines different grades of steel are used. On pre-war J2 engines and post-war J, J2 engines the inlet valve head is *larger* than the exhaust valve head and assists identification. Besides being careful

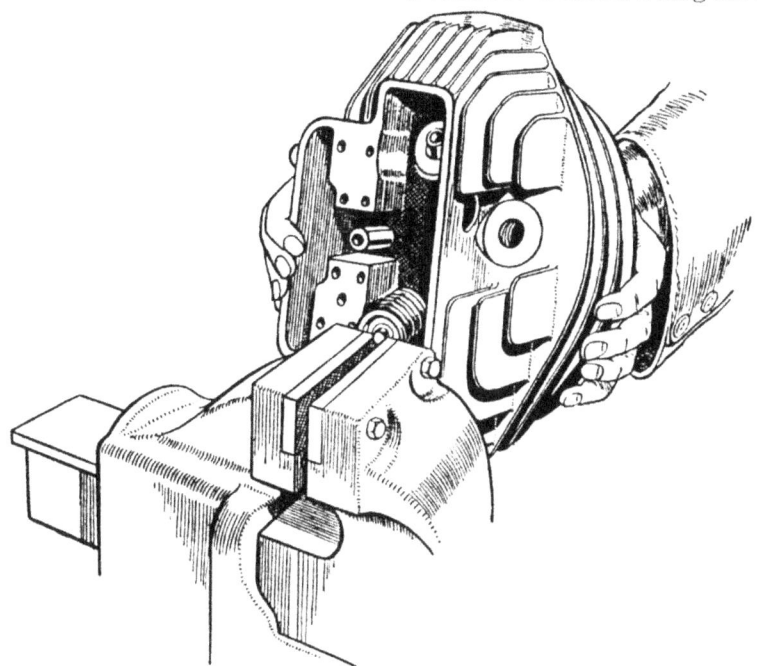

FIG. 81. A GOOD METHOD OF REMOVING VALVE STEM END CAPS
(*The Enfield Cycle Co., Ltd.*)
If an end cap is stuck, compress the valve spring slightly and grip the end cap in a vice as shown

not to interchange the valves, it is also desirable always to keep the split collets and the upper valve spring collars paired up with their respective valves.

Grinding-in the Valves. Should the valve faces or seats show signs of serious pitting, the valves will have to be ground-in. Valves of the side-by-side and overhead type have, of course, to be rotated and lightly pressed down on their seatings with a screwdriver inserted in the slot in the valve head.

Only grind in valves *when necessary*, using a ready-made compound such as Richford's grinding paste; only a small quantity is necessary, and do not revolve the valves round and round, but rotate the valve about a third of a turn in one direction and then an equal amount in the opposite direction. About every six oscillations lift the valve, rotate it $\frac{1}{8}$ to $\frac{1}{4}$ of a revolution and proceed as before, stopping when no "cut" can be felt to redistribute the grinding paste and examine the valve face and seat. Continue grinding-in until both the valve face and seat have a bright ring. It will facilitate grinding-in the valves if a small compression spring is inserted under the valve head. This avoids

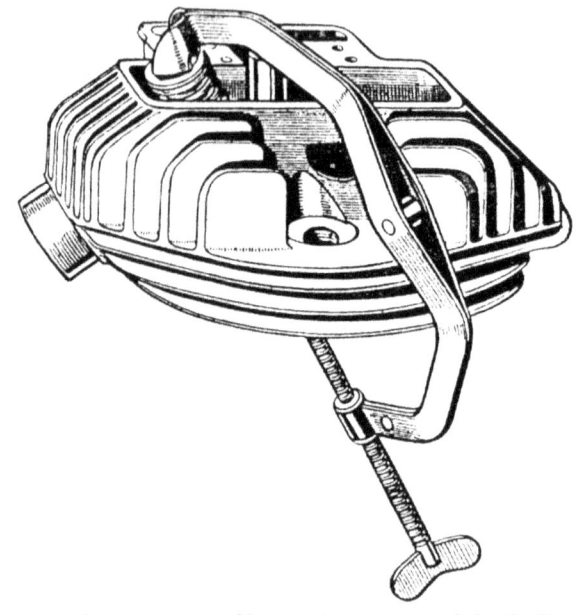

FIG. 82. COMPRESSING VALVE SPRING ON O.H.V. ENGINE
(*The Enfield Cycle Co., Ltd.*)
The spring compressor shown in use is the Terry illustrated in Fig. 80 (B)

the nuisance of having repeatedly to lift the valve by hand to change it to a new position.

Very great care must be taken after grinding-in to remove all traces of valve-grinding compound. The valve stems may be cleaned with *very fine* or worn emery cloth. Do not use coarse grinding compound for grinding valves in unless the pitting is very extensive. A little fine paste smeared very lightly over the valve face is far better. Care should be taken to avoid burring the valve stems, otherwise unnecessary wear will take place in the valve guides.

Do not grind-in the valves to an unnecessary extent, as this eventually causes them to become seriously "pocketed" with

ADJUSTMENTS AND OVERHAULING 151

the result that resistance is offered to the flow of the incoming and outgoing gases. See that all pitting is removed from each valve face and seat, but if the valves and their seats happen to be very badly pitted the proper course is to send the cylinder (or head) and valves to Redditch in order to have new faces cut.

On Some 250, 350 c.c. "Bullets." The valves are not slotted to take a screwdriver and to grind them it is necessary to attach a holder to the valve stem. The cylinder head joint on the 1939 Model G "350 Bullet" is of the metal-to-metal type and the joint should be lightly scraped to remove all traces of jointing compound. If there is evidence of "blowing," remove the six head retaining studs and lap the cylinder head on to the barrel face, using some fine grinding paste thinned down with a little metal polish.

Reassembling Valves. All is now ready for assembling. When replacing the valves see that the springs (duplex on O.H.V.), collars and cotters or split collets bed down properly. Replacing the valve springs is considerably helped on the single-cylinder engines by applying grease to the tapered portion of the valve stem as this enables the split collets to be held in place while compressing the springs with a "Terry" compressor or other suitable tool. On all engines make sure that the individual valves are fitted into the seats into which they have been ground.

After Reassembling the Valves. It is an excellent plan to test the seats by pouring some petrol into the ports and watching for leakage past the valves. Not the slightest trace of moisture should creep past the valves until a very considerable time has elapsed. If some petrol does get past quickly it indicates that the valves have not been properly ground-in and the remedy is obvious—carry on.

Refitting Cylinder Barrel (S.V. and O.H.V.). Before reassembling, clean thoroughly all the parts with paraffin and clean rags. To refit the cylinder it is necessary to adopt roughly the reverse order of dismantling. Smear the cylinder wall, piston, and rings with clean engine oil before replacing the cylinder and see that the gudgeon-pin circlip which has previously been removed is replaced by a new one and properly bedded down in the piston boss groove. Gudgeon-pin circlips should *always* be renewed after removal as they are apt to become distorted during removal. The 1937–9 Model C has copper end pads.

Fit a new cylinder base washer (where provided). The paper washer should be oiled before fitting and it is important on engines having a double-acting type feed pump (see page 65) to fit the washer such that the small hole in it registers with the oil feed hole to the rear of the cylinder barrel. Place the piston at B.D.C. and offer it up to the cylinder barrel. To ensure proper entry of the rings, squeeze each ring as it enters the mouth of the barrel. Be very careful not to impose any side strain on the piston. When tightening down the nuts at the base of the cylinder, give each a successive turn in a diagonal order, otherwise there is a risk of distorting the cylinder base and preventing its bedding down properly on the crankcase. This method of tightening also applies to the cylinder head nuts or bolts (Big Twins).

Final Assembly (S.V. Engines). Assembly should be effected in the reverse order of dismantling. When replacing the cylinder head it is advisable to anneal the old copper washer by heating it to a red heat and then plunging it into cold water. It is a good plan to smear the washer with some shellac varnish or a similar jointing compound. As in the case of the cylinder barrel retaining nuts (see previous paragraph), tighten down the cylinder head securing nuts evenly. To complete the reassembly of a S.V. engine, replace the carburettor, also the exhaust pipe, silencer and sparking plug. Finally check the tappet adjustment, replace the valve chest cover, and warm up the engine thoroughly. Then again check the cylinder head and barrel retaining nuts for tightness. On the pre-war Big Twins the above-mentioned parts (except the carburettor) are, of course, duplicated. Each cylinder head should be dealt with in turn.

Final Assembly (O.H.V. Engines). Reassemble the engine in the reverse order of dismantling, after refitting the cylinder barrel as described on page 151. Certain points should be carefully noted. Before replacing the cylinder head and push-rod cover tubes, replace the copper washer for the cylinder head joint. This should be heated red hot and then quenched in water.

In the case of the 1939 Model G "350 Bullet" if the cylinder barrel and head are not fitted together, it is necessary (in order to obtain sufficient clearance) to turn the front side of the cylinder barrel to the timing side of the engine prior to fitting the cylinder head. When remaking the metal-to-metal cylinder head joint, apply a little thin shellac jointing between the faces.

To avoid oil leakage it is important on all engines to remake the push-rod cover tube joints properly. Except on a few earlier engines of small capacity, Hallite washers are provided. Fit new washers and paint them with gold size or shellac. Tighten down the cylinder head retaining nuts in the proper manner. On 1937–8 and earlier 1939 O.H.V. engines apply a spanner to each cylinder head nut in turn. On later 1939, all military machines, and all post-war models, the insides of the Hallite washers are supported

ADJUSTMENTS AND OVERHAULING

by ferrules as shown in Fig. 83. Where ferrules are fitted, first tighten the two nuts on the push-rod side of the engine. This will compress the Hallite washers thoroughly and also create even pressure on the copper gasket of the cylinder head.

Oil the push-rod ends before fitting the push-rods in their cover tubes, and on earlier engines see that the rocker housing support bolts are tightened evenly and securely. It is a good plan to insert the push-rods before refitting the cylinder head, as this

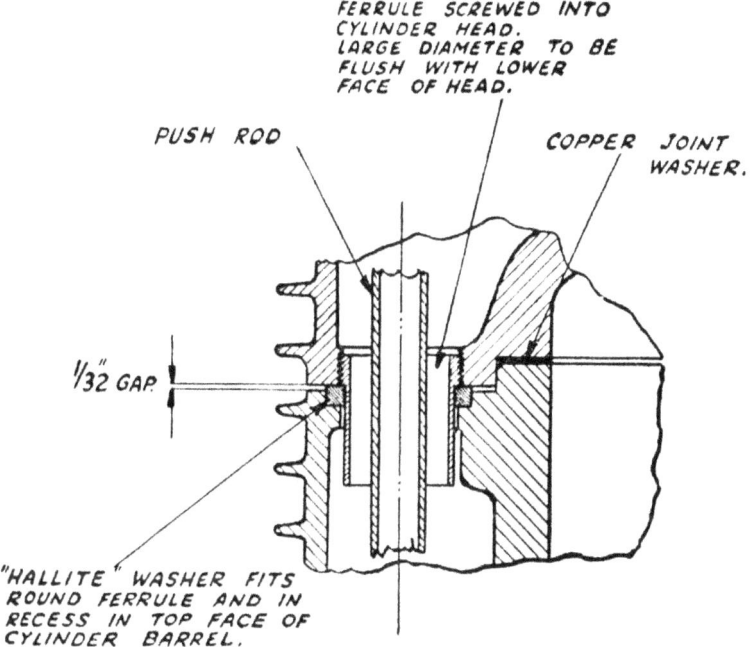

Fig. 83. Sectional Drawing showing Details of Push-rod Cover Tube Joints
(*The Enfield Cycle Co., Ltd.*)

ensures that no difficulty is experienced due to spreading of the soft washers sealing the push-rod cover tube joints. On some earlier O.H.V. engines the push-rods have cups which are deeper at the top than at the bottom. On these engines make sure that the deeper cups *are* uppermost.

To simplify assembly of the overhead valve gear on the 1937–8 four-valve Model JF engine, engage the push-rods with the valves *before* fitting the near-side rocker plate. On this machine see that both push-rods are properly located before replacing the front half of the off-side plate, and remember to fit the distance piece behind the back half of the off-side plate. When reassembling the exhaust valve lifter on Model JF and the 250, 350 c.c. "Bullets" it is important to replace the length of outer casing over the cable inside the return spring. This functions as a stop and prevents excessive lifting of the exhaust rocker.

On replacing the valve rockers and caps on 1937–9 Models G, G2, J, JM, J2, and the 1946–9 Models G, J, J2, CO (and WD/CO), apply a little oil to each overhead rocker and see that the rocker is quite free after its cap has been retightened. If the rocker is stiff, tap its end sharply to free it.

After assembly of the cylinder barrel, cylinder head, and overhead valve gear is complete, check the push-rod adjustment (see page 113), replace the carburettor, sparking plug, valve chest cover, exhaust pipe, silencer, etc. Also reconnect the exhaust valve lifter. Then warm up the engine thoroughly and again check for tightness the nuts securing the cylinder barrel and head.

Refitting Cylinder (Model A Two-stroke). See that all bits are clean and smear a little oil on the piston and cylinder before assembly. Then proceed to reverse the process of dismantling. See that the piston is fitted the right way round (the steep side of the deflector head to the rear). It is necessary to make an absolutely air-tight joint between the cylinder base and the crankcase (on the two-stroke the mixture is compressed in the crankcase), and the contacting faces must therefore be quite clean and free from any traces of the old joint washer, which must be renewed. A paper washer is used and it should be oiled before insertion. When tightening the holding down bolts, tighten them diagonally and each a few turns at a time. Refit the carburettor, plug, exhaust pipe and silencer and you are "all set."

Final Reassembly (Models RE, WD/RE). When reassembling the 125 c.c. two-stroke engine see that all parts are quite clean and oil the piston, particularly the rings. See that the piston ring gaps are correctly positioned relatively to the ring stops (see Fig. 76) prior to replacing the cylinder barrel with or without the head. A gas-tight joint at the base of the cylinder is vital and the paper washer must be renewed if damaged in the slightest degree. Scrape off all traces of the old washer. Before replacing the cylinder barrel also make quite sure that the piston is fitted with the *small deflectors at the rear*. Renew the gudgeon-pin circlip.

If the cylinder head has been removed from the barrel, remake the metal-to-metal joint, using shellac, gold size, or a similar jointing compound. See that there are no burrs or other marks on the cylinder barrel and head joint surfaces. These are liable to cause leakage. If it is found difficult to make a good joint, remove the four studs from the cylinder barrel and lap the two surfaces together with some *fine* grade valve grinding paste. Be careful to remove all traces of paste afterwards.

When replacing the cylinder head retaining nuts do not forget the washers below the nuts. These nuts and those retaining the cylinder barrel to the crankcase must be tightened in a diagonal order and checked for tightness with a spanner after thoroughly warming up the engine. On connecting up the compression release valve, see that the head of the bolt (Fig. 57) is fitted beneath the clip welded to the handlebars. Adjust the control by means of the adjuster screw at the lower end (see Fig. 58) until there is a little slackness in the control cable. Check the adjustment with the handlebars central and also turned to full lock on either side. In general, the reassembly of the 125 c.c. engine is a reversal of the procedure for dismantling.

THE COMPLETE OVERHAUL

After a big mileage some keen motor-cyclists strip down their "buses" and examine all the components, effecting such replacements and adjustments as an expert eye deems necessary. This complete overhaul, which of course, involves removing the engine and gearbox from the frame, is not a job to be undertaken lightheartedly by any except expert owner-drivers, and the following hints, necessarily brief, are only intended for those riders who have had some considerable experience. Others should entrust the work to The Enfield Cycle Co., Ltd., or a good service agent.

Frame. Alignment, existence of flaws or cracks, play in fork links, looseness of steering head, wear caused by friction of all attached parts, condition of enamel.

Wheels. Condition of journal bearings or balls, cones, and cups; truth of wheels, alignment, loose spokes, condition of rims, wear of tyres, condition of valve "insides," wear of brake linings.

Chains. Excessive wear, cracked or broken rollers, joints, tension.

Engine. Oil leaks, compression leaks, main bearings, valves, valve guides and tappets, overhead valve rockers, valve springs, valve seats and faces, cotters, condition of cylinder bore, piston, piston rings, play in big-end and small-end bearings, timing wheels, shafts and bearings, cams, condition of plug and contact-breaker.

Gears. Condition of teeth on sprockets and pinions, damaged ball races and loose parts generally.

The examination should also include all control rods and cables, tank filters, clutch and brake linings, etc. To sum up, everything should be dismantled and readjusted or renewed.

Removing Engine from Frame (1937-49 S.V. and O.H.V. Singles). The following is the procedure for machines other than those referred to in subsequent paragraphs. As a rule it should *not* be necessary to remove the engine except when it is necessary to return it to Redditch or an agent in order to have new bearings fitted or in order to have it completely overhauled.

Remove the exhaust pipe(s) and silencer(s), chain case, chain, and all external fittings. On "Magdyno" models remove the four leads to the "Magdyno." To remove the front half of the chain case, unscrew the nut holding the near-side footrest, remove the footrest and brake pedal, and pull the front of the chain case away from the rear half. To remove the rear half of the case, first take off the engine sprocket, clutch, and primary chain. Then unscrew the small pin securing the case to the engine and the two nuts securing it to the gearbox attachment bolts and lift the case away. Now remove the bolts holding the engine into its plates. Remove the two rear engine plates and lift the engine out of the frame. In the case of Model CO and the later type Model WD/CO machines with frames having tank rails, remove one front and one rear engine plate, and then lift the engine out sideways.

On 1939 Machines with Circular Crankcases. On these 225 c.c. machines (Models WD, D, DC, S, SF), to take the engine out of the frame, first remove the exhaust pipe and silencer, the primary chain cover, chain, and all external fittings. Now remove the cover for the dynamo driving chain, the dynamo or "Magdyno" (where fitted), the generator driving chain, and the platform for the generator. Disconnect the oil pipes, remove the bolts which secure the engine to the frame, and then lift the crankcase forwards and upwards until it clears the engine plates.

To Remove Engine from Frame (1937-9 O.H.V. Model T). On this 148 c.c. model first remove the exhaust pipe and silencer, the primary chain cover, chain, rear brake pedal, the footrests, and all external fittings. Then remove the off-side rear engine plate. Leave the large securing bolts still pushed through the near-side plate and the frame lugs so as to hold the frame together. Now withdraw the bolts which secure the engine to its plates, and gently lower the engine on to the ground.

Removing Engine from Frame (1939-41 S.V. Model WD/C). First remove the gearbox in the following manner. Remove the near-side footrest and the front half of the primary chain case.

ADJUSTMENTS AND OVERHAULING

Next disconnect the primary chain, dismantle the multi-plate clutch, and withdraw the engine sprocket and the clutch centre, using the special extractors provided. Remove the rear half of the primary chain case and the top attachment stud for the gearbox. Slacken the nuts on the gearbox bottom attachment stud, and remove the gearbox.

Having removed the gearbox, take off the exhaust pipe, silencer, and carburettor. Jack up the machine by inserting a suitable

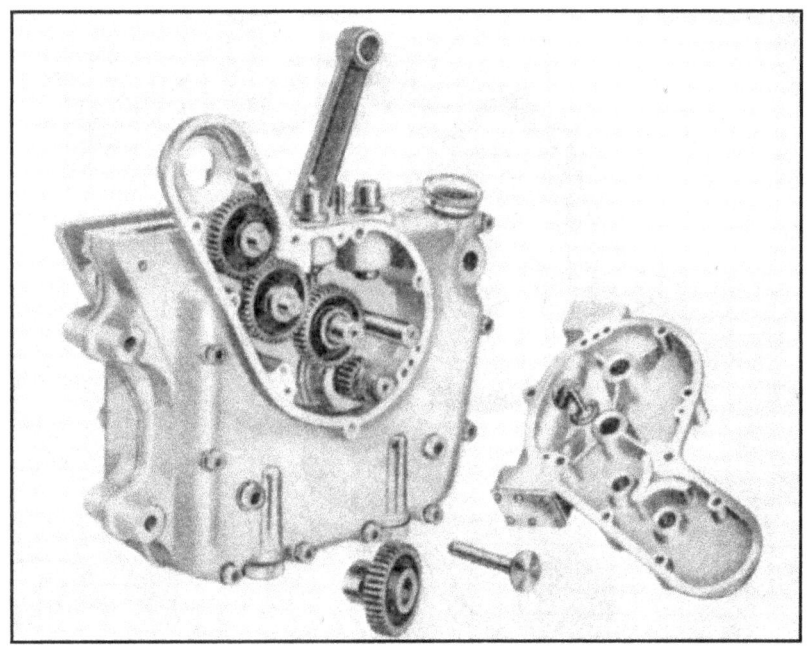

FIG. 84. ROYAL ENFIELD TWIN CAMWHEEL TIMING GEAR

The exhaust camwheel and flat base tappet are shown removed. On 1939 250 c.c. models with circular crankcases a single camwheel with twin cams is used

box below the cradle tubes and remove the off-side engine plate. Finally remove the front engine securing bolt and take the engine out of the frame.

To Remove Engine from Frame (1937-9 S.V. Models K, KX).

On the Big Twins remove the primary chain case, the "Magdyno" driving chain cover, the driving chain and both sprockets, and the "Magdyno" itself together with its mounting platform. Withdraw the near-side engine plate and remove the gearbox. Then remove the off-side engine plate, the front main engine-securing bolt, and carefully lift out the complete engine. Owing to the size of the twin-cylinder engine, the clearance between the engine and frame is small, and the engine can only be removed in *one* position. Furthermore the power unit is rather heavy. Consequently the author advises the preliminary removal of both cylinders and pistons.

Removing Engine and Gearbox (1937-9 Model A Two-stroke). Removal of the engine and gearbox on this 225 c.c. model presents

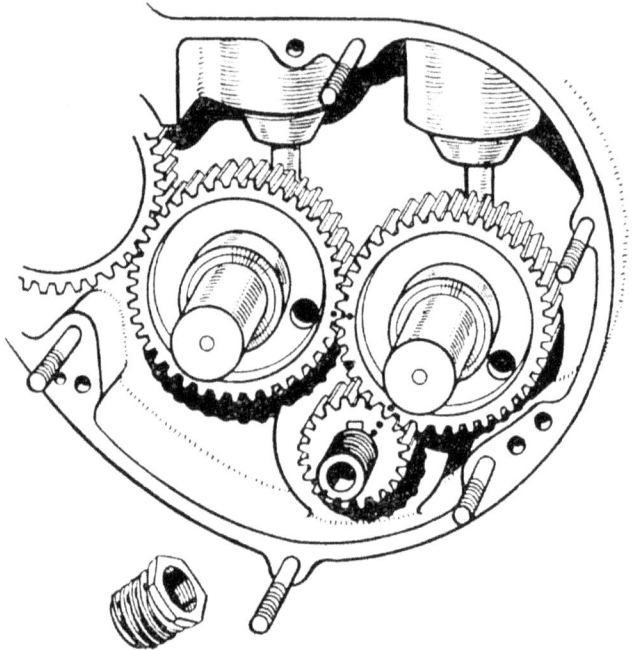

FIG. 85. SHOWING THE DOT SYSTEM USED FOR MARKING THE VALVE TIMING (1937-49 SINGLES)

(*The Enfield Cycle Co., Ltd.*)

(This applies to all engines except those with circular crankcases and a single camwheel timing gear)

no special difficulties, but two points should be observed. First disconnect the secondary chain before removing the chain guard. Secondly when removing the gearbox do not forget to jack up the crankcase with a suitable box. One of the gearbox securing bolts is also used to secure the chain stays to the engine plates. You do not want the machine to disintegrate!

To Remove Engine and Gear Unit from Frame (Models RE, WD/RE Two-stroke). Take off the carburettor, exhaust pipe, and the compression release valve. Also remove the sparking plug.

ADJUSTMENTS AND OVERHAULING

Remove the secondary chain and disconnect the clutch and gear controls. Then remove the four bolts securing the engine and gearbox unit to the frame and lift out the unit.

Dismantling the Crankcase (1937-49 S.V. and O.H.V. Singles).
On removal of a single-cylinder engine from the frame, drain the oil tank and remove the cylinder and piston, if not already done. Next unscrew the timing cover nuts and tap off the cover; then remove the "Magdyno" (or dynamo) driving pinion. This is a taper fit on its shaft and is tapped for a small extractor, which will be found in the tool kit. Now lift out the two cam wheels and the intermediate driving pinion(s) for the "Magdyno" or dynamo drive.

To remove the tappets and guides, tap them gently from underneath with a brass or aluminium drift (having first removed the tappet guide securing clamp on the side valve engines). Now loosen the dynamo (or "Magdyno") securing strap and lift the complete instrument away. Remove the timing pinion nut which has a left-hand thread. The pinion can now be drawn off the taper shaft, preferably using a sprocket drawer. If one is not available, wedge a screwdriver behind the pinion and tap the end of the shaft, but take great care not to damage the shaft. It is now only necessary to remove the bolts holding the two halves of the crankcase together, when these can be separated. Do not lose the rollers from the main bearings as these fall out. Do not attempt to separate the flywheels.

To Dismantle Crankcase (1937-9 S.V. Models K, KX).
The general procedure for dismantling the crankcase of a Big Twin is similar to that already described for the S.V. and O.H.V. singles, but a single camwheel timing gear (Fig. 29) is used. When removing the timing pinion nut (and engine sprocket), insert a $\frac{3}{8}$ in. rod through the hole in the camwheel bush. This will engage the crankpin boss and prevent the flywheels from rotating when the nut is loosened.

On Machines with Circular Crankcases.
To dismantle the crankcase, first remove the engine from the frame (see page 156). Then remove the cylinder and piston if this has not already been attended to. Now remove the timing cover securing screws and tap off the cover. Lift out the camwheel and rockers from the timing case and remove the nuts securing the engine sprocket and timing pinion. This latter nut has a left-hand thread. Withdraw the sprocket and pinion from their tapers. Then to separate the crankcase halves, remove the bolts which hold them together. Be careful not to lose the rollers of the main bearings as they come away, and do not attempt to part the flywheels.

To Dismantle Engine and Gear Unit (Models RE, WD/RE). On the unit construction 125 c.c. two-stroke model first remove the cam from the contact-breaker and also the flywheel cover plate (see Fig. 73). A taper, key, and nut (R.H. thread) secure the flywheel to the engine main shaft, and the boss of the flywheel is threaded to take a special extractor obtainable from The Enfield Cycle Co., Ltd.

Take off the primary chain cover. Also unscrew the six pins which secure the clutch springs, and dismantle the clutch. Disconnect the primary chain. The use of extractors is necessary to withdraw the engine sprocket and clutch centre which are secured to tapered shafts by nuts having a right-hand thread. Remove the nuts securing the halves of the crankcase together and split the crankcase after first removing the cylinder and piston.

It should be noted that the crankcase has three studs with nuts on both ends, five with nuts on the driving side, and one with the nut on the kick-starter side. The kick-starter mechanism and the countershaft sprocket can be left undisturbed.

Reassembling Engine and Gear Unit (Models RE, WD/RE). See that all components are quite clean and free from any grit. Smear some clean engine oil on all moving parts. Then reassemble in the reverse order of dismantling, previously described. For instructions on retiming the magneto, see page 53. Prior to replacing the back half of the chain case and the clutch, fit the rear chain on the countershaft sprocket. Cleanliness between the joint surfaces of the crankcase is essential and some seccotine, varnish or shellac should be used for this joint. Do not forget partly to fill the gearbox and chain case with soft grease. Some engine oil should be added when the assembly is completed.

Permissible Play in Engine Bearings. With the big-end and mainshaft roller bearings a small amount of end play is permissible, as is a little "shake" in the connecting-rod. If, however, quite appreciable up and down play can be felt it is advisable to send the crankcase, flywheels and connecting-rod to Redditch for attention as special appliances are wanted to ensure the correct assembly of new parts. The foregoing applies to all 1937-49 four-stroke models. The big-end bearing on 1937-8 engines is of the cageless roller type, but the later 1939 and all subsequent engines have a white-metal lined floating bush. The main bearings are of the caged roller type. The camshaft bearings comprise phosphor-bronze bushes. If these bushes require renewal, the crankcase should be returned to the makers.

The gudgeon-pin should be a free working fit in the small-end and a push fit in the piston bosses with the engine cold.

ADJUSTMENTS AND OVERHAULING

Valve Timing. No difficulty should be experienced when reassembling the crankcase (S.V., O.H.V.), but care should be taken to see that all parts are quite clean and that the cams and bearings are oiled. The valve timing should be checked if the small engine pinion has been *removed* because it has three key-ways cut on it to enable the timing to be varied by one-third of a tooth (by using one or other of the key-ways), so enabling the exact timing to be obtained. Checking, however, can be dispensed with if note is taken of the key-way used prior to dismantling and if the dot system of marking the engine pinion, inlet and exhaust camwheels (see Fig. 85) is used to obtain the correct relative positions of the three wheels. All post-war engine pinions have one key-way.

On machines having circular type crankcases (1939 Models WD, D, DC, S, SF) a single camwheel timing gear is provided. The camwheel should be assembled so that the marks on the engine pinion are in line with those on the camwheel. This applies also to the S.V. Big Twins, Models K, KX. On all other 1937–49 four-stroke S.V. and O.H.V. engines a twin camwheel timing gear (Fig. 85) is used. In this case the inlet and exhaust camwheels should be assembled so that the two dots on the small engine pinion are in line with the two dots on the exhaust camwheel, while the single dot on the exhaust camwheel is in line with the single dot on the inlet camwheel.

CORRECT 1937–49 VALVE TIMINGS*
(0·005 in. VALVE CLEARANCE)

Enfield Models	Inlet Opens	Inlet Closes	Exhaust Opens	Exhaust Closes
1937–9 Models B, BCO, BM, C, CO, CM, G, G2, H, HM, L, J, JF, JM, J2, S, SM, S2, T, TM, 250, 350 c.c. "Bullets"	30° B.T.D.C.	60° A.B.D.C.	75° B.B.D.C.	35° A.T.D.C.
1937–9 Models K, KX	20° B.T.D.C.	60° A.B.D.C.	65° B.B.D.C.	38° A.T.D.C.
1939 Models† D, DC, WD, S, SF	22° B.T.D.C.	60° A.B.D.C.	60° B.B.D.C.	22° A.T.D.C.
1939–45 Models WD/C, WD/CO	30° B.T.D.C.	60° A.B.D.C.	75° B.B.D.C.	35° A.T.D.C.
1946–9 Models CO, G, J, J2	30° B.T.D.C.	60° A.B.D.C.	75° B.B.D.C.	35° A.T.D.C.

* The abbreviations B.T.D.C., A.B.D.C., B.B.D.C., and A.T.D.C. imply before top dead centre, after bottom dead centre, before bottom dead centre, and after top dead centre respectively.

† The engines of these machines have circular type crankcases with a single camwheel timing gear.

The valve timings for the 1937–49 Models are tabulated on page 161 and if in any doubt it is wise to check up the timing. Note that these timings are for checking with a valve clearance of 0·005 in., not the running clearances given on pages 109–114.

Making Crankcase Joints. Use shellac, seccotine or any good proprietary jointing compound for the joint between the crankcase halves, and see that the special washer is used for the timing cover joint. A *paper* washer is required for the timing case joint on engines with circular type crankcases. On these engines it is also very important that the leather washer which seals the joint in the oil passage from the pump is in sound condition. The same applies to the cork bush in which the end of the timing shaft runs. Do not omit to replace the steel washer located beneath the cork bush.

When Refitting Tappets. When refitting tappets and guides observe that the longer pair are for the exhaust valve.

Oil Pump Assembly. See notes on page 72. Note that on earlier 1939 models with a single-acting feed pump and a double-acting return pump, the diameter of both pump plungers is the same, namely $\frac{3}{8}$ in.

How to Dismantle Telescopic Front Forks. It should not be necessary to dismantle the telescopic front forks except in order to renew the springs, oil seals, or bearing bushes. Referring to Fig. 86, the following dismantling procedure should be used for dismantling each fork leg.

To remove the spring G from the fork leg, unscrew the nut A and remove the washer from below. Unscrew the filter body B and detach it together with the filter C. Unscrew the oil level plug S and remove the plug and the fibre washer over it. Next unscrew the nut R after positioning a suitable receptacle to catch the hydraulic fluid as it drains away. Then pull the spring G from the upper end of the fork leg. The top stud and the bottom stud O will come away with the spring.

To remove the bottom tube N, withdraw the spring G as previously described. Next take the weight off the front wheel by placing some packing beneath the crankcase and remove the front wheel from the fork end T. The front brake control cable must, of course, first be disconnected. Unscrew the outer tube I from the fork crown H and slide it downward until the gland nut J is exposed. Unscrew the gland nut and then pull the bottom tube N downward until it comes away. This leaves the bottom tube bush L, the oil seal K, and the gland nut J on the main tube E. Make no attempt to detach the fork end T from the bottom tube.

ADJUSTMENTS AND OVERHAULING 163

To detach the main tube *E*, first remove the spring *G* and the bottom tube *N* as previously described. Next slacken the clip

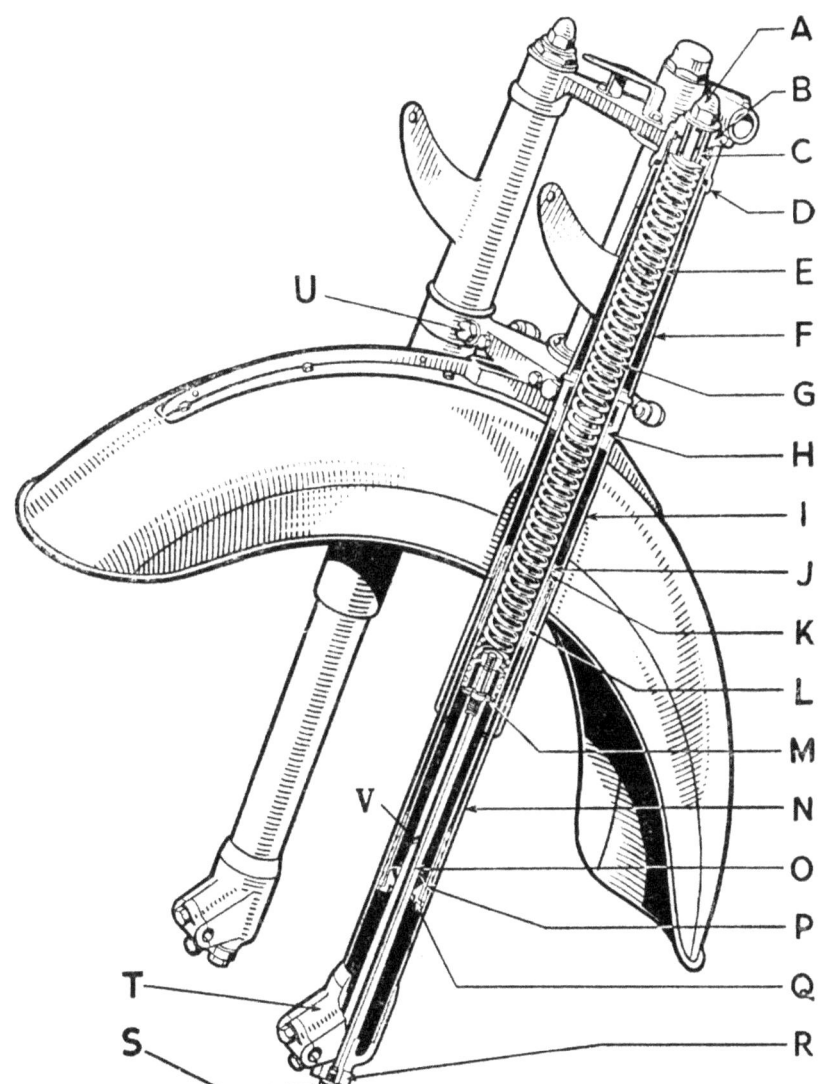

Fig. 86. The Royal Enfield Telescopic Front Forks with One Leg Cut Away to Reveal Details
(*The Enfield Cycle Co., Ltd.*)

screw *U* and pull the main tube *E* downwards out of the ball head clip *D* and the fork crown *H*. Then lift the gland nut *J*, oil seal

K, and bottom tube bush L from the main tube E. The main tube bush O should not be removed. If it requires renewing, a main tube complete with bush must be fitted.

To remove the lamp bracket tubes F, slacken the clamp bolt through the ball head clip. Unscrew the large nut from the top of the steering stem and also the two smaller nuts A. Now unscrew both filter bodies B and tap the ball head clip D carefully upwards until it is clear of the steering head stem. Be careful when doing this not to lose any of the balls from the upper steering head race. The lamp bracket tubes can then be detached.

Dismantling Four-speed Gearbox. The gears on the four-speed gearbox cannot be removed until the mainshaft has been withdrawn, and to do this the clutch must be taken off.

Remove two bolts holding on bearing cap and remove cap complete with clutch actuating lever. The mainshaft nut is *left hand*, and must therefore be unscrewed in a clockwise direction. The cover bolts may now be removed and the cover lifted off. Do not prise cover by means of a screwdriver, as this damages the face of the cover and destroys the joint, causing oil leaks. A gentle tap on the clutch end of the spindle with a mallet will loosen it. The kick-starter mechanism comes away with the cover. The mainshaft can now be withdrawn, followed by the layshaft, layshaft gears, mainshaft sliding gears and fork in one block. The withdrawal of the mainshaft sleeve and sleeve gear completes the dismantling as far as is necessary for practically everything.

In all cases, when assembling, make sure that the ball of the operator, which juts out of the box, fits into the operator lever which is in the cover. The chain sprocket is mounted on the high gear sleeve by means of splines and locked down by a key washer and lock-ring. These are unscrewed with an anti-clockwise movement.

Maintenance and Overhaul of 1950-3 Models. See notes in Preface regarding 1950-3 Models G, J2, RE.

INDEX

Accessory firms, 107
Acid level, 87
Air filters, 40-1
Alignment—
  headlamp, 93
  wheel, 105
Amal non-needle carburettor, 29-32
  single-lever needle-jet carburettor, 32-7
  two-lever needle-jet carburettor, 19-29
Ammeter, 82
Assembling—
  engine, 152-5
  valves, 151

Battery maintenance, 86-8
Brakes, 124
Brushes, commutator, 82, 85
Bulb replacements, 91
Bulbs, fitting, 93

Cables, identifying, 85
Carbon—
  deposits, 134
  removing, 145
Carburettor—
  dismantling, 27, 32, 36, 38
  settings, 23, 26
Chain adjustment, 122-4
Changing down, 12
  up, 11
Chromium, cleaning, 108
Cleaning—
  commutator, 82
  lamps, 94
  motor-cycle, 108
  silencer, 146
  sparking plugs, 43-5
Clutch—
  control adjustment, 118-21
  slip, 121, 122
Coil, attention to, 50
Colloidal graphite, 17, 68

Commercial potash, 146
Commutator brushes, 82, 85
Compensated voltage control, 54, 82-4
Complete overhaul, 155
Compression-release valve, 7, 114-17
Condenser, testing, 50
Connections, making, 85
Contact-breaker, coil ignition, 47
  face-cam, 45
  gap, 46, 48, 52
Controls, 4-7
Covers, tyre, examining, 102
Crankcase—
  dismantling, 159
  flooding, 10
  joints, 162
Cush-drive rear hub, 129
Cylinder—
  barrel removal, 139-41
  replacing, 151
  head removal, 137-9

Decarbonizing, 133
Detachable rear mudguard, 126-7
Diagnosing ignition trouble, 50
Difficulty in starting, 10
Dipped beam filament, 91
Dipper switch lubrication, 80
Double-acting feed pump, 63
Driving—
  licence, 3, 4
  hints, 18
Dry sump lubrication, 62-72
Dunlop valve, 100
Dynamo chain, adjusting, 123
  lubrication, 73, 82

Electric horn, faulty, 95
Engine bearings, play in, 160
  oils, suitable, 60
Exhaust valve lifter backlash, 114
Exide batteries, 88
"Export" batteries, 88

FACE cam contact-breaker, 45
Felt filter, cleaning, 71
Final engine assembly, 152–5
Flooding—
  carburettor, 28
  crankcase, 10
Flywheel—
  generator, Miller, 86
  magneto, 51–3, 55–8
  lubrication, 73
Focusing headlamp, 93
Foot gear control, adjusting, 118
Foot-lever position, 118
Four-speed gearbox, dismantling, 164
Four-stroke controls, 4
Front—
  fork adjustment, 130
  wheel, removing, 125

GEAR control, adjusting, 117
Gearbox, four-speed, dismantling, 164
Gearbox lubrication, 74
Grease on brake linings, 124
Greases, suitable, 79
Greasing, 77
Grinding-in—
  compression release valve, 115
  valves, 149
Gudgeon-pin removal, 142

HAND gear control, adjusting, 117
Handling a Royal Enfield, 1–18
Headlamp alignment, 93
Hill climbing, 12
Hydrometer, 87

IGNITION system, 42–59
  timings, 53–9
Inflation pressures, 100–101
Insurance, 1

KNOCK-OUT rear spindle, 127

LICENCES, obtaining, 3
Lighting—
  circuit, Miller, testing, 86
  equipment, 81
Lubrication charts, 75, 78

Lucas—
  dynamo, 81–5
  "Lucas-Nife" battery, 84

"MAGDYNO"—
  chain, adjusting, 123
  contact-breaker, 45–6
  lubrication, 72
Miller contact-breaker, 48–51
  dynamo, 85–6
Mixture, correct, 22, 34, 37
Moving off, 11

NEUTRALIZING—
  lever, 14
  adjustment, 118

OIL—
  bath, replenishing, 76
  circulation, verifying, 68
  pump assembly, 162
  pumps, stripping down, 72
  return pump, 64
  tank, draining, 70, 72
    replenishing, 68
Overhead valve gear, lubricating, 68

PARKING machine, 15
Petroil lubrication, 60–2
Petrol—
  obtaining, 3
  tank removal, 136–7
Piston—
  removal, 142
  rings, 143–5
  seizure, 17
Plug gap, 43
Pressed steel forks, 130
Pressure gauge, 70, 100
Price's engine oils, 60
Primary—
  chain, adjusting, 122
  lubrication, 76
Push-rod adjustment, 113
  cover tube joints, 153

REAR wheel removal, 127–8
Removing engine from frame, 156–8
Repair stand, 107
Riding comfort, 133

INDEX

Ring-cam contact-breaker, 46
Ring gap dimensions, 144
Running-in, 16–17

SECONDARY—
  chain, adjusting, 123
  lubrication, 77
Shock-absorber adjustment, 133
Short-circuiting, avoiding, 81
Sidecar lamp, 95
  wheel alignment, 105
Silencer, cleaning, 146–7
Smooth tyres, 103
Sparking plugs, suitable, 43, 59
Specific gravity, electrolyte, 87–8
Speedometer light, 93
Spring link, chain, 124
Starting procedure, 7–10
Steering—
  damper, use of, 133
  head adjustment, 131–2
Stopping—
  engine, 15
  machine, 14
Storing battery, 87
Sump, draining, 70
Switch positions, Lucas and Miller, 89–91

TAIL lamps, 94
Tappet adjustment, 110–113
Tappets, refitting, 162
Telescopic—
  forks, dismantling, 162
  front forks, 79, 80

Testing plug, 45
Timing—
  case, draining, 70
  ignition, 53–9
Topping-up—
  battery, 87, 88
  telescopic forks, 79, 80
Tyre—
  pressures, 100–101
  removal and fitting, 103–104
  repairs, 104
Tubular forks, 130
Tuning carburettor, 22, 31, 35, 37
Two-stroke controls, 6

VALVE—
  clearances, checking, 109–114
  removal, 148
  spring compressors, 148
  timing, 161
Valves, removing, 147
Villiers single-lever carburettor, 37

WARMING-UP engine, 70
Warning lamp, 53, 92
Weatherproof plugs, 59
Wheel—
  alignment, 105–106
  bearing adjustment, 125
  hubs, greasing, 77
  removal, 125–9
Wiring—
  diagrams, 96–9
  examining, 84

ARE YOU:
INTERESTED IN EUROPEAN, IMPORT & EXOTIC AUTOMOBILES?

DO YOU:
DO YOUR OWN MAINTENANCE?

If you answered yes to either of these questions, then you should check out our automobile books and manuals. We have included a sample listing of some of our featured marques. However, for complete details and the most up-to-date information, please visit our website.

────── www.VelocePress.com ──────

The fastest growing specialist USA publisher of niche market automotive books and manuals.

All VelocePress titles are available through your local independent bookseller, Amazon.com or direct from VelocePress. Wholesale customers may also purchase direct or from the Ingram Book Group.

AUTOBOOKS WORKSHOP MANUALS

ALFA ROMEO GIULIA 1300, 1600, 1750, 2000 1962-1978 WSM
AUSTIN HEALEY SPRITE, MG MIDGET 1958-1980 WSM
BMW 1600 1966-1973 WSM
BMW 2000 & 2002 1966-1976 WSM
BMW 2500, 2800, 3.0 & 3.3 1968-1977 WSM
BMW 316, 320, 320i 1975-1977 WSM
BMW 518, 520, 520i 1973-1981 WSM
FIAT 1100, 1100D, 1100R & 1200 1957-1969 WSM
FIAT 124 1966-1974 WSM
FIAT 124 SPORT 1966-1975 WSM
FIAT 125 & 125 SPECIAL 1967-1973 WSM
FIAT 126, 126L, 126 DV, 126/650 & 126/650 DV 1972-1982 WSM
FIAT 127 SALOON, SPECIAL & SPORT, 900, 1050 1971-1981 WSM
FIAT 128 1969-1982 WSM
FIAT 1300, 1500 1961-1967 WSM
FIAT 131 MIRAFIORI 1975-1982 WSM
FIAT 132 1972-1982 WSM
FIAT 500 1957-1973 WSM
FIAT 600, 600D & MULTIPLA 1955-1969 WSM
FIAT 850 1964-1972 WSM
JAGUAR E-TYPE 1961-1972 WSM
JAGUAR MK 1, 2 1955-1969 WSM
JAGUAR S TYPE, 420 1963-1968 WSM
JAGUAR XK 120, 140, 150 MK 7, 8, 9 1948-1961 WSM
LAND ROVER 1, 2 1948-1961 WSM
MERCEDES-BENZ 190 1959-1968 WSM
MERCEDES-BENZ 220/8 1968-1972 WSM
MERCEDES-BENZ 220B 1959-1965 WSM
MERCEDES-BENZ 230 1963-1968 WSM
MERCEDES-BENZ 250 1968-1972 WSM
MERCEDES-BENZ 280 1968-1972 WSM
MG MIDGET TA-TF 1936-1955 WSM
MINI 1959-1980 WSM
MORRIS MINOR 1952-1971 WSM
PEUGEOT 404 1960-1975 WSM
PORSCHE 911 1964-1973 WSM
PORSCHE 911 1970-1977 WSM
RENAULT 16 1965-1979 WSM
RENAULT 8, 10, 1100 1962-1971 WSM
ROVER 3500, 3500S 1968-1976 WSM
SUNBEAM RAPIER, ALPINE 1955-1969 WSM
TRIUMPH SPITFIRE, GT6, VITESSE 1962-1968 WSM
TRIUMPH TR2, TR3, TR3A 1952-1962 WSM
TRIUMPH TR4, TR4A 1961-1967 WSM
VOLKSWAGEN BEETLE 1968-1977 WSM

BROOKLANDS BOOKS & ROAD TEST PORTFOLIOS (RTP)

AC CARS 1904-2009
ALFA ROMEO 1920-1933 ROAD TEST PORTFOLIO
ALFA ROMEO 1934-1940 ROAD TEST PORTFOLIO
BRABHAM RALT HONDA THE RON TAURANAC STORY
BUGATTI TYPE 10 TO TYPE 40 ROAD TEST PORTFOLIO
BUGATTI TYPE 10 TO TYPE 251 ROAD TEST PORTFOLIO
BUGATTI TYPE 41 TO TYPE 55 ROAD TEST PORTFOLIO
BUGATTI TYPE 57 TO TYPE 251 ROAD TEST PORTFOLIO
DELAHAYE ROAD TEST PORTFOLIO
FERRARI ROAD CARS 1946-1956 ROAD TEST PORTFOLIO
FIAT 500 1936-1972 ROAD TEST PORTFOLIO
FIAT DINO ROAD TEST PORTFOLIO
HISPANO SUIZA ROAD TEST PORTFOLIO
HONDA ST1100/ST1300 PAN EUROPEAN 1990-2002 RTP
JAGUAR MK1 & MK2 ROAD TEST PORTFOLIO
LOTUS CORTINA ROAD TEST PORTFOLIO
MV AGUSTA F4 750 & 1000 1997-2007 ROAD TEST PORTFOLIO
TATRA CARS ROAD TEST PORTFOLIO

VELOCEPRESS AUTOMOBILE BOOKS & MANUALS

ABARTH BUYERS GUIDE
AUSTIN-HEALEY 6-CYLINDER WSM
BMW 600 LIMOUSINE FACTORY WSM
BMW 600 LIMOUSINE OWNERS HAND BOOK & SERVICE MANUAL
BMW ISETTA FACTORY WSM
BOOK OF THE CARRERA PANAMERICANA - MEXICAN ROAD RACE
COMPLETE CATALOG OF JAPANESE MOTOR VEHICLES
DIALED IN - THE JAN OPPERMAN STORY
FERRARI 250/GT SERVICE AND MAINTENANCE
FERRARI 308 SERIES BUYER'S AND OWNER'S GUIDE
FERRARI BERLINETTA LUSSO
FERRARI BROCHURES AND SALES LITERATURE 1946-1967
FERRARI BROCHURES AND SALES LITERATURE 1968-1989
FERRARI GUIDE TO PERFORMANCE
FERRARI OPP. MAINTENANCE & SERVICE H/BOOKS 1948-1963
FERRARI OWNER'S HANDBOOK
FERRARI SERIAL NUMBERS PART I - ODD NUMBERS TO 21399
FERRARI SERIAL NUMBERS PART II - EVEN NUMBERS TO 1050
FERRARI SPYDER CALIFORNIA
FERRARI TUNING TIPS & MAINTENANCE TECHNIQUES
HENRY'S FABULOUS MODEL "A" FORD
HOW TO BUILD A FIBERGLASS CAR
HOW TO BUILD A RACING CAR
HOW TO RESTORE THE MODEL 'A' FORD
IF HEMINGWAY HAD WRITTEN A RACING NOVEL
JAGUAR E-TYPE 3.8 & 4.2 WSM
LE MANS 24 (THE BOOK THAT THE FILM WAS BASED ON)
MASERATI BROCHURES AND SALES LITERATURE
MASERATI OWNER'S HANDBOOK
METROPOLITAN FACTORY WSM
MGA & MGB OWNERS HANDBOOK & WSM
OBERT'S FIAT GUIDE
PERFORMANCE TUNING THE SUNBEAM TIGER
PORSCHE 356 1948-1965 WSM
PORSCHE 912 WSM
SOUPING THE VOLKSWAGEN
TRIUMPH TR2, TR3, TR4 1953-1965 WSM
VEDA ORR'S NEW REVISED HOT ROD PICTORIAL
VOLKSWAGEN TRANSPORTER, TRUCKS, STATION WAGONS WSM
VOLVO 1944-1968 ALL MODELS WSM

VELOCEPRESS MOTORCYCLE BOOKS & MANUALS

AJS SINGLES 1955-65 350cc & 500cc (BOOK OF)
ARIEL 1939-1960 4 STROKE SINGLES (BOOK OF)
ARIEL LEADER & ARROW 1958-1964 (BOOK OF)
ARIEL MOTORCYCLES 1933-1951 WSM
ARIEL PREWAR MODELS 1932-1939 (BOOK OF)
BMW M/CYCLES R26 R27 (1956-1967) FACTORY WSM
BMW M/CYCLES R50 R50S R60 R69S (1955-1969) FACTORY WSM
BSA BANTAM (BOOK OF)
BSA ALL FOUR-STROKE SINGLES & V-TWINS 1936-1952 (BOOK OF)
BSA OHV & SV SINGLES - 250cc 1954-1970 (BOOK OF)
BSA OHV & SV SINGLES 1945-54 250-600cc (BOOK OF)
BSA OHV SINGLES 350 & 500cc 1955-1967 (BOOK OF)
BSA PRE-WAR MODELS TO 1939 (BOOK OF)
BSA TWINS 1948-1962 (BOOK OF)
BSA TWINS 1962-1969 (SECOND BOOK OF)
CATALOG OF BRITISH MOTORCYCLES (1951 MODELS)
DOUGLAS PRE-WAR ALL MODELS 1929-1939 (BOOK OF)
DOUGLAS POST-WAR ALL MODELS 1948-1957 FACTORY WSM
DUCATI 160cc, 250cc & 350cc OHC MODELS FACTORY WSM
HONDA 50 ALL MODELS UP TO 1970 INC MONKEY & TRAIL (BOOK OF)
HONDA 90 ALL MODELS UP TO 1966 (BOOK OF)
HONDA MOTORCYCLES 125-150 TWINS C/CS/CB/CA WSM
HONDA MOTORCYCLES 250-305 TWINS C/CS/CB WSM
HONDA MOTORCYCLES C100 SUPER CUB WSM
HONDA MOTORCYCLES C110 SPORT CUB 1962-1969 WSM
HONDA TWINS & SINGLES 50cc to 305cc 1960-1966 (BOOK OF)
HONDA TWINS ALL MODELS 125cc THRU 450cc UP TO 1968 (BOOK OF)
INDIAN PONYBIKE, BOY RACER & PAPOOSE ILL PARTS LIST & SALES LIT
LAMBRETTA ALL 125 & 150cc MODELS 1947-1957 (BOOK OF)
LAMBRETTA LI & TV MODELS 1957-1970 (SECOND BOOK OF)
MATCHLESS 350 & 500cc SINGLES 1945-1956 (BOOK OF)
MATCHLESS 350 & 500cc SINGLES 1955-1966 (BOOK OF)
NORTON 1938-1956 (BOOK OF)
NORTON DOMINATOR TWINS 1955-1965 (BOOK OF)
NORTON MODELS 19, 50 & ES2 1955-1963 (BOOK OF)
NORTON MOTORCYCLES 1957-1970 FACTORY WSM
NORTON PREWAR MODELS 1932-1939 (BOOK OF)
ROYAL ENFIELD SINGLES & V TWINS 1937-1953 (BOOK OF)
ROYAL ENFIELD 736cc INTERCEPTOR FACTORY WSM
ROYAL ENFIELD 250cc & 350cc SINGLES 1958-1966 (SECOND BOOK OF)
SUZUKI 50cc & 80cc UP TO 1966 (BOOK OF)
SUZUKI T10 1963-1967 FACTORY WSM
SUZUKI T20 & T200 1965-1969 FACTORY WSM
TRIUMPH PRE-WAR MOTORCYCLE 1935-1939 (BOOK OF)
TRIUMPH MOTORCYCLES 1937-1951 WSM
TRIUMPH MOTORCYCLES 1945-1955 FACTORY WSM
TRIUMPH TWINS 1956-1969 (BOOK OF)
VELOCETTE ALL SINGLES & TWINS 1925-1970 (BOOK OF)
VESPA 1951-1961 (BOOK OF)
VESPA GS & SS 1955-1968 (BOOK OF)
VINCENT MOTORCYCLES 1935-1955 WSM

www.VelocePress.com

www.ingramcontent.com/pod-product-compliance
Lightning Source LLC
Chambersburg PA
CBHW070549170426
43201CB00012B/1774